Screwball Comedy
and Film Noir

CU00704474

ALSO BY THOMAS C. RENZI
AND FROM MCFARLAND

Cornell Woolrich from Pulp Noir to Film Noir (2006)

*Jules Verne on Film: A Filmography of the Cinematic
Adaptations of His Works, 1902 through 1997*
(2004; paperback 1998)

Screwball Comedy and Film Noir

Unexpected Connections

Thomas C. Renzi

McFarland & Company, Inc., Publishers
Jefferson, North Carolina, and London

LIBRARY OF CONGRESS CATALOGUING-IN-PUBLICATION DATA

Renzi, Thomas C., 1948–
    Screwball comedy and film noir : unexpected connections /
Thomas C. Renzi.
        p.   cm.
    Includes bibliographical references and index.

    ISBN 978-0-7864-6672-6
    softcover : acid free paper ∞

    1. Screwball comedy films—United States—History and
criticism.   2. Film noir—United States—History and
criticism.   I. Title.
PN1995.9.C55R47 2012
791.43'617—dc23   2011053527

BRITISH LIBRARY CATALOGUING DATA ARE AVAILABLE

© 2012 Thomas C. Renzi. All rights reserved

*No part of this book may be reproduced or transmitted in any form
or by any means, electronic or mechanical, including photocopying
or recording, or by any information storage and retrieval system,
without permission in writing from the publisher.*

On the cover: Barbara Stanwyck in *The Lady Eve* (1941)
Paramount Pictures/Photofest; Rita Hayworth in *Gilda* (1946)
Columbia Pictures/Photofest.

Manufactured in the United States of America

McFarland & Company, Inc., Publishers
    Box 611, Jefferson, North Carolina 28640
        www.mcfarlandpub.com

For Deb,
my angel, my love

Acknowledgments

My research in the areas of screwball comedy and film noir, in addition to involving written publications, depended very much on two unique sources, Turner Classic Movies (both the website and the cable television network) and the Internet Movie Database. The information they provided was invaluable, TCM for its many impossible-to-find films from the pre–Code, screwball, and noir eras, and the Internet Movie Database for its extensive personnel and production data for virtually every film ever made.

Contents

Preface

Screwball comedy and film noir—the very names suggest genres that are diametrically opposed to one another. The term "screwball comedy" instantly conjures up images of outrageous characters with amusing idiosyncrasies, and hilarious plots filled with enough ironic twists to confound a pretzel-maker. Film noir, on the other hand, christened "black film" by French cineastes, suggests that we are about to experience a film "black" in mood, character, and theme. And of course, we do. All kinds of evils—theft, blackmail, adultery, murder—are perpetrated in the dark shadows of smoke-filled nightclubs and cheerless dwellings, in the dismal gloom of city streets and debris-strewn alleyways. The innocent along with the guilty are drawn into a corrosive web of corruption and chaos, and all humanity seems doomed to succumb to the dark side, no matter how valiantly it fights and struggles and resists. Comparing film noir with screwball comedy, how can we even consider that there is any relation between the two?

Yet there is—and more than just a distant kinship.

As an instructor at Buffalo State College in Buffalo, New York, I have taught various English courses in the areas of literature, composition, and reading, and occasionally I get the opportunity to teach a film course. Most often, I choose as my subject my favorite area of study, film noir. One semester a situation occurred where I was offered a second film course. I could have duplicated the first class and taught film noir in both, but I decided to teach different film genres in the two classes. One class would, of course, deal with film noir; the other would focus on screwball comedy. I thought that screwball made a nice contrast to noir, the lighter fare contrasting the gritty, seamy world of doomed and desperate characters.

Up to then, I was familiar with the more famous screwball films, *It Happened One Night*, *My Man Godfrey*, *Bringing Up Baby*, *Nothing Sacred*.

Before deciding on my complete curriculum, I researched the watershed films, those most critical to the period and most representative of the genre. As I watched what were supposed to be comic films, I became suddenly aware of darker elements in them. I attributed this to the fact that I had been concentrating on noir for so long that I was watching the comedies through a noir lens. Noir images, motifs, and characterizations appeared superimposed on the comedies. The clever and conniving woman in screwball was actually a comical sister of the self-serving seductress in noir. The screwball male, when portrayed as the object of the female's intentions, was oftentimes as hapless a figure as the doomed noir protagonist. There was a similarity in the complexity of plot construction. It became apparent that an undercurrent of cynicism ran like a continuum from the screwball comedies of the 1930s directly into the films noirs of the 1940s. I wondered if I was forcing this comparison, if I was imposing noir sensibilities and techniques on these comic entries.

At the same time that I was viewing the screwball comedies, I delved into some notable books on the genre, among them Stanley Cavell's *Pursuits of Happiness*, Ed Sikov's *Screwball*, and Molly Haskell's *From Reverence to Rape*. Another author, Wes D. Gehring, had devoted a great deal of critical study to romantic and screwball comedies and had written several books on the subject. In one of his books, *Screwball Comedy: A Genre of Madcap Romance*, he offers observations that were ironically relevant to my current area of inquiry:

> In many ways—particularly female domination—screwball comedy of the 1930s and early 1940s anticipates the more sinister woman-as-predator film noir movies of the 1940s. One might even call screwball comedy an upbeat flipside of noir—in both cases it is a frequently irrational world with women hunting vulnerable men.... In fact, the quasi-screwball comedy *Thin Man* series ... might be seen as a bridge between the two genres, especially with the original novel being penned by Dashiell Hammett, also author of *The Maltese Falcon*, which [was] closely adapted in 1941 [and] became an early noir prototype [60–61].

After my excitement over what I thought had been an original inference on my part, I felt suddenly humbled. It was as if I had planned to scale a high mountain, expecting to be the first man to gain the summit, and then learned that someone had already planted a small flag there. Gehring later adds that screwball and noir

> have manipulative women, moldable men, suppressed sexuality, an antiheroic worldview, involvement of important screwball comedy people, and the overlapping time periods (1930s and 1940s) with which both genres are so heavily associated [145–146].

Noir, he concludes, is apparently the "dark side" of screwball's lighter fare. Fortunately for me, Gehring's observations were limited to these few generalizations. My intention was to compare much more detailed aspects of the two genres.

There are arguments as to whether screwball comedy and film noir are actually genres, whether the one is simply the offshoot of romantic comedy and the other is a stylistic movement confined to a specific time frame. In one respect, screwball and noir appear to be genres: they have distinct, definable conventions that can still be reproduced today by current filmmakers. Yet in another respect, because modern contexts and attitudes impose themselves on the films so that content and purpose must be different from those of the classical era, screwball and noir of the 1930s through the 1950s cannot be recreated exactly. At that time, certain social, political, and cultural events gave rise to these two genres that reflect the attitudes of this particular period, and without the intersection of those identical circumstances, modern replicas of those films can never be made or viewed again in quite the same way.

The chapters that follow focus on the classical periods of screwball comedy and film noir, approximately 1930 to 1960, the epoch that shaped and defined these two genres. We will look at aspects of the historical contexts that spawned them, justify the films' designation as genres, and compare the filmmaking techniques and elements that link them so closely together and verify their affiliation as two distinct yet complementary forms of film.

1

Toward Definitions of Screwball Comedy and Film Noir

According to the philosophical principle of yin yang, the natural world is comprised of a system of interconnected forces, one force necessarily giving rise to an opposite and equal force. Yang, the male principle, embodies such things as heat, light, and dominance, while yin, the female principle, is associated with opposing concepts of cold, darkness, and submission. In the early- and mid–20th century, two particular film genres emerged which seem, because of their sequential appearance, to follow the yin yang principle. Screwball comedy, according to film historians, was "officially" born in 1934, followed shortly thereafter by film noir in 1941—although cinematic precursors in both categories blur the specificity of those years. (Calling screwball and noir "genres" requires some justification, which is discussed in Chapter 3.) At first glance, screwball and noir appear to be two radically different genres that have nothing to do with each other: after all, one is frothy romantic comedy while the other is grim crime drama. It is, however, this very antithetical tone and content which connects them, and if we compare the two genres more closely, we see that the light comedies have an ironic kinship with their darker counterpart, anticipating similar images, motifs, and characterizations: the clever, self-confident woman in screwball is a forerunner of noir's dangerous, self-serving seductress; the screwball male, destined to mate with the charming female, is confounded by fate as often as the doomed noir protagonist (even if he enjoys a more favorable outcome); and the sarcastic humor in screwball contains an undercurrent of cynicism that becomes more pronounced in the despondent tone of film noir.

Before discussing the ironic parallels, we should consider possible definitions of screwball comedy and film noir, a difficult task that, nonetheless, needs addressing. Although both genres display certain standard conventions that enable us to classify individual films in their respective categories, trying to construct neatly worded definitions that encompass all facets of every screwball comedy and all facets of every film noir is like trying to pour sawdust through a straw—stray particles inevitably run over the side, failing to flow neatly into the conduit.

Ever since screwball was identified as a hybrid of the romantic comedy and noir was designated an offshoot of the crime film, attempts to define their specific qualities have met with only partial success—definitions may catalog certain conventions that distinguish these two genres, but they have difficulty allowing for the many anomalies to which these genres are susceptible. When Raymond Durgnat writes his seminal "Paint It Black: The Family Tree of the *Film Noir*" (1970), dividing noirs into 11 main categories, each containing various sub-categories, he is in effect proving the difficulty of restricting the genre to one precise definition. And the same is true of screwball comedy. Most definitions successfully capture the general nature of these genres, but no single definition can encompass all of the variations and cram them satisfactorily under one neatly prescribed label.

Film historian Lewis Jacobs offered one of the first attempts to define screwball in its earliest years. Referring to films made between 1934 and 1938, he observed a trend in certain romantic comedies:

> The loss of credibility in former values, the breakdown of the smugness and self-confidence of the jazz era, the growing bewilderment and dissatisfaction in a "crazy" world that does not make sense, has been reflected in the revival of comedies of satire and self-ridicule.
>
> "Daffy" comedies became the fashion. Here the genteel tradition is "knocked for a loop": heroes and heroines are neither ladylike and gentlemanly. They hit each other, throw each other down, mock each other, play with each other.... [These films] lampooned the dignified and accepted. These films were all sophisticated, mature, full of violence—hitting, falling, throwing, acrobatics—bright dialogue, slapstick action—all imbued with terrific energy.
>
> In these films the rebel, the individualist, is once more respected. The artist, the eccentric, the unaccountable, who was once a poor and lazy good-for-nothing in films, now is the sane person in a chaotic world... [535–536].

When Jacobs wrote this, he had viewed but a handful of the earliest screwballs, among them *It Happened One Night, Twentieth Century, My Man Godfrey,* and *Theodora Goes Wild.* Yet he manages to identify some of the key elements found in the screwball genre: daffiness, eccentricity, self-deprecation, satire, and physical and verbal battles between the sexes.

Noted film analyst and critic Andrew Sarris, reacting in large part to Jacobs's observations about screwball comedy, offers some insights of his own in his monumental opus *You Ain't Heard Nothin' Yet.* He states that "the thirties, more than any decade before or since, transformed the star system into the co-star system" (93). He refers to the fact that screwball, as a kind of romantic comedy, depends on two equal adversaries, a man and a woman, locked in a love-hate relationship, the traditional battle of the sexes: "An inordinately large proportion of movies made in America has

It Happened One Night (1934, Columbia; Frank Capra, director)—Peter Warne (Clark Gable) and Ellie Andrews (Claudette Colbert) create the prototype of the screwball couple. The carrot that Warne carelessly pares becomes a symbol of humility for Ellie, for she will reach the point of desperation to where, despite her highbrow tastes that prefer to have carrots cooked, she gives in and eats them raw.

dealt with issues arising during the periods of courtship and early marriage in the lives of extraordinarily photogenic men and women. This is particularly true of screwball comedies, each of which is based scrupulously on male and female polarities" (93).

In citing Richard Griffith and Arthur Mayer, co-authors of the pictorial book *The Movies*, Sarris appreciates that, with the screwball comedy, they "at least acknowledge courtship and marriage as the dominant narrative elements, and their correlation of slapstick and violence with frustration." (94). These elements, too, are critical to the genre, and Sarris goes on to identify what becomes one of the central conflicts in screwball comedy:

> What then is the source of "frustration" in the screwball comedies? I would suggest that this frustration arises inevitably from a situation in which the censors have removed the sex from sex comedies. Here we have all these beautiful people with nothing to do. Let us invent some substitutes for sex. The aforementioned wisecracks multiply beyond measure, and when the audience tires of verbal sublimation, the performers do somersaults and pratfalls and funny faces.... From 1934 on it does not matter whether the couple is married or not: the act and fact of sex are verboten. The nice naughtiness which characterized such early thirties comedies as *Laughter* (1930) and *Trouble in Paradise* (1932) ... were supplanted by the subterfuges of screwballism [95].

Sarris later will concisely describe screwball as "a self-contradictory genre, the sex comedy without the sex," a phrase that singles out one of the core ingredients of the genre. However, he is sparing in identifying additional trademarks of these films:

> There are a few constants for screwball comedy. First, children almost never exist, and babies absolutely never.... *The Thin Man* notwithstanding, the great majority of screwball comedies save marriage for the final fadeout or even beyond. Screwball comedies are therefore generally comedies of courtship.
> Howard Hawks ... stuck with the primal man-woman struggle throughout his career, and his comedies remain the most audacious in examining the possibilities of role-reversal and sexual metaphor [two elements which appear in many screwball films]....
> But if we are to isolate one factor above all others it would have to be the presence in Hollywood at one time of an incredible assortment of gifted comediennes with a variety of trick voices, insinuating mannerisms, and unearthly beauty. There was Irene Dunne ... Jean Arthur ... Myrna Loy ... Barbara Stanwyck, and ... Rosalind Russell ... [along with] Ginger Rogers and Katharine Hepburn [97, 98].

For all this, Sarris admits that "it remains difficult to establish hard and fast boundaries for the genre" (98). When one of our hallowed pundits is willing to make this confession, we have to appreciate the challenge of trying to confine screwball comedy within precise parameters. One of the reasons is that every critic emphasizes certain criteria over others, which in turn affects his or her definition. Even here, Sarris's firm dictum that "children almost never exist, and babies absolutely never" may fit most screwball comedies, but it is a generalization that meets with frequent exceptions: *My Favorite Wife, And So They Were Married,* and *The Impatient Years* involve children of the combative couple; and babies contribute to the complications in *Bachelor Mother, Christmas in Connecticut, Theodora Goes Wild,* and *The Miracle of Morgan's Creek.* There are those films, too, where a dog serves as the surrogate child, such as in *The Awful Truth* and *Theodora Goes Wild*—and in *The Thin Man* where the canine Asta plays the Charles' offspring until the human one appears later in the series (as Sarris notes).

One author who has made a lifelong study of the genre has an inventive approach to a definition. Wes D. Gehring sees the genre in the context of the evolution of American comedy, particularly in the way the protagonist presents himself and in the way the audience perceives him. He proposes that early American humor was the province of the "homespun philosopher" or the "rustic wiseman" (*Screwball Comedy* 15). This character, called a "cracker-barrel philosopher," gradually gave way in the 20th century to a new kind of comic antihero who exhibited specific traits while situating himself at the heart of screwball comedies: "This antihero is characterized by his abundant leisure time, childlike nature, urban life, apolitical outlook, and basic frustration (especially in relationships with women)" (15). Gehring implies that these five traits, some or all of which are found in the central character (primarily the male but often applicable to the romantically entangled couple), encapsulate the essence of screwball comedy. It is noteworthy that he is attributing to the character(s) some of the traits that both Jacobs and Sarris apply to screwball in general, particularly the "eccentric" nature of the characters, their frequent "childlike" behavior, and the general "frustration" felt especially in romantic relationships. By extension, the dominant traits of the comic antihero actually delineate the main elements of screwball comedy. Thus, Gehring's focus on the male protagonist works fairly well to explain most of what comprises screwball plots as a whole. (In treating this subject in his book *Romantic vs. Screwball Comedy,* Gehring drops "urban lifestyle" and "apolitical outlook" in favor of two other criteria, "physical comedy" and "a proclivity for parody and satire." The two original characteristics contribute satisfactorily to the definition of the genre; why he chose to supplant them instead of merely adding the new aspects to his updated analysis is not clear.)

Another leading writer on screwball comedy lists a number of general characteristics of the genre. Ed Sikov begins with an imaginative prelude to a definition, discussing how the word "screwball" entered the English lexicon, how it referred to "an erratic pitch that is produced in an elaborate and deliberate way ... the point of the pitch is that the batter is supposed to be confused" (*Screwball* 19). Further, "the word *screwball* entered the language in the 1930s not only to describe a baseball pitch, but also as an adjective meaning insane or eccentric and as a nominal term for lunatic ... [and it] brought together a number of connotations in a single slang and streetwise term: lunacy, speed, unpredictability, unconventionality, giddiness, drunkenness, flight, and adversarial sport" (19). Clearly, this list of connotations applies to the essence of screwball comedies as well.

Sikov expands on these attributes. He notes that "one of the qualities that distinguish screwball comedy is a sense of confusion about romance and human relations usually expressed by verbal and sometimes physical sparring" (19). The tempo of these films is often "fast-paced, contentious" (20) and the dialogue shows "cleverness and technical dexterity" (24). Sikov states that the romantically paired male and female, copied from characters drawn by the likes of Noel Coward, are "battling, strong-willed couples whose wrangling was the very essence of their love" (24–25). One basis for the wrangling is that "the heroine's relative independence is countered all too often by punishing, resentful heroes whose punching fists, spanking palms, and generally threatening mouths serve as the forces of masculine reaction" (28). In respect to setting, "One of the most striking features of screwball comedies is that so many of them are set in New York, the city that not only epitomized the sophistication of urban America, but had also served as the stomping ground of many screwball scriptwriters" (23). Screwball often displays a "visual clash between good taste and bad manners" in "a world of rampant conflict, an uneasy social vision that fills the gap between lofty goals (love and marriage) and warped reality (love and marriage)" (28). Screwball couples are sandwiched between sex and society so that their "antic adventures make fun of a greater cultural distress. Although their discontents are often masked by charm, screwball couples reflect a sense of literal disease, inner turmoil that is often made physical in manic gestures and attitudes" (28).

We see that many of screwball's qualities singled out by Sikov iterate those proposed in others' definitions. He especially reinforces the notion that the "battling" and "wrangling" between the two romantically paired lovers are symptoms of displaced love, symbolic acts that make the screwball genre a "sex comedy without the [explicit] sex."

John Belton in *American Cinema/American Culture* also provides a definition that generalizes screwball's main features, many of which have already been noted:

> Various strains and styles of comedy [of the 1930s] found their way into a single hybrid form, known as the screwball comedy. The screwball comedy combined high comedy, such as romantic comedy and comedy of manners, with low slapstick comedy. It does not rely on clowns who looked funny, wore comic costumes, or possessed a recognizable comic persona. Instead, it took romantic leading men and women such as Irene Dunne, Katharine Hepburn, John Barrymore, and Cary Grant, who had established themselves in serious drama, and plunged them into the madcap world of vulgar slapstick routines [180].

Interesting is the fact that Belton echoes Andrew Sarris by anchoring his definition of screwball with a roster of key players who keep reappearing in these comedies, as if a few popular actors put a familiar face on the genre. This consideration is not unique to Belton and Sarris. Gehring and Sikov also devote some discussion to the recurring presence of specific actors who are associated with the genre and give it its identity.

Besides the actors, there are other key film personnel who contributed substantially to defining the genre. Prominent directors such as Howard Hawks, W. S. Van Dyke, George Cukor, Mitchell Leisen, and Preston Sturges, along with outstanding writers such as Ben Hecht, Billy Wilder, Charles Lederer, and Charles Brackett, imbued the screwball films of the thirties and forties with qualities that were consistent and recognizable.

Screwball comedy experienced its classical period during those years when the Motion Picture Production Code of 1934 had pervasive influence over film content, most specifically its sexual innuendoes. With that in mind, Andrew Sarris gives screwball only a brief shelf life, between 1934 and perhaps 1939. However, writers like Gehring and Sikov flirt with later dates. In *Screwball Comedy: A Genre of Madcap Romance,* Gehring ends screwball's classical cycle with Capra's *Arsenic and Old Lace* in 1944 (a comic farce that is debatably screwball) and then lists a number of "Notable Post-1944 Screwball Comedies," taking us from the late forties and into the eighties. Subsequent to this book, Gehring, six years later, published *Romantic vs. Screwball Comedy,* in which he makes a case for later screwball comedies produced into the 21st century and starring the likes of Sandra Bullock, Hugh Grant, Meg Ryan, Tom Hanks, and Julia Roberts. The modern films he selects continue the screwball tradition, but time and the obsolescence of the MPPC of 1934 have changed the dynamics and ethos in these films, so that even if they are direct descendants of screwball, they have evolved into different entities from their predecessors.

There are two films that, depending on how they fit into the cycle, may arguably represent the swan song of the classical screwball era: Preston Sturges's 1948 *Unfaithfully Yours* and Howard Hawks's 1952 *Monkey Business.* In a similar way that Welles's *Touch of Evil* signals the climactic end of noir's classical period (the flawed and ignoble Sheriff Quinlan devolving from the flawed but noble hardboiled detective), both screwball films, in different ways, take their genre to the furthest limits of its established conventions. *Unfaithfully Yours* has the battle of the sexes escalating into an extreme emotional conflict: a jealous husband (Rex Harrison) imagines the possible outcomes in three successive fantasies: how he might murder his wife (Linda Darnell) and frame her lover (Kurt Kreuger) for the crime; how he might divorce her in a flourish of magnanimous self-pity; and finally how he might kill himself with a display of flippant bravado. Inspired by these daydreams, he tries unsuccessfully—and absurdly—to carry out each scenario, yet threatening to negate the comedy and turn the film into a noir crime drama. Symbolically, *Unfaithfully Yours*, with its potential to transition from comedy to tragedy, suggests that screwball has been pushed to its limits and cannot go any further without destroying itself.

At the same time, a case can be made for *Monkey Business* as the last of the classical screwball comedies. The two screwball lovers (Cary Grant and Ginger Rogers, definitive actors of the screwball genre) have aged and mellowed into a dignified, sedate married couple. Grant plays a scientist whose lab monkey accidentally concocts an elixir that acts like the fountain of youth. The couple, after inadvertently drinking it, reverts to their younger, less inhibited selves in which state they resume their childish battle of the sexes. That is, the screwball couple can no longer behave like the classical screwball couple without help from science, and even that is a one-time accident that cannot be recreated. So the former vivacious, dynamic screwball couple represents what most (all?) married couples are doomed to become—contented, tolerant, stodgy, and inert.

Although *Unfaithfully Yours* is a valid choice to close screwball comedy's classical period—after all, it is written and directed by a major director who crafted six key films that defined the genre—*Monkey Business*—also the product of a major director who helped to establish screwball—deserves precedence. Like noir's Captain Quinlan, an old, fat, and jaded character who has outlived his welcome, the staid married couple represents all the aged screwball characters who have matured and moved beyond their former reckless and riotous selves to become model members of conventional society.

However, there is still a third rationale for determining what marks the end of the classical screwball period—and this may work best because it is less arbitrary and offers a definite sign of closure. With the initiation of the MPPC of 1934 was born the Production Code Administration (PCA), the Code's judicial and enforcement mechanism headed by Joseph I. Breen. Breen was the heart and soul of the PCA. He was notorious for running his office with an authoritarian style that dictated how films were to be handled, which of them contained objectionable scenes that needed slashing, and which of them had improper scripts that needed revision. After 20 years as the conscience of the film industry, he retired in 1954 and was replaced by Geoffrey Shurlock, who showed more flexibility and tolerance than his predecessor. This date then, 1954, seems the logical cut-off date for classic screwball because it ends that first era of the Code when censorship was strictest and when one man defined the spirit and policies of that enforcement agency.

Around 1954 and shortly thereafter, a number of events occurred to change the public's attitude toward censorship. In 1952, the U.S. Supreme Court ruled in the case of *Joseph Burstyn, Inc. v. Wilson*, in what became notoriously known as the "Miracle Decision," that motion pictures were protected under the First Amendment, and that the New York Board of Regents had no legal right to prevent the screening of Rossellini's *The Miracle* (1948, a segment from *L'amore*). This encouraged the importation of more foreign films to America, films which ignored the guidelines of the PCA. Swedish films were especially incendiary because they often included nude love scenes.

Television was already competing with feature films as a mode of popular entertainment, and filmmakers tried to overshadow the new medium by making their fare more distinctive. One of the ways to do this was to include provocative subjects and dialogue forbidden on the smaller screen. Several films directed by Otto Preminger violated the MPPC outright, yet even without the Production Code seal of approval, the movies earned a profit. *The Moon Is Blue* (1953) included the verboten words "virgin," "seduce," and "mistress"; *The Man with the Golden Arm* (1955) was a graphically morbid study of the proscribed theme of drug abuse; and *Anatomy of a Murder* (1959), while dealing with the unmentionable subject of rape, mentioned the word "panties" in the dialogue. When these and other films achieved commercial success in the face of protests from the Legion of Decency, that august body lost its bite.

Any comedy produced between 1934 and 1954, during Joseph I. Breen's 20 year tenure, may be classified as screwball comedy if it meets most of the following criteria cited by the several film analysts previously noted.

Battle of the Sexes Motif—The main characters are always a man and woman, married or not, whose relationship or interaction depends on a rivalry (*There's Always a Woman, Adam's Rib*), mutual dislike (*It Happened One Night, The Bride Came C.O.D.*), running argument (*I Love You Again, The Ex-Mrs. Bradford*), common but tempestuous history (*Mr. & Mrs. Smith, His Girl Friday*), or some misunderstanding or hidden truth that alienates the couple and delays their final union (*Christmas in Connecticut, The Whole Town's Talking*). This friction should be a central, if not *the* central, element in the story. Physical altercation often occurs, whether explicitly executed (*The Footloose Heiress, Nothing Sacred*) or implied as a threat (*It Happened One Night, The Thin Man*), and verbal sparring abounds (*Twentieth Century, Theodora Goes Wild, His Girl Friday*).

Convoluted Plot—The plot usually contains a considerable degree of complexity and confusion. The story takes some peculiar turns that make the exact direction of the narrative unpredictable, even when the final outcome, marriage or reconciliation between the two lovers, is obvious from the beginning. Despite all the battling and bickering throughout the story, the warring couple must, in the end, achieve some form or semblance of resolution, even if it is implied that their battling will continue beyond the final frame of the film.

Eccentric Characters—The story showcases characters who exhibit odd, outlandish, or quirky behavior. These characters can be one or both of the screwball lovers, who may show bizarre traits all the way through the story (*Twentieth Century, Bringing Up Baby*) or only at appropriate moments (*My Man Godfrey, Mr. & Mrs. Smith, Theodora Goes Wild*), or they can be from among the supporting characters (Roscoe Karns as Oscar Shapeley in *It Happened One Night*, Luis Alberni as Mr. Louis Louis in *Easy Living*).

Romantic Triangles—Nearly all screwball comedies rely on the eternal triangle to add another dimension to the conflict, complicate the plot, and delay the ultimate uniting of the two lovers. This third party, as an alternative love interest for the male or female protagonist, acts like a foil to the first love interest, calling for a comparison between the right and wrong choices a person can make in choosing a life-long partner.

Very often the story begins with a man and woman already engaged to be married when the new lover enters and, intentionally or not, breaks up that union and replaces the fiancé or fiancée. *Bringing Up Baby, The More the Merrier, Christmas in Connecticut, Vivacious Lady, The Footloose Heiress, The Major and the Minor,* and *The Bride Came C.O.D.* are some examples. Sometimes a third party enters the lives of two people who are or have been married, but are now estranged or divorced. That new arrival may either pose obstacles to their eventual reconciliation, or actually become the new spouse. In *It Happened One Night* and *Theodora Goes Wild,* the interloper replaces the previous lover. In *The Awful Truth, The Palm Beach Story, Mr. & Mrs. Smith,* and *The Philadelphia Story,* the battling couples, in their process of reconciling, manage to ease the unsuitable third party out of the running. *My Favorite Wife* and *Too Many Husbands* fit both the pre- and post-marital situations. A unique situation occurs in *Design for Living,* a 1933 pre-screwball directed by Ernst Lubitsch. A woman (Miriam Hopkins) falls in love with two male friends (Gary Cooper, Fredric March) who do not let their attraction for the lady interfere with their friendship. The result is an eternal triangle based on mutual acceptance of the unorthodox relationship.

City Rat Race vs. Country Retreat—Screwball protagonists are products of the modern metropolis. Their lives and routines are governed by the stone and steel monolith where they work, that beehive of law offices, brokerage firms, banking organizations, investment companies, and newspaper industries. As Gehring points out, the comic antihero adheres to an urban lifestyle. This is generally true, but screwball plots often imply, if only cursorily, that the city can stifle a relationship, while the country can nurture it. There are many examples where circumstances lead the screwball couple out of the city, whether briefly or for an extended length of time, as if, for them to discover their love for the first time or to reclaim a love that they thought was lost, they must interact within a curative, invigorating environment to give their inhibitions a chance to dissolve, their pent-up hostilities a chance to dissipate. The rural (or any non-urban) locale in screwball has the effect of the pastoral setting in Shakespeare, such as the Forest of Arden or the woodland in *A Midsummer Night's Dream*, in which the characters can escape the rigid strictures of the urban center and open themselves up to unlimited intimate possibilities in their new surroundings. *It Happened One Night, Christmas in Connecticut, Next Time I Marry,* and *Theodora Goes Wild* show what happens when two potential lovers spend considerable time away from their calcified urban routine. A shorter hiatus occurs in *Tell It to the Judge, Mr. & Mrs. Smith, My Favorite Wife,* and *Adam's Rib,* but the outcome is the same: love is restored. An interesting variation occurs in *Topper,* in which George and Marion Kerby are killed while driving along a country road. On one hand, the suggestion is that they are safer living their reckless and carefree lives in the city. On the other hand, their death not only enables them to continue their eccentric lifestyle, but it also gives them more options for doing mischief.

His Girl Friday is one exception where a contrast between city and country is not an obvious issue, but even here, Hildy (Rosalind Russell) rejects a marriage that will take her from her fast-paced journalistic life in the big city (New York) to a more sedentary life in a provincial locale (Albany). *The Talk of the Town* and *Unfaithfully Yours* are additional examples of screwballs that sidestep the city-country theme. *The Thin Man* series focuses on events in the city until the last entry, *The Thin Man Goes Home* (1944), which takes Nick and Nora back to his small-town roots.

Sexual Innuendoes—References to sex or sexual activity either through innuendo (Irene inviting Godfrey to sit on her bed in *My Man Godfrey*), wordplay ("sexagenarian" in *The Thin Man;* de Carter's "little wand" in *Unfaithfully Yours*), symbolism (the Walls of Jericho in *It Happened One Night*), or explicit discussion (Trudy Kockenlocker's premarital pregnancy in *The Miracle of Morgan's Creek*) represent screwball's attempt to flout the Production Code of 1934. In the 1930s and '40s, society was more compliant with the Puritanical rules governing conduct and propriety than it is in the modern era. Films like *Design for Living* and *The Miracle of Morgan's Creek* provoked more controversial reaction when they appeared back then than if they were produced today. Because the social context has changed, modern screwball comedies cannot recapture the mystique they once had, although many later comedies, such as *When Harry Met Sally* (1989) and *You've Got Mail* (1998), with battling lovers struggling through their intricate plots, contain remnants of the former screwball formula.

Sexual consummation of a marriage or relationship often becomes a running gag in screwball comedy. Even while the MPPC of 1934 discouraged allusions to sexual activity—thus the necessity for twin beds and the one-foot-on-the-floor rule—screwball comedies delayed the consummation

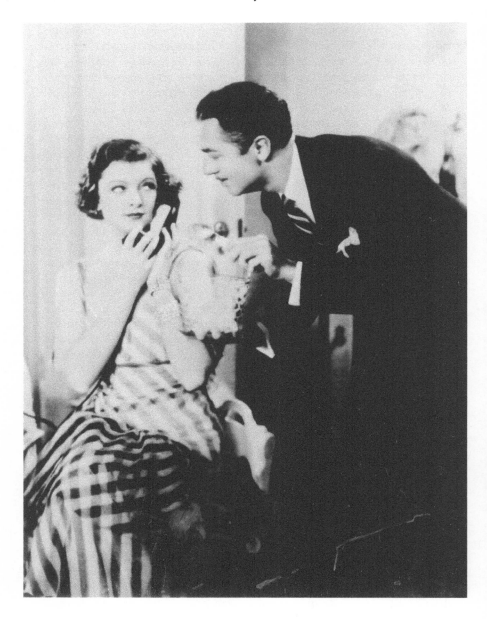

The Thin Man **(1934, MGM; W.S. Van Dyke II, director)—Although he proves himself a sleuth with exceptional skills for solving a crime, Nick Charles (William Powell) is seldom far from a drink and an ice bucket as he prepares a libation for his wife, Nora (Myrna Loy).**

to remind the audience of the lovers' primary objective and to create situations for humorous effect. In *Vivacious Lady,* for instance, James Stewart and Ginger Rogers take a train to Stewart's college in Old Sharon and are forced to sleep in the public lounge on their wedding night. Once they get to Old Sharon, they have to live apart because Stewart needs time to break the news gently to his former fiancée and his parents. In Rogers's apartment, the Murphy bed, whimsically called Walter, is prone to falling out of the wall when least expected, and this unpredictability melds humor with suspense. In *Next Time I Marry,* Lucille Ball pays James Ellison to marry her in order to fulfill a requirement for her inheritance. The business arrangement precludes any romantic entanglements, but Ellison abducts her, and even though they are married and travel together, consummation is suspended indefinitely. In *It Happened One Night,* there are the auto camps where Clark Gable and Claudette Colbert, though unmarried, register as husband and wife. In one scene, they sleep in a field of haystacks, and at two particular moments, they nearly kiss as they become conscious of their attraction to each other. These are sexually charged scenes that tease the viewer and prudently delay the consummation that comes in the final scene when marriage entitles them to the proper union.

Toward the end of the cycle, filmmakers assumed more liberties. Preston Sturges, for instance, manages to incite the audience and at the same time openly defy the Code in *Unfaithfully Yours.* In an early scene, Sir Alfred de Carter (Rex Harrison) and his wife, Daphne (Linda Darnell), retire to their bedroom behind closed doors while several of their associates loiter outside the room, waiting for them and *knowing* that the two are engaged in the connubial act. Inside the room, we see Daphne lying across a bed but with one foot on the floor to appease the Code's stricture on modesty. Yet shockingly, their discussion clearly implies that they have, in fact, just made love together. So much for complying with the do's and don'ts of the Code.

Film noir is as elusive as screwball comedy when it comes to wedging it within the strictures of a precise definition. As with screwball, noir definitions vary, although commonalities keep reappearing.

Nino Frank is credited with being among the first to apply the word "noir" when, in his seminal article "A New Kind of Police Drama: The Criminal Adventure" (1946), he discusses this particular kind of crime drama: "These 'noir' films no longer have any common ground with run-of-the-mill police dramas. Markedly psychological plots, violent or emotional action, have less impact [than] facial expressions, gestures, utterances—rendering the truth of the characters.... After films such as these the figures in the usual cop movie seem like mannequins.... Today's viewers are more responsive to this stamp of verisimilitude, of 'true to life'" (Silver and Ursini, *Film Noir Reader 2,* 18). Frank notices that these newer crime films deviate from earlier ones because of their added psychological dimension, the doubts that force the protagonist to undergo an ethical self-examination, a mental process that gives him greater depth and ambiguity than his gangster predecessors. What Frank is pointing out is perhaps one of the key elements of noir, the existential factor whereby the noir protagonist questions his motives and behavior and must reconcile them with his conscience: "The essential question is no longer 'who-done-it?' but how does this protagonist act" (Silver and Ursini, *Film Noir Reader 2*, 16).

Related to this internal strife of the noir protagonist is another key element highlighted by Nino Frank, namely, the narrative voiceover that is often imposed on these stories: "There is another, purely formal, change in expository style, the intervention of a narrator or commentator permits the fragmentation of the narrative, to quickly gloss over the traditional plot elements and to accentuate the 'true-to-life' side. It's clear that this method permits ... the insertion of a dynamic element into an otherwise static, psychological portrait" (Silver and Ursini, 18). The narrative voiceover is important for several reasons: it exposes the internal thought process of the narrator (who most frequently is the protagonist); it can enhance the pace of the story; and it reinforces the general disorientation faced by the protagonist and felt by the audience, especially when the narrative involves digressive flashbacks.

Raymond Borde and Etienne Chaumeton offer one of the earliest in-depth analyses of noir in their book *A Panorama of American Film Noir, 1941–1953*. Their intent is to examine those films classified as noir and to identify the common denominators. Their deliberate quest to define the genre concentrates on "the single emotional attitude all the works in the series tend to bring into play" (5).

First, they agree with Nino Frank's phrase that describes noir as "'the dynamism of violent death'.... Blackmail, informing, theft, or drug trafficking weave the plot of an adventure whose final stake is death" (5). They note that noir contains "all the ambiguity of a criminal milieu in which the power relationships continuously change" (8). This ambiguity applies to all the principal characters, the detective, the criminal, and the victim, and invites us to study "a psychology of crime" (7).

Another common thread running through these films: "In genuine film noir, strangeness is inseparable from what could be called the *uncertainty of the motives*" (11). The "emotional attitude" that Borde and Chaumeton set out to find is intertwined with the characters' ambiguities and this pervading strangeness, all of which create incoherence and confusion. These films obfuscate conventional logic and traditional expectations and assume an "oneiric quality specific to the series" (11), in turn producing a general disorientation for the audience. The authors' conclusion: "The moral ambivalence, criminal violence, and contradictory complexity of the situations and motives, all combine to give the public a shared feeling of anguish or insecurity.... All the works in this [noir] series exhibit a consistency of an emotional sort; *namely, the state of tension created in the spectators by the disappearance of the psychological bearings.* The vocation of film noir has been to create *a specific sense of malaise*" (13).

In *Film Noir: An Encyclopedic Reference to the American Style*, editors Alain Silver and Elizabeth Ward concede that these films share some commonalities, such as their taking place in a contemporary urban setting and their liberal borrowing of "visual conventions, iconic notations, or character types from other extrinsic sources" (3), but they also argue that film noir is not defined like other genres by conventional iconography. Rather, one salient feature found from noir to noir is the "cohesive visual style": "A side-lit close-up may reveal a face, half in shadow, half in light, at the precise narrative moment of indecision. A sustained moving camera may forge a link between characters or events simultaneously with a parallel narrative connection" (3). Like Nino Frank and Borde and Chaumeton, Silver and Ward single out character as the central common denominator for classifying noir: "The most consistent aspect of film noir, apart from its visual style, is its protagonist. If a usable definition of the noir protagonist is to be formulated, it must encompass two key character motifs. Of the two, alienation is perhaps the more intrinsic.... [There is also] the second key emotion in the noir universe: obsession" (3–4). Silver and Ward go on to show how these two qualities emanate from the noir protagonist in a way that affects all aspects of the noir world.

Foster Hirsch offers a comprehensive study of noir in *The Dark Side of the Screen: Film Noir.* Following Borde and Chaumeton, he notes many of the same identifying features related to the natures of the three principal characters, the "sleuth, the criminal, the middle-class victim and scapegoat" (13), and he discusses some of the devices, iconography, and themes that recur in noir. One mainstay is how all characters, whether morally upright or not, are subject to an indifferent fate that governs their actions and affects outcomes. As for iconography, Hirsch singles out the labyrinth as a key image embodying the "contradictory complexity of the situations and motives" mentioned by Borde and Chaumeton. He explains that the labyrinth frequently has not only a physical presence in the story, but also signifies the characters' psychological states of mind and the complexities of the plot. Related to the labyrinth is noir's primary setting of "the American big city ... its throbbing presence an integral part of the drama" (78). And convoluted flashbacks, usually associated with the voice-over, can contribute to a "jumbled time sequence ... [and] support the characterizations, which are also ... crooked rather than straight, devious rather than forthright" (74). Hirsch may iterate what others have said before, but he elaborates on their observations and clarifies them with additional explanations and a range of examples.

Hirsch is echoed, in large part, by Andrew Dickos who, in *Street with No Name*, itemizes "the paraphernalia of the nighttime noir milieu" (174)—nightclubs, empty offices, rain-washed streets, cigarettes, fedoras, trench coats, and so on. He goes on to explain the main purpose of the voice-over: "It functions as an aural 'remembrance of things past' in search of answers to an inscrutable present...." (177). And related to the voice-over is the flashback device, which "allows the noir protagonist to revisit the past and square the record with his or her perception of the truth in an attempt to make the present clear" (179). Dickos also discusses the peculiar nature of certain noir characters, the harried noir protagonist, the ambiguous hard-boiled detective, and the treacherous femme fatale.

The same criteria that define screwball comedy can be applied to the definition of film noir:

Conflict between the Noir Protagonist and Femme Fatale—Noir inverts screwball's "battle of the sexes": whereas screwball lovers begin their association in discord and gradually progress toward harmony, noir couples are often drawn together by a feverish infatuation that deteriorates into conflict. The "battle of the sexes," which in screwball comedy implies a comical confrontation between the male and female protagonists is, in noir, a serious, dangerous, and often fatal altercation. As in screwball, this conflict can take many different forms.

In *The Maltese Falcon*, for instance, Sam Spade (Humphrey Bogart) succumbs early to the allure of Brigid O'Shaughnessy (Mary Astor) and he allies himself with her in an effort to locate and attain the titular object. He quickly realizes, however, that she is a chronic liar, and their pursuit of the bejeweled rara avis becomes more of a competition between them. He obtains the falcon first, and in the end, after discovering that she is untrustworthy and dangerous, he wisely abandons her. In *Out of the Past*, Jeff Markham (Robert Mitchum) initially forsakes his professional ethics for femme fatale Kathie Moffat (Jane Greer) who exploits his gullibility for her own selfish purposes, and then betrays him when he outlives his usefulness; conversely, he also betrays her, an act that leads to both their deaths. In *Double Indemnity*, Walter Neff (Fred MacMurray) becomes obsessed with a married woman, Phyllis Dietrichson (Barbara Stanwyck). She infects him with her desire to murder her husband (Tom Powers), but once the crime is completed, fear and distrust cause their relationship to collapse, and each plots to break their pact by murdering the other. In *Scarlet Street*, naïve Chris Cross (Edward G. Robinson) believes he shares an ideal platonic relationship with Kitty March (Joan Bennett) when in fact she feigns admiration to siphon money out of him. The revelation of her deceit proves too devastating for his fragile ego, and in a vengeful jealous rage, he kills her and exiles himself into the city streets as a guilt-ridden pariah.

The Window (1949, RKO; Ted Tetzlaff, director)—Tommy Woodry (child-star Bobby Driscoll) tries to convince police detective Ross (Anthony Ross, standing) that he has seen a murder, but with his reputation as the boy who cried wolf, he has difficulty getting people to believe him. The film is based on Cornell Woolrich's short story "The Boy Who Cried Murder."

Convoluted Plot—Just like screwball, noir imposes a complex plot on its characters, with twists and turns that reflect their lost and confused state of mind. Noir protagonists often encounter a literal labyrinth of some sort to reinforce this abstract concept: winding streets and alleyways (*Phantom Lady, Night and the City*), angled walkways and stairways (*The Lady from Shanghai, Kiss Me Deadly*), long corridors (*Murder My Sweet, D.O.A.*). Peripheral characters, who are not what they seem to be or are not who they say they are, contribute to the surreal, oneiric quality of the protagonist's dilemma (Dr. Lilith Ritter in *Nightmare Alley;* the Kellersons in *The Window*).

Eccentric Characters—Like screwball, noir has its share of idiosyncratic characters, both main and minor. Odd behavior obviously reflects something of their personality, but it can also reveal something of their social class and point to key motifs in the story. For instance, Albuquerque newspaper editor Jacob Q. Boot (Porter Hall) in *Ace in the Hole* is a minor character who holds up his pants with a belt and suspenders and has a sampler on his office wall iterating his singularly all-important motto, "Tell the Truth." Charles Tatum (Kirk Douglas) is an unscrupulous, out-of-work reporter who, while tapping Boot for a job, recognizes these clues to the man's personality: "I'd never be so stupid as to lie to a man who wears both belt and suspenders.... You strike me as a cautious man, a man who checks and double checks." Tatum gets the job and, for a time, wears both belt and suspenders, but when he gets a chance to exploit a story, he cannot help reverting to his old devious ways. Dispensing with a cautious approach to the facts and distorting the truth to suit his purpose, he equivocates in his coverage of a story, trying to heighten the sensationalism, and he becomes responsible for a man's death and his own downfall. In *Scene of the Crime,* the police stoolie Sleeper (Norman Lloyd) has the habit of ending his spiel with a dry mock laugh, "Nyuk, nyuk." While this idiosyncrasy serves as his trademark, it also suggests how Sleeper, a traitor to his peers and pariah to the police, is a humorless joke.

Noir protagonists, subject to some degree of alienation from society, may exhibit traits of eccentricity that separate them from the mainstream population. Frank Bigelow (Edmond O'Brien in *D.O.A.*) ignores a commitment to his girlfriend (Paula Gibson) and plans a solo vacation in San Francisco where he expects to find excitement from fresh female companionship. It is not his immoral motives alone that suggest unconventional behavior but his juvenile manner and emotional giddiness as he anticipates his erotic spree and the women he will meet. When he arrives at his hotel and stands in the lobby, his head is on a swivel. Every time he ogles a pretty woman, an asynchronous simulated wolf whistle indicates his puerile state of mind and his depraved intentions. This sudden obsession that brought him to San Francisco is also the cause of his death, as it gives his murderer the opportunity to poison him.

The hardboiled detective usually displays some attitudinal idiosyncrasies that mark him as a loner, a law unto himself. Sam Spade (*The Maltese Falcon*), Jeff Bailey (*Out of the Past*), Philip Marlowe (*Murder My Sweet, The Big Sleep*), Mike Hammer (*Kiss Me Deadly*), and Captain Hank Quinlan (*Touch of Evil*) may get occasional help from an associate, but most of their success depends on their working independently. At times, marginal characters enter the story and bring with them an assortment of unusual quirks and mannerisms: Tommy Udo (Richard Widmark) in *Kiss of Death* has a snide, sadistic laugh; Dr. Soberin (Albert Dekker) in *Kiss Me Deadly* speaks with inflated literary jargon; Jefty Robbins (Richard Widmark) in *Road House* has a neurotic, frenetic edge to his mannerisms; Willard Gates (Laird Cregar) in *This Gun for Hire* gorges on mints and cringes when anyone talks of killing, even though he is the one who gives the orders to kill.

D.O.A. (1950, United Artists; Rudy Maté, director)—Frank Bigelow (Edmond O'Brien, left) approaches two men (Phillip Pine, center, and Ivan Triesault) about a photograph taken at their studio. The noir protagonist must often piece together scraps of information to learn how and why he became entangled in a strange predicament.

Romantic Triangles—Screwball comedy uses the eternal triangle to diversify the conflicts in the battle of the sexes. There is never a doubt as to which one of the three will be factored out of the equation and which two are destined to pair off and pursue their happiness together. That third party, if not overtly repellent, possesses some obnoxious trait—such as smugness or rigid intolerance—that discourages any feelings of pity we might have had for him or her. Meanwhile, the true lovers, even if idiosyncratic, display endearing qualities that enable us to sympathize with them and cheer for their ultimate union. The same dynamics occur with regularity in this three-cornered conflict, as is apparent, for example, in *Mr. & Mrs. Smith, My Favorite Wife, Bringing Up Baby, The Awful Truth,* and *The Bachelor and the Bobby-Soxer.*

Noirs invert and pervert screwball's treatment of the love triangle. In those noirs where a triangle exists, the third party usually enters to disrupt a stable relationship between two people who are already married or have a well-established affiliation. This introduces moral and ethical questions not broached in screwball: Is it wrong—or even a crime—for that third party to impose on that relationship? Or is it wrong for the man or woman already committed to a relationship to betray his or her partner and pursue an obsessive whim?

In screwball's *The Philadelphia Story*, C.K. Dexter Haven (Cary Grant), the ex-husband of Tracy Lord (Katharine Hepburn), interferes with her wedding to George Kittredge (John Howard), yet it is obvious that the publicity-hungry Kittredge is not as well suited for Tracy as Haven is, and so he becomes expendable and Haven gets to remarry his ex-wife. No one feels sorry for Kittredge and the Lord-Haven union seems fitting and right. The happy ending justifies both the breakup of the inappropriate pair and the reconciliation of the estranged couple.

Such a simple resolution is not possible in noir. There are always dire consequences. Ethical issues arise when someone violates the sanctity of a legitimate—if not thriving—relationship, whether that someone is already in the relationship and goes outside of it to seek excitement, or is outside the relationship and trespasses on the couple's realm. In *Angel Face*, Diane Tremayne (Jean Simmons) finagles her way into the life of Frank Jessup (Robert Mitchum), who yields to her seduction and deserts his longtime loyal girlfriend Mary Wilton (Mona Freeman). Diane's actions are suspect because of her selfish motives, and Frank's are dishonest because he lies to Mary, breaking dates so he can be with Diane. As their relationship becomes more intense and more complicated, Diane and Frank move closer to obliteration, the inevitable outcome. In *Double Indemnity*, Neff is the outsider who consorts with a married woman who wants to kill her husband. Phyllis Dietrichson may not be in an ideal marriage, but murder seems an extreme means of dissolving it. Neff is obsessed with her and she is obsessed with the money she can get from the insurance. Their deranged motives contribute to an unbalanced, unnatural relationship that eventually self-destructs. There are numerous noirs in which deviance and obsession are introduced into the lovers' triangle, producing tragic results. Among such films are *Where Danger Lives, Pitfall, Possessed, Murder My Sweet, Out of the Past, The Two Mrs. Carrolls, Nightmare Alley,* and *The Chase.*

City Rat Race vs. Country Retreat—Like their screwball counterparts, noir protagonists are generally rooted in an urban lifestyle that nurtures their street smarts and edgy attitudes. Yet for them, the city presents even greater negative implications. In screwball, characters are affected by the hectic pace that one must adopt while living their lives in a modern industrialized world. Life moves quickly, people talk rapidly, situations change faster than configurations in a kaleidoscope. In *Easy Living*, a fur coat falls from the sky into the lap of Mary Smith (Jean Arthur) and, in an instant, her life is completely transformed. In *Midnight*, penniless Eve Peabody

Deadline at Dawn (1945, RKO; Harold Clurman, director)—June Goth (exquisitely beautiful Susan Hayward) is a worldly-wise taxi dancer who overcomes her cynical outlook to help a troubled young sailor, Alex Winkley (Bill Williams).

(Claudette Colbert) stumbles into a bridge game with rich aristocrats and her life takes a sudden and unpredictable turn. Yes, the city may complicate matters for screwball characters, but any obstacles it poses are momentary, often amusing, and eventually overcome.

Noir's urban environment has a more insidious and corrosive effect on its denizens. The noir city is an "asphalt or concrete jungle" where Darwin's natural laws freely apply—the struggle for survival, survival of the fittest. The city has little if any redeeming value, for it corrupts, undermines, and debilitates the people who contend there for the right to exist, let alone for the opportunity to succeed in a career and romance. In *Deadline at Dawn,* June Goth (Susan Hayward) is a young taxi dancer, older than her years, who comments on the city's demoralizing hopelessness: "This is New York, where hello means good-bye." She meets a sailor (Bill Williams), who is unwittingly implicated in a murder, and she offers to help him with the understanding that, if they can clear him of the crime, they will get themselves clear of the city together.

Many, if not most, films noirs generally begin with a high-angle establishing shot of the city—New York, San Francisco, Chicago—portending the impact the urban sprawl will have on events and on the characters and their aspirations. *Kiss of Death, Force of Evil, The Lady from Shanghai, The Maltese Falcon, Side Street,* and so on, all open with that panorama of skyscrapers rising majestically yet ominously toward the sky, foreshadowing a stark contrast between the grand view one sees from a distance and the harsh reality facing the inhabitants whose dreams will be ground into dust by the indifferent monolith.

In *The Sweet Smell of Success,* Sidney Falco (Tony Curtis) has the despicable job of defaming a young musician whose only crime is that he wants to marry the sister of powerful newspaper columnist J. J. Hunsecker (Burt Lancaster). Falco has adopted the philosophy that it is a dog-eat-dog world and he is willing to do whatever it takes to secure the power and money that Hunsecker promises him. In the end, he learns that, despite his calculated choices and best efforts, the city has sabotaged his ambitions even when they seemed like a sure thing.

Contrasting the city is the country which offers opportunities and freedoms not accessible in the urban fray. In *On Dangerous Ground,* a city-hardened cop (Robert Ryan) recovers his humanity when he trails a murder suspect to a farm and meets the man's sister (Ida Lupino) who, although physically blind, possesses a keen spiritual insight that helps him see himself more clearly. In *Out of the Past,* private detective Jeff Markham and femme fatale Kathie Moffat enjoy their most intimate, most liberated moments while hiding away in a cabin in the woods. The romance is short-lived, however, and Markham temporarily escapes his past when he adopts the alias Jeff Bailey, opens a gas station in a small quiet town, and courts a local beauty, innocent Ann Miller. His respite is interrupted when a henchman of his former employer passes through town, recognizes him, and pulls him back into his previous sordid routine. Implied is that no safe haven exists that is permanent and impervious enough to withstand attacks from life's insidious influences. This is a pervasive notion in noir and occurs in numerous films: *Kansas City Confidential, Road House, The Lady from Shanghai, Ace in the Hole, Shadow of a Doubt,* and *Cape Fear,* to name a few. Lawlessness and corruption, usually originating in the city, can invade and contaminate even the simplest and most idyllic of rustic places.

Sexual Innuendoes—Film noir and screwball comedy were subject to the same restrictions dictated by the Motion Picture Production Code of 1934. In some ways, noir trod a trickier path than screwball because its content included more of those situations and themes that fell into the MPPC's cautionary categories. Plus, noir treated these situations seriously, supposedly a more realistic reflection of life than screwball which, with its humorous spin, could extenuate a serious topic and make it appear light and droll. We find amusement in the scene in *Nothing Sacred* where Wally

Cook (Fredric March) punches Hazel Flagg (Carole Lombard) on the jaw, but we more likely cringe in horror when Vince Stone (Lee Marvin in *The Big Heat*) flings scalding hot water in the face of Debby Marsh (Gloria Grahame), leaving her scarred. The battle of the sexes takes on different tonal implications for the two genres.

Although many noirs make explicit references to sex, especially associating it with lascivious or perverted behavior (*Sunset Boulevard, The Blue Gardenia, Kiss Me Deadly*), they also practice screwball's more subtle approaches by using symbolism and verbal innuendo. Joel Cairo (Peter Lorre in *The Maltese Falcon*) carries a cane with a bent handle which he fondles while talking to Spade for the first time. When we learn of his artistic temperament and observe his effeminate mannerisms, the bent cane handle takes on more specific connotations. In the same film, Spade calls gun-toting Wilmer Cook (Elisha Cook, Jr.) a "gunsel" (a word which, incidentally, comes directly from Hammett's novel). On one level, the term means a gunman, but it can also refer to a young boy who is exploited for

Fear in the Night (1947, Paramount; Maxwell Shane, director)—Holding the gun, Vince Grayson (DeForest Kelley) thinks he controls the situation, but hypnotist Lewis Belknap (Robert Emmett Keane) knows that he holds the greater power because he can control Vince's mind.

sexual purposes. This double meaning gives multiple implications to the relationship between Wilmer and his employer, Kasper Gutman (Sydney Greenstreet). In *Fear in the Night,* Vince Grayson (DeForest Kelley) wakes from a nightmare in which he killed a stranger, and he fears he might have done so in reality. Plagued by doubt, he visits his brother-in-law Cliff Herlihy (Paul Kelly), a police detective. He stays the night, and in one scene, Cliff enters Vince's bedroom, and the dialogue, positions, and movements of the characters give the impression that there is some secret sexual collusion between the two men. This is reinforced in a final scene where Cliff pulls a drowning Vince from the water, and while trying to resuscitate him, he performs actions that carry strong homosexual connotations.

It is ironic that these story elements that connect screwball comedy with film noir are antithetical in nature, as if noir emerged to counteract screwball's facetious treatment of the subject matter. Instead of following screwball's formula of moving from enmity to marriage, noir inverts the progress of the screwball couple's relationship, taking them from intense passion to divisive animosity. Intricate plot lines are common in both genres: in screwball, complexity adds to the farce and humor of the situation; in noir, it augments an already complicated intrigue and signifies the fateful circumstances from which characters cannot easily extricate themselves. Duplicity and disguise also occur frequently in the two genres, but whereas screwball uses them to complicate and enhance the comedy, noir uses them as devices for self-serving treachery and fraud. Both screwball and noir are set primarily in modern urban locales to reflect the mores and attitudes of contemporary society and to show what effect city-living has on its inhabitants. Tonal shadings differ between the two genres: noir is overcast with shadow and gloom to intensify the inescapable fatalistic doom hovering over every individual; screwball, ostensibly lighter and more cheerful, uses wit and humor to offset its underlying cynicism. More detailed examination of these conventions appears in Chapter 4.

In Chapters 2 and 3, we will examine screwball comedy and film noir for their historical and generic origins. In the process, we will see to what extent they are connected despite their differences in tone and intention: the pessimistically dark and despair-laden mood of film noir acts as counterpoint to the playful, mischievous, and energetic spirit of screwball comedy.

2

Historical Context of Classical Screwball Comedy and Classical Film Noir

The conundrum posed by the chicken and the egg applies, in a way, to the connection between art and history: Do historical events precede and influence art, or does art precede and influence historical events? The likely answer is that they affect each other mutually. Art derives its subject matter from the world, and in turn, acts like a mirror on the world, reflecting literally and metaphorically the events, trends, and attitudes that define contemporary society. At the same time, by holding up that mirror to society, art forces society to look at itself, which can influence behavior and effect change. It is natural, then, that film, as one form of art, should serve this function. The first half of the 20th century was a tumultuous period in American history, and American cinema responded by reflecting the human condition associated with the times. Screwball comedy and film noir, emerging one after the other, were affected by many of the same historical events, which led to some ironic connections between the two genres despite their antithetical themes, tones and intentions.

Classical screwball, pigeonholed loosely between 1934 and 1954, shares a 14-year overlap with classical noir which critics generally slot between 1941 and 1960. Parallels between the comedies and films noirs suggest that, even though they treat their subject matter in different ways, the two genres at that time derive their ideas, plots, characterizations, and themes from similar cultural, social, economic, and political events—among them, the Great Depression, the post–Roaring Twenties era, the threat of war so soon after the armistice following World War I, women's increased incursions in the workforce, women's suffrage and independence movements, World

War II, Hiroshima, the growth of urban populations, and restraints on artistic license from the tougher Motion Picture Production Code of 1934.

Motion Picture Production Code of 1934

Film historians single out the Motion Picture Production Code of 1934 (MPPC) as one of the most significant influences on film content through the 1930s and 40s. Screwball comedy and film noir show direct signs of that influence.

The year 1934 was not the first time that the film industry attempted self-censorship in order to quell public outcry against its immoral and dissolute practices. Whenever the movie-going public seemed exceptionally unified in their vociferous disapproval of screen content, film producers worried about a shortfall in profits, and so they made an effort (or at least the pretense of one) to comply with the public's wishes. The first time the moral majority voiced a collective reprimand was in the years between 1907 and 1909 (Cook 34–35; Belton 11–12). Another short-lived reformation was revived in 1922 when more serious charges were brought against the industry because of a series of shocking scandals. The previous year, popular silent film comedian Roscoe "Fatty" Arbuckle was indicted in the death of actress Virginia Rappé. Allegedly, he had raped her and accidentally killed her by crushing her under his enormous bulk. After enduring three grueling and sensationalized trials, he was finally acquitted, but the notoriety destroyed his career (Mast 130–131; Cook 215). In 1922, two additional scandals broke. The public learned that matinee idol Wallace Reid was a drug addict (Mast 131; Cook 215–216). Early in 1922, William Desmond Taylor, a director with Famous Players-Lasky, who was also serving as president of the Screen Directors Guild, was mysteriously murdered. During the investigation, the tabloids discovered that he was associated with two women simultaneously. What may have been innocent friendships the tabloids turned into salacious entanglements. The result was that the careers of the two actresses, Mabel Normand (a frequent co-star with Arbuckle) and Mary Miles Minter, careened into oblivion (Mast 131; Cook 215). These shocking tragedies, compounded by stories of decadent, depraved lifestyles, gave the public cause to rage against Hollywood Babylon.

In 1922, the film industry opted for self-regulation with the formation of the Motion Picture Producers and Distributors Association (MPPDA). This organization gave the impression that self-censorship was motivated primarily by a genuine sense of ethics and right-thinking, when in fact it more likely "was to adjust the industrial and moral disputes amicably and thus forestall federal interference or federal censorship" (Jacobs 290). The MPPDA promptly recruited Will H. Hays as its first president. Postmaster General in Warren G. Harding's cabinet, Hays was a stalwart citizen with the credentials of a veritable saint, "an ultraconservative Republican, Mason, Kiwanian, Rotarian, and Presbyterian elder" (Cook 216). The MPPDA, more familiarly called the Hays Office, acted less as a stringent instrument of censorship than as a lobbying machine and public relations bureau for the film industry (Cook 216). Lewis Jacobs positions Will Hays as "the buffer between industry and the public" (291).

In the way of moral guidance, the Hays Office published a litany of "recommendations" called a "Purity Code" that was euphemistically termed the "Don'ts and Be Carefuls." However, the Code was summarily ignored; filmmakers held it in as much regard as a housefly, a pesky but harmless nuisance. Although the Hays Office was borne out of a need for self-censorship, its purpose was more "to stave off the threat of government censorship by mollifying pressure groups, managing news, deflecting scandal, and generally discouraging close scrutiny of the industry" (Cook 217).

The difference between the "Purity Code" of 1922 and the Motion Picture Production Code first drafted in 1930 is the degree to which they were enforced. The 1922 code was nothing more than a panacea for priggish protestors. When blatant sexual situations and risqué dialogue resurfaced in 1920s' films as infractions against the code, the public once again mounted a righteous attack. In 1930, a new code, the MPPC, was outlined by Father Daniel Lord, S. J., and Martin Quigley, a Catholic publisher of the *Motion Picture Herald* (Ellis 154). Despite the dictatorial Ten-Commandment tone of the code, the 12 main sections telling filmmakers what *not* to do lacked any leverage to force compliance, and as a result, transgressions against the toothless law were prevalent. In 1933, however, the "first large-scale, social-scientific studies of the effects of mass media on the social attitudes and behavior of audiences were published: the twelve-volume *Motion Pictures and Youth,* sponsored by the Payne Fund.... In 1934 Catholic forces, particularly unhappy about Hollywood flouting a Code drafted by two of their own, formed the Legion of Decency" (Ellis 154).

Roger Maltby mitigates the negative reputation of the MPPC, saying that, despite the Code's being "held responsible for the trivialization of American movies and blamed for Hollywood's timidity and lack of realism," it "contributed significantly to Hollywood's avoidance of contentious subject matter" and "was a determining force on the construction of narrative and the delineation of character in every studio-produced film after 1931" (38). What Maltby asserts is that the Code derived its power not from the Hays Office where it originated, but from the film industry itself that treated it as "the instrument of an agreed industry-wide policy..." (38). The industry was fearful of boycotts by morally conscious congregations, and consequently, the Legion of Decency, strongly endorsed by both Catholic and Jewish organizations, was able to wield some powerful influence. Hays established the Production Code Administration (PCA) and appointed as its first director Joseph I. Breen, a Catholic (Cook 282). The result was the creation of the Code seal, an imprimatur stamped on Hollywood's films, which without it were barred from distribution and exhibition. Since the members of the MPPDA included all the major studios, and consequently meant those studios controlling the greatest share of production, distribution, and exhibition of films, such a penalty had more clout. In addition, the MPPDA agreed to enforce a $25,000 penalty against anyone guilty of non-compliance with the Code.

In the Preamble of the Production Code, members of the MPPDA "recognize the high trust and confidence which have been placed in them by the people of the world.... They recognize their responsibility to the public because of this trust and because entertainment and art are important influences in the life of a nation.... They know that the motion picture within its own field of entertainment may be directly responsible for spiritual or moral progress, for higher types of social life, and for much correct thinking" (Phillips 386).

The Code goes on to cite guidelines for topics related to crime, sex, vulgarity, religion, and so on. The following contains excerpts from the Code's comments on specific issues that will later affect the way screwball comedies and films noirs are produced:

GENERAL PRINCIPLES
1. No picture shall be produced which will lower the moral standards of those who see it. Hence the sympathy of the audience shall never be thrown to the side of crime, wrongdoing, evil or sin....

I. CRIMES AGAINST THE LAW

These shall never be presented in such a way as to throw sympathy with the crime as against law and justice or to inspire others with a desire for imitation.
1. Murder
a) The technique of murder must be presented in a way that will not inspire imitation.
b) Brutal killings are not to be presented in detail.
c) Revenge in modern times shall not be justified....

II. SEX

The sanctity of the institution of marriage and the home shall be upheld. Pictures shall not infer that low forms of sex relationship are the accepted or common thing.
1. Adultery and illicit sex, sometimes necessary plot material, must not be explicitly treated or justified, or presented attractively.
2. Scenes of passion
a) These should not be introduced except where they are definitely essential to the plot.
b) Excessive and lustful kissing, lustful embraces, suggestive postures and gestures are not to be shown.
c) In general, passion should be treated in such manner as not to stimulate the lower and baser emotions.

3. Seduction or rape
    a) These should never be more than suggested, and then only when essential for the plot. They must never be shown by explicit method.
    b) They are never the proper subject for comedy.

    ....

6. Miscegenation (sex relationship between the white and black races) is forbidden [Phillips 386].

In addition, provisions for vulgarity urge filmmakers to cater to "the dictates of good taste." Obscenity is expressly forbidden, as is profanity, especially demeaning terms and ethnic slurs.

All of these issues have implications for screwball and noir. Yet many filmmakers refused to feel daunted or suppressed, and they responded to the Code like upstart teenagers dealing with strict authoritative parents: they pretended to adhere to its tenets while actually testing its limits, devising ingenious ways of circumventing it with innuendo and symbolism.

One idiosyncrasy of the Hays Office was its seemingly arbitrary and enigmatic way of enforcing the Code. In *Two-Faced Woman*, Greta Garbo tries to teach husband Melvyn Douglas a lesson by pretending to be her own twin sister. Originally, she was supposed to succeed in fooling him while he tried to seduce her, but the Hays Office insisted that he must know that she is actually his wife before he carried out his seduction. A scene was inserted to accommodate the censors (Douglas makes a phone call to verify his wife's true identity), but this greatly undercut what could have been some humorous irony for the story. And in Sturges's *Unfaithfully Yours*, Rex Harrison was originally supposed to go through a litany of sarcastic comments about the four wives he divorced before he married Linda Darnell. This diatribe was censored for its puns and insinuations. On the other hand, the censors allowed Sturges, in *The Miracle of Morgan's Creek*, to use the premise that a woman not only becomes pregnant from a one-night fling with a G.I., but that she can't even recall his name or what he looked like, only the blurred—and dubious—recollection that they had married. And McCarey's *The Awful Truth* was permitted to begin its story with a man telling his wife he had to go to California on business, when all the time he had remained in New York, using his few days of reclaimed bachelorhood to engage in whatever extramarital adventures our imaginations could conjure.

The caveats against overt sexual exploitation were a challenge to both screwball and noir, which incorporated imaginative symbolism to sidestep the constrictive parameters. To preserve the virginity of his female roommate in *It Happened One Night*, for instance, Peter Warne concocts the Walls of Jericho by hanging a blanket between their beds (symbolizing that her maidenhead remains intact); yet the "discreet" attempt to protect her

The Awful Truth (1937, Columbia; Leo McCarey, director)—Jerry Warriner (Cary Grant) assumes a position of dominance over his ex-wife Lucy (sophisticated Irene Dunne), but this is only a momentary triumph. In the battle of the sexes, the screwball couple take turns outdoing each other.

reputation calls attention to the very subject the Code wanted to keep hushed. There is also the scene in Ellie's bedroom when her father (Walter Connolly) sits next to her on her bed and tells her that his "pump isn't what it used to be." The remark plays on the ambiguity of the word "pump" to conjure up sexual suggestions, possibly with a wink at incestuous conduct.

David Huxley in *Bringing Up Baby* becomes ecstatic after losing and then finding his intercostal clavicle—a perfectly legitimate appendage for a dinosaur that takes on proscribed implications when referred to as Huxley's "bone." In *The Lady Eve*, Jean Harrington (Barbara Stanwyck) may quip as if she had the loose morals of a world-wise con artist, but her flippancy merely shields her more vulnerable nature, for she reveals a fear of losing her chastity when she runs screaming from Hopsie's (Henry Fonda) snake— that is, the less than subtle phallic symbol wriggling in his bed. And in addition to its suggestive title *Come Live with Me* is the scene in which Bill Smith (James Stewart) takes Johnny Jones (Hedy Lamarr's Americanized name for her Austrian character Johanna Janns) to his apartment thinking that she is a prostitute (although he thinks wrongly and never voices this thought aloud). As they exit their taxi, the car's radiator suddenly overheats and spews water and vapor into the air, the image connoting Bill Smith's anticipation of things to come.

Finding its stride soon after talkies became the standard of the industry, screwball comedy camouflaged its sexual subtext in the physical abuse and verbal tirades that the two lovers heaped on one another. "The restrictions of the Production Code and the demands of a new technology gave birth to new forms and figures of speech: to romantic comedies in which love was disguised as antagonism and sexual readiness as repartee" (Haskell 124). In *Nothing Sacred*, Wally Cook not only lands a love punch on Hazel Flagg's chin, but takes care that, when she falls, she lands comfortably on the double bed in her hotel suite. Later, Hazel returns the favor. In *His Girl Friday*, the glib, rapid-fire repartee between Walter Burns and Hildy Johnson suggests more about their personalities and their volatile relationship than do the words themselves.

Noir is just as replete with similar examples. Even from the first, noir filmmakers tested the strength of the Code. In *The Maltese Falcon*, at a time when homosexuality was viewed as abnormal, perverted, and deviant behavior, Joel Cairo, with his bent cane handle, gardenia perfume, and partiality for the theater, is earmarked as gay. In *Double Indemnity*, during Phyllis Dietrichson's first visit to Neff's apartment, the two lovers sit on the couch in an amorous embrace while the camera tracks back and then dissolves to the frame story in which the wounded Walter Neff is narrating his confession into a Dictaphone. After he winds up his soliloquy, the camera returns to the previous scene in Neff's apartment and tracks in to a complacent Neff smoking and lying on one side of the couch while Phyllis, sitting on the other, applies fresh make-up—the interval implies the tacit consummation of a sexual interlude while the narrator was confessing his dream of crooking the house. And also in filmdom's record of notable verbal exchanges is the scene in Hawks's *The Big Sleep* wherein Philip Marlowe and Vivian Rutledge trade double entendres in the guise of a horse-racing analogy.

The Big Sleep (1945, Warner Bros.; Howard Hawks, director)—Philip Marlowe (Humphrey Bogart) has reason to be worried about his dilemma, but he can depend on Mrs. Vivian Rutledge (Lauren Bacall), the Femme Blanche, to help him out of this tight situation.

Gruesome violence in early noirs is visually muted but often horrifically implied. In *The Maltese Falcon,* Wilmer kills at least two people, both shootings taking place off screen. In the murder scene in *Double Indemnity,* the camera stays focused on Phyllis's smug, gloating countenance the whole time that Neff is struggling to break Mr. Dietrichson's neck. And in *Murder, My Sweet,* the dreadful ordeal that Philip Marlowe endures at the hands of Jules Amthor is filtered through a surrealistic dream sequence. Later noirs take more liberties. In *Kiss Me Deadly* (1955), director Robert Aldrich blatantly depicts sadistic violence and viciousness in several scenes—detective Mike Hammer pounds a man's head against a brick wall then pushes him down a long stairway; Hammer crushes the medical examiner's hand in a drawer, making him squeal in pain. At other times, he brings us to the very brink of graphic violence before pulling back and only suggesting the ghastly, grisly brutality—we hear Christina's screams and see her bare legs dangling from a table while she is tortured; Hammer's friend Nick is crushed under a car.

By the time Welles directs *Touch of Evil* in 1958, it is evident that filmmakers have already stretched the envelope well past the Code's acceptable limits. In the scenes at Grande's motel in the remote countryside, we see Susie Vargas (Janet Leigh) strolling around her room in her brassiere and slip while being subjected to an intense level of sadistic psychological brutality (Leigh will reprise her exhibitionism two years later in Hitchcock's *Psycho*); and later, in a hotel room located in town, Quinlan (Welles) attacks and strangles Uncle Joe Grande (Akim Tamiroff) in a graphic murder scene that directly challenges the Code's dictum that "brutal killings are not to be presented in detail."

The kind of latitude that Welles and others were achieving in the later noir films, Preston Sturges had already enjoyed in his screwball comedies of the forties, such as *The Miracle of Morgan's Creek* (1944, unwed motherhood) and *Unfaithfully Yours* (1948, detailed planning of a murder—first treated seriously, then humorously). This is to say that, although Welles's film 24 years after the inception of the MPPC, seems to show how much latitude filmmakers were given by that time, the truth is that filmmakers rebelled against the Code right from the beginning. They dealt with prohibited controversial subjects, and even if they had to present them in a subtle, indirect way, they did not have to present them in a saccharine way. They invented means to express violent and sexually charged content despite the Code's ominous admonitions. Adherence to the Code was, from the very beginning, a pretense—film production had more to do with *how* the details were displayed on the screen than with *what kind* of content was actually included. Sex and violence were always prominent elements in these films, even where they were addressed more by suggestion and allusion than by overt presentation. What might be called an eventual shift or deviation from the strictures of the Code has more to do with graphic explicitness of certain situations and actions than with the essential subject matter that appeared in the films.

The Great Depression and Wealth-Consciousness

Another historical event having significant influence on screwball comedy and film noir is the Great Depression. In the first years after Black Tuesday, October 29, 1929, Hollywood seemed depression-proof: production thrived and audiences continued to frequent theaters. There was a brief slump between 1933 and 1934, but the industry quickly rebounded in production and attendance (Mast 273, 274). Most historians believe that film served a practical social purpose during these trying times: it provided a portal to new worlds where the masses could escape their mundane strife; where viewers could see people who, confronted with worse difficulties, were able to resolve their problems; where good conquered evil; where dreams came true; and where life played itself out just as it should, scripted with a satisfying, if not always happy, ending. As prima donna Lina Lamont (Jean Hagen) tells her audience in the finale of *Singin' in the Rain:* "If we bring a little joy into your humdrum lives, it makes us feel as though our hard work ain't been in vain for nothing." The musical was made in 1952, well after the depression years, yet it incisively captures the tenor of the movie industry while undergoing its transition from silent to sound films, and although Lisa Lamont speaks condescendingly, her words ironically voice what the movie industry must have assumed was its public service during that era.

To iterate this notion, Preston Sturges presents his 1941 satire, *Sullivan's Travels*. The dedication after the film's opening credits makes clear his intention:

> To the memory of those who made us laugh: the motley mountebanks, the clowns, the buffoons, in all times and in all nations, whose efforts have lightened our burden a little, this picture is affectionately dedicated.

The subsequent story demonstrates the significant contribution that comedy makes to society. Well-known director John L. Sullivan (Joel McCrea as Sturges's surrogate) has become disenchanted with producing only comedy films and aspires to make a great American drama that will call attention to society's ills and motivate people to correct them. He befriends "The Girl" (Veronica Lake) and, together, they dress in rags and live the life of tramps to experience firsthand the hardships facing the destitute. When the harsh living conditions become unbearable, they forsake their willful penury to reclaim their more prosperous state. Sullivan feels grateful for what the poor have taught him and he returns to the slums to give a handout to every indigent he meets. In an ironic turn of events, he gets waylaid by a thieving vagrant, who packs him into a boxcar. When Sullivan regains consciousness, he has an altercation with a railroad guard, gets arrested, and ends up on a chain gang. Living under the harshest conditions, he becomes extremely bitter, until he and his fellow prisoners are brought into a black gospel church where they view a Disney cartoon and he learns to laugh again. The experience awakens Sullivan's appreciation of humor's therapeutic qualities. He is able to escape his prison ordeal, and he returns to his studio, cured of his obsession to make a pretentious melodrama and intent on directing only comedies.

Films were themselves a reaction to and reflection of the attitudes, ideals, impulses, beliefs, and emotions spawned by the dire economic straits facing the nation and the world. The cynical attitudes of many characters found in both screwball and noir may have come out of the protracted despondency brought on by the Great Depression. As is often noted, "depression" might have been an economic term, but it aptly described the mood and mentality of the people struggling with financial afflictions.

For many, the Depression stifled faith in the American dream, challenged the conviction that America was the land of opportunity, that anyone with desire and industry could achieve and become anything he or she wished. Americans were suddenly deprived of what was considered a birthright. The belief that "prosperity is just around the corner" may have endured briefly, but reality must have quickly undermined this unrealistically optimistic slogan, for it is ridiculed several times in 1932's *Trouble in Paradise* and 1936's *My Man Godfrey*. Yet even with optimism tainted and hope stymied, screwball comedies during the Depression years managed to be cynical without being pessimistic. People could still cling to the idea that these economic woes would end and circumstances would improve.

Money might have been the cause of the crisis, but money was also the solution to the problem, so in many films, money takes the form of deus ex machina. In screwball comedies where wealth is at issue (and it often is), money sometimes assumes a paradoxical quality, simultaneously bearing the mark of the devil while appearing like manna from heaven. Ultimately, however, having money turns out to be a good thing, although to ensure the empathy of the film audience, the romantic pair, in resolving their differences, must both realize that money is less fulfilling than the true love they found or rediscovered.

Not all screwball comedies involve money as part of the central conflict, but the many that do generally fall into five main categories defined by the relationship between the screwball male and female. The first category can be labeled "The Rich Woman Meets the Working-class Man," where the screwball lovers include a wealthy woman, often an heiress, whose fortune has insulated her and fostered a naïveté about life, and a man, more experienced in the ways of the world, who is pressured by some economic quandary. Frank Capra's *It Happened One Night* is the prototype. Reporter Peter Warne has just lost his job on a New York paper when he encounters runaway heiress Ellie Andrews and sees the potential for a profitable story. He is a principled and resolute supporter of the working middle class, and constantly belittles Ellie for being a spoiled brat, blaming her wealth and status for her pretensions (according to his prejudiced perception of the rich). Yet Peter cannot deny the necessity of money when he sees Ellie forced to eat the raw carrots she formerly refused, when he lies to the manager of an auto camp to get a room, and when he asks his editor to advance him the thousand dollars he needs to marry Ellie. The ironic upshot of his marriage is that, as the husband of the runaway heiress, he will have attained enormous wealth in spite of his deep-seated working-class principles—and the audience revels vicariously in his good fortune.

In another film of this type, *Next Time I Marry*, spoiled heiress Nancy Crocker Fleming (Lucille Ball) can expect her inheritance only if she weds a "plain American" (according to her father's will). Her present engagement to a foreigner (Lee Bowman) could nullify her rights to the money, so she strikes a deal with WPA road worker Tony Anthony (James Ellison), offering him a thousand dollars if he will marry her temporarily. Afterwards, to secure a divorce, they travel to Reno together in his car and trailer. Anthony is indifferent to excessive wealth (an important trait of the highly principled, self-confident working man, with or without a job), content with his free, unfettered way of life. The rebellious heiress resists the blue-collar laborer at first, but then her feelings soften toward him as she gradually comes to accept the vagabond lifestyle, eating hamburgers and cooking food on a campfire. She learns to love him for his modest wants and expectations, and he, at the same time, merits both her and the fringe benefits of her inheritance.

In *Holiday*, wealthy businessman Edward Seton (Henry Kolker) outlines a logical career path for his future son-in-law Johnny Case (Cary Grant) that will guarantee a secure, successful future for him and daughter Julia (Doris Nolan). Though practical and promising, the offer would be for the young man a joyless, stifling occupation harnessing his uninhibited spirit at a time when Case, penniless but carefree, wants to travel and experience life before resigning himself to the fetters of a steady job.

Other films that adopt this formula are *Love on the Run, Cross-Country Romance, The Bride Came C.O.D., Take a Letter, Darling,* and *Live, Love, and Learn.* Curtis Bernhardt's *Million Dollar Baby* (1941) fits here, too, with the added twist that the woman begins the story as a department-store clerk and suddenly becomes rich. Initially, Pamela McAllister (Priscilla Lane) and Peter Rowan (Ronald Reagan), a struggling musician, live in a boarding house, content with their relationship despite their financial dearth. Enter wealthy heiress Cornelia Wheelwright (May Robson) who has learned that the millions she inherited from her father were the result of his cheating his business partner. To make amends, she has her lawyer James Amory (Jeffrey Lynn) seek out the defrauded partner's descendants, who she believes are entitled to some remuneration. Pamela is the only living relative and Miss Wheelwright, anonymously through Amory, gives her a million dollars. The windfall would seem a blessing, except that the upright Rowan adheres to the conventional belief that the man must be the breadwinner in the family. He leaves New York to work with a dance band in Detroit. Although Amory, wealthy, successful, and interested in Pamela himself, appears as Peter's logical replacement, Pamela concludes that money is not as important as love. She gives away her fortune and reclaims her proper position beside Peter, who continues to play piano in the traveling band, satisfied with earning $75 a week of "real money."

Million Dollar Baby is interesting because it works from two angles at once. Headstrong Peter Rowan represents the proud working class that adheres to the belief that the American dream must be attained through hard work, perseverance, and developing one's unique skills, that "real money" is deserved by working for it, not by having it land in one's lap without some tangible achievement. Pamela McAllister represents those who gain the wealth too easily without earning it; they have to learn that, without being attached to some sense of accomplishment, wealth cannot offer fulfillment and happiness.

Howard Hawks's *Bringing Up Baby* also fits the category, although there are marked deviations in the formula. David Huxley (Cary Grant), far from being a blue-collar worker, is a paleontologist employed by a museum. He is not privy to the true identity of Susan Vance (Katharine Hepburn) until the very end, when he discovers that she is the niece of the woman who has offered to finance his museum project. Although she comes from money, Susan does not have to learn the lesson that love is more important than wealth because she already embraces that maxim as she strives to convince David that he belongs with her more than he does with the woman to whom he is presently engaged.

A reversal on the first category, the second type of screwball comedy where wealth-consciousness interferes in the relationship of the screwball couple is "The Rich Man Meets the Working-class Woman." The woman, employed or not, comes from a middle- or lower-class background and meets a man who has money and status. Like the rich woman in the first category, the rich man may parade his pretentiousness until he learns that love with the right woman is worth more than his wealth and position. Such is the case in *Bachelor Mother* and *5th Ave. Girl* in which self-important males (David Niven and Tim Holt) must rid themselves of their stuffy pomposity before they merit the love of an admirable woman (Ginger Rogers in both films). *Vivacious Lady* and *You Can't Take It with You* also fit this category, although the screwball male (James Stewart in each case) is, at the outset of both films, a noble, grounded character genuinely in love with a deserving young lady (Ginger Rogers and Jean Arthur). Complications ensue—perhaps having more to do with status and reputation than with money—and the two lovers become alienated, so that the two films follow the classic formula of boy-meets-girl, boy-loses-girl, boy-finds-girl.

You Can't Take It with You varies the situation somewhat in that both screwball lovers share a mutual attitude toward love and a minimal interest in riches—rather, the complication is created by the young man's parents whose fixation on money and affluence has turned them into malcontented snobs. Anthony P. Kirby (Edward Arnold) is a high-powered Wall Street banker, financially successful but ulcer-ridden. The girl, Alice Sycamore (Jean Arthur), has a grandfather, Grandpa Vanderhof (Lionel Barrymore), who is patriarch of the eccentric and quixotic Vanderhof-Sycamore family. He spouts his middle-class philosophy that people, if they intend to enjoy life, must pursue whatever it is that makes them happy, even if it brings no financial reward. His maxim is presented in a way to appear more attractive

You Can't Take It with You (1938, Columbia; Frank Capra, director)—Screwball comedies end with the male and female settling their differences. While Tony Kirby, Jr. (James Stewart), and Alice Sycamore (Jean Arthur) resolve their romantic differences in an embrace, Grandpa Vanderhof (Lionel Barrymore, left) and Anthony Kirby, Sr. (Edward Arnold), symbolize a resolving of the differences between classes.

than Kirby's vain, money-grubbing ambitions. Kirby has forfeited his humanity for an account ledger with a profitable bottom line. He expects his son to follow in his footsteps until Anthony, Jr. (James Stewart), confesses indifference toward business matters and shows a stronger interest in Vanderhof's granddaughter. In the finale, Alice and Anthony, Jr., reunite with the intention to marry, thus signifying a compromise between the two conflicting classes. The senior Kirby joins Grandpa Vanderhof in a harmonica duet, suggesting the banker's contrition for his callousness and his potential redemption from monetary greed.

The third category of film where wealth plays a significant role might be called "The Rich Man Meets the Gold Digger." Unlike the two previous categories where the wealthy party has lost sight of his or her humanity and has to be redeemed, here the woman from the middle or lower class suffers the same attitude as the smugly rich. Her obsession with marrying money (personified by the classic millionaire) blinds her to the true essence of love and marriage, and she must learn that loving the man takes precedence over the wealthy lifestyle he can afford her.

Jean Harlow as *The Girl from Missouri* plays one of these first gold diggers in the screwball cycle. Eadie Chapman (Harlow) has become disgusted with having to fend off lecherous men at the road house run by her mother and stepfather. Watching her mother from outside the window, she gives her a sad and private farewell and runs off to New York with her friend Kitty (Patsy Kelly) to meet and marry a millionaire. A life of deprivation and shoddy experiences have ingrained in her the attitude developed by most gold diggers, namely, the necessity of placing money before love. Despite this materialistic attitude, she vows outright to Kitty that she will "play it straight"; that is, she intends to win a husband while keeping her virtue intact.

Working as a chorus girl, she gets to perform at a private party hosted by elderly millionaire Frank Cousins (Lewis Stone). She flirts with Cousins, who asks her to marry him. But the millionaire is toying with her. He is actually a ruined man, and when she steps out of the room, he shoots himself. Eadie would have gotten into trouble with the police if not for help from another millionaire, T. R. Paige (Lionel Barrymore). She later seeks him out and becomes obnoxiously aggressive trying to coax him into marriage. Paige rejects her gold-digging efforts, not wanting anything to do with a woman he stereotypes as promiscuous and immoral. She follows him down to Palm Beach where she meets his son, Tom Paige (Franchot Tone). This is a common situation in gold-digger screwballs: the woman suddenly finds herself positioned between her targeted spouse and a new suitor who offers her true love. Tom is enamored with her, and she is attracted to him, but he wants a relationship without marriage and she refuses to squander her virginity without the promise of a permanent—and profitable—arrangement.

The elder Paige tries to discourage his son from getting involved with her, and when Tom tells him he plans to marry her, Paige has her framed on a prostitution charge. Another elderly millionaire, Charlie Turner (Hale Hamilton), posts her bail. Eadie learns that Paige, who was recently appointed international ambassador, is sailing off on a peace mission. She arranges with a news photographer to take a picture of her with him in a compromising position, thus framing him as he did her. Eadie goes with Turner to his house, drunk and prepared to lose her virginity. However, Tom arrives in time to stop her. Paige also shows up, the victim of a scandal. He explains that he has already denounced Eadie's photos as contrived by political rivals. He told reporters that Eadie was already married to Tom— which means that she and Tom have to marry right away to legitimize the lie. Paige provides the license and the justice of the peace and welcomes Eadie into the family because he admires her fighting spirit.

The critical point in Harlow's film occurs just before her arrest: she tells Kitty that she loves Tom and would marry him even if his father dis-

The Girl from Missouri (1934, MGM; Jack Conway, director)—Eadie (Jean Harlow) is, paradoxically, a gold digger with scruples. Although she likes Tom Paige (Franchot Tone), her ethical values cause her to take offense when he attempts to buy her favor and turn their relationship into something sordid.

inherited him for loving her. In all these films, the gold digger learns that love is more important than money. Either she forsakes her future spouse for a working stiff who offers her true love (*Midnight, The Palm Beach Story*) or she realizes she actually loves her wealthy quarry before she marries him (*Smartest Girl in Town, Woman Chases Man,* and, with some variation, *The Lady Eve*). *Hands Across the Table* creates parallel situations where both a man and a woman act like gold diggers at the same time. Theodore Drew III (Fred MacMurray), once rich, now bankrupt, meets manicurist Regi Allen (Carole Lombard). Both agree that the only sure way to attain wealth is to marry it. Drew is already engaged to a wealthy woman (Astrid Allwyn) and Regi forms a friendship with a millionaire (Ralph Bellamy), but love proves stronger than lucre and they abandon their prospects to marry each other.

The fourth category of the wealth-conscious theme is "The Rich Man Disguised as a Working-class Male Meets the Working-class Woman." The male protagonist is rich, yes, but the screwball female does not know this because a mistake or misunderstanding delays the revelation of his identity, such as occurs with John Ball, Jr. (Ray Milland), in *Easy Living*, or because he deliberately conceals his background, like John Merrick (Charles Coburn) in *The Devil and Miss Jones*.

In *The Devil and Miss Jones*, millionaire department store owner John P. Merrick takes a job as a clerk in one of his own stores to discover the identity of those protesting the store's policy against unionizing. Instead of confronting the belligerent workers he expected to find, he is befriended by compassionate Mary Jones (Jean Arthur), her boyfriend Joe O'Brien (Robert Cummings), and Elizabeth Ellis (Spring Byington), who becomes Merrick's love interest. While on a beach picnic together, he treats them to a bottle of exquisite wine that he sequestered from his private cellar. They all make sour faces and declare that the wine tastes terrible and that he was cheated. The implication is that something more than money separates the classes from one another, the rich possessing cultivated tastes unappreciated and misunderstood by the lower strata. When he finally reveals to them who he is, he does so apologetically, embarrassed by his status and afraid they will reject him. The irony is that he represents the upper-class nabobs who value their position of authority and do not expect to kowtow to anyone, yet here he is groveling for acceptance by less affluent people who are quite content with who they are and with what they have.

When a screwball comedy attempts to sermonize on the tendencies of the rich to cling to Mammon at the expense of their humanity, the story either satirizes their hubris and prodigality, as it does with the Bullocks in *My Man Godfrey* and Tracy Lord in *The Philadelphia Story*, or contrasts the foolishness of the status-conscious upper class with the more worldly-wise middle or lower class, as it does in *The Devil and Miss Jones*. The man's "disguise" enables the woman to learn about him as a peer and the man has the chance to learn about the attitudes and habits of those people he may not have considered before. Two people, one from the upper class and one from a lower class, get to learn about each other and appreciate each other on a personal level. Eventually they marry, their union signifying the ability of the two extreme classes to reconcile their prejudices and make allowances for their differences. Other examples of this fourth type of wealth-conscious screwball film are *If You Could Only Cook* and *Maid's Night Out*.

Finally, the fifth category, "The Rich Man in Disguise Meets the Rich Woman," shares some similarities with the previous category. Again, the man's disguise may be intentional or a matter of a misunderstanding or mistaken identity. However, while the woman assumes a comfortable superiority over the man, the man's fuller knowledge of their true relationship enables him to manipulate the situation more deliberately. *My Man Godfrey* serves as the model for this group of screwball comedies. While on a socialite scavenger hunt for a "forgotten man," Irene Bullock (Carole Lombard) discovers the tramp Godfrey (William Powell) living in a garbage dump. She decides to hire him as the family butler despite resistance from her mother (Alice Brady) and sister Cornelia (Gail Patrick). Godfrey proves to be exceptionally proficient at his job. In reality, he comes from wealthy New England blue-bloods. A failed love affair left him despondent and he sunk into the life of a homeless tramp. While working for the Bullocks, he invests money in the stock market and saves the family from ruin. Observing Cornelia's pretentious and devious behavior, he finds his moral principles awakened and he decides to return to society as an active participant. He uses his money to turn the garbage dump into a swank restaurant and hotel, hiring the tramps he befriended to fill the positions. Irene had never hidden her romantic intentions from Godfrey, and although he previously refused her proposal to marry, she visits him at The Dump and this time does not take no for an answer.

The reference to the "forgotten man" comes from the Warren and Dubin song "Remember My Forgotten Man" that appeared a few years earlier in the musical *Gold Diggers of 1933*. Godfrey, as the "forgotten man," is a person with unrealized potential, biding his time until he is ready to demonstrate his real power. The irony is in people's erroneous notion of who he is and their underestimation of his capabilities. After he endures unfair treatment from a number of individuals, he finally decides to rise from the ashes to prove that he is more than he was thought to be. A similar pattern occurs in *The Footloose Heiress* and *Merrily We Live*, where a family mistakes a cultured, well-educated, and well-connected man for an uncouth, destitute hobo.

We might allow for a sixth situation, "The Rich Man and the Rich Woman," where wealth is an organic element in the comedy, a contributing factor to both the setting and the lifestyle of the characters. However, because the battle of the sexes is fought within the one class and the combatants are less concerned with financial gain than with retaliation and redress for personal wrongs done to each other, wealth ironically does not emerge as an issue in the conflict. For instance, at their divorce trial in *The Awful Truth*, rich socialites Jerry and Lucy Warriner (Cary Grant and Irene Dunne) are more interested in who gets custody of their dog, Mr. Smith, their surrogate child, than they are with any financial settlement. Their story is a series of efforts to sabotage each other's attempt to find a new mate. Similar is *Mr. & Mrs. Smith*, in which an argumentative married couple (Robert Montgomery and Carole Lombard) learns that they are not legally joined and become suddenly an argumentative unmarried couple. Again, the feud has nothing to do with money and everything to do with rivalry and reconciliation.

Breakfast for Two at first seems concerned with money. Jonathan Blair (Herbert Marshall), absorbed in a carefree life of dissipation, neglects his business and loses his fortune. Rich heiress Valentine Ransome (Barbara Stanwyck), after a one-night fling with Blair, has fallen in love with him. To save him, she buys up all the stock to his shipping line, assumes the presidency of the company, and makes Blair vice-president. Blair rebels against her presumption to run his business. Valentine lets the shipping line go into receivership to give Blair a chance to prove his mettle, and he does, arguing before the board of directors to let him return as principal director of the shipping line. Although money is an important concern for Blair, it never emerges as a critical divisive issue for him and Valentine. The conflict depends more on their sexist rivalry, on her control of his company and his attempt to recover that control.

There are several reasons screwball comedy addresses this contrast between secure affluence and financial strife. One is to show how the rich, impervious to the Depression and perceived as unsympathetic to the condition of the less fortunate, may in fact possess more humanity than is generally assumed. Another is that, if the rich appear initially unsympathetic in these films, it does not mean they cannot rediscover their lost humanity. Ellie's father, Alexander Andrews (Walter Connolly), in *It Happened One Night* and Hopsie's father, Horace Pike (Eugene Pallette), in *The Lady Eve* are examples of the former. John P. Merrick (Charles Coburn) in *The Devil and Miss Jones* and Anthony Kirby, Sr. (Edward Arnold), in *You Can't Take It with You* are examples of the latter.

A third reason for including the wealth issue is that it automatically creates another level of conflict since one of the two romantically enmeshed lovers comes from money, while the other has more modest roots. *The Palm Beach Story, The Philadelphia Story, It Happened One Night, Double Wedding, The Footloose Heiress,* and *Holiday* are a few titles wherein this situation occurs as a crucial element in the story. Symbolically, the marriage (or conjoining) of the two battling lovers suggests that the upper and lower classes they represent can resolve their differences, that the compromise between the screwball couple can serve to bridge the gap between the two opposing factions. (Such was the wishful thinking of Friar Laurence in *Romeo and Juliet*. In the same way that Shakespeare's drama ends with a fragile truce, screwball comedies often end with a reconciliation that is accepted as expeditious and temporary.)

The films of Frank Capra retain that connection to wholesomeness, to right-thinking homespun philosophy, and to innate goodness, by having the childlike hero oppose and overcome the monolithic forces corrupted by money and power. His screwball comedy *You Can't Take It with You* and the borderline screwballs *Mr. Deeds Goes to Town* (1936) and *Mr. Smith Goes to Washington* (1939) present characters who initially appear eccentric, but eventually reveal themselves to be saner (even if fanatically idealistic) than the society that condemns their behavior. It is society that has become perverted, has lost its moral compass and turned into a wayward, directionless, apathetic mass. Capra's heroes try to remind society of its forsaken values and to restore that lost direction.

In film noir, money is one of the prime motivations for committing a crime (along with three other passions: lust, power, and vengeance). All throughout the genre there lurks the industrious criminal who adopts the tenet expressed by Alonzo D. Emmerich (Louis Calhern) in *The Asphalt Jungle:* "Crime is only a left-handed form of human endeavor." In one of the earliest examples of monetary greed, the rogues' gallery of *The Maltese Falcon,* in concerted pursuit of the jewel-encrusted idol, is willing to lie, cheat, steal, and kill for the extraordinary wealth attached to the black bird. Men and women from all walks of life "go bad" when they sell out their friends, their families, and their souls for a pot of gold. Numerous noirs, such as *Force of Evil, Criss Cross, Kansas City Confidential, The Lady from Shanghai, The Asphalt Jungle, 711 Ocean Drive, Roadblock,* and *Shield for Murder,* involve characters who once upheld idealistic values, but are blinded by money's bright allure. They end up hurting not only themselves, but others around them. Often, the lust for wealth is complicated by the lust for a woman. In *Double Indemnity,* for example, Walter Neff killed a man to satisfy that dual temptation, but like all of the doomed noir protagonists he represents, he laments: "I didn't get the money and I didn't get the woman."

In screwball comedy, the male and female protagonists never show so intense an obsession for wealth that they alienate the audience's sympathy for them. Born out of Depression-era anxieties, most screwball comedies cater to the viewpoint of the middle and lower classes, extolling the virtues of their ordinary lifestyle and underrating the significance of living amid extraordinary wealth. Screwball's protagonists have (or learn to have) modest ambitions: financial security without a surfeit of riches brings happiness and contentment enough. Yet ironically, circumstances often lead the pure-hearted protagonist to unsought-for wealth, the material reward for loving the right person for the right reasons. Thus, Peter Warne, a newspaperman, marries heiress Ellie Andrews in *It Happened One Night;* Alice Sycamore, a secretary, unites with a banker's son, Anthony Kirby, Jr., in *You Can't Take It with You;* and Polly Parrish, a department store clerk, plans to marry David Merlin, son of the store's owner, in *Bachelor Mother.*

The noir protagonist, on the other hand, has abandoned the idealistic belief that economic promises of the American dream come to everyone, and he (or she) knows that only devious and unethical means can attain it. *Force of Evil, The Killers, Criss Cross, Nightmare Alley,* and *Night in the City* expose this warped mindset of characters whose grandiose designs must eventually disintegrate into dust.

Interestingly, in both screwball and noir, the American dream suffers some distortion, some unsettling refraction that causes the pursuer to pause and waiver with question and doubt. Screwball characters, to surmount these uncertain moments, often become idealistic philosophers who explain away the unreachable dream with self-consoling euphemisms about money not buying happiness (Grandpa Vanderhof in *You Can't Take It with You*) or who assert that the simple life has greater appeal than the life of the rich (Godfrey in *My Man Godfrey;* Peter Warne in *It Happened One Night;* Butch Baeder in *The Footloose Heiress*). In a few situations, screwball protagonists may actually face dire circumstances similar to those of their noir counter-parts. Only their own stoicism or some unexpected fateful event enables them to recover before they sink into the quagmire of utter desperation. In *Come Live with Me,* down-and-out writer Bill Smith (James Stewart) is one dime away from becoming a professional vagrant until he meets illegal immigrant Johnny Jones (Hedy Lamarr), marries her to keep her from being deported, and treats their relationship as the inspiration for a new novel that rescues him from poverty. In *5th Ave Girl,* Mary Grey (Ginger Rogers) has no job and no prospects. By accident, she meets millionaire businessman Timothy Borden (Walter Connolly), who hires her as his nightly escort, hoping to make his wife jealous so she will pay more attention to him. Mary's new role leads to a romance with Borden's son Tim (Tim Holt), the once irresponsible youth now reformed to cover his prodigal father's absence from the business. And in *The Bride Came C.O.D.,* Steve Collins (James Cagney) is about to lose his private airline because he cannot make the latest payment on it. When heiress Joan Winfield (Bette Davis) coin-cidentally hires his plane to take her and her fiancé (Jack Carson) to Las Vegas to get married, Steve makes a secret deal with her father, millionaire Lucius K. Winfield (Eugene Pallette), to sabotage the wedding for the money he needs to pay his creditor. The ordeal of their having to endure each other's company leads the feisty couple, of course, to love, and in the end, Steve succeeds not only in earning the necessary money but also in marrying Winfield's daughter.

Screwball treats wealth as an ambiguous symbol—for all its attractive aspects, wealth is an inadequate or misleading measure of success and hap-piness—yet the protagonist often attains this very prize after a hard-fought romantic conflict. Like screwball, film noir treats wealth as an ambiguous symbol but one related to the contradictory concepts of success and avarice. Objectively, wealth is one way that society measures success, and noir pro-tagonists, perhaps burning a little more feverishly than most people about securing the brass ring, pay homage to the golden idol. Frustrated in their inability to make their fortune legitimately, they willingly sell their souls to the devil to reach their goal by any means possible. Wanton venality is displayed by Walter Neff and Phyllis Dietrichson in *Double Indemnity,* Joe Morse (John Garfield) in *Force of Evil,* Det. Lt. Barney Nolan (Edmond

O'Brien) in *Shield for Murder,* and Lt. Jim Cordell (Charles McGraw) in *Armored Car Robbery.* In their monomaniacal pursuit of wealth, noir characters fall into the same trap that snared Macbeth: Impatience fuels their mistrust of Time and Fate, and so they are compelled to "screw [their] courage to the sticking place" and take a drastic, violent, and illicit first step to secure their destiny, a step that conversely takes them across the threshold into catastrophe.

Ambitious Women: Competing with Men Professionally, Socially and Domestically

The women's suffrage movement of the late nineteenth and early 20th centuries was more than a clamor for the right to vote; it symbolized women's claim for general equality with men, a demand for comparable consideration in a wide range of social and professional endeavors. Although a true "liberation movement" was never openly declared until the 1960s, women of this earlier period grew bolder about seeking recognition for their intelligence and talents that earned them the right to compete with men in traditionally male-dominated arenas. Women were shattering socially repressive stereotypes by deciding for themselves whether they wanted to forsake the conventional path of the housewife and follow, instead, a professional career.

World War II provided a greater opportunity for women to fulfill their deferred ambitions. At that time, the American workforce suffered from a vacuum in manpower that could be filled by the one main demographic group still available: females. In her book *From Reverence to Rape,* Molly Haskell notes the trenchant impact the war had on women, socially and mentally:

> A poll of working women taken during the war [showed] that 80 percent wanted to keep their jobs after it was over. After a sharp drop-off following the end of the war ... married women *did* go back to work, although as late as 1949 it was still frowned upon. This, of course, is the source of the tremendous tension in films of the time [221–222].

When the men returned from overseas, either they could not get work because women had replaced them in their former jobs, or if they found employment, it was at the expense of women who had settled into new productive roles outside the home. Either way, one gender might feel animosity toward the other: men frustrated because they lost their jobs to women; women defiant because they were displaced by men.

The competitive attitude between men and women in the workplace spread to their general relationships, a trend that is reflected in the conflicts the characters face in screwball and noir. The first screwball comedies of 1934 depicted strong women in roles where they did not merely interact with men, but displayed attributes that enabled them to challenge their male counterpart and the traditional sexist stereotypes. *It Happened One Night* begins with rich heiress Ellie Andrews already married against her father's wishes. She displays her spunk and independence by leaping from his yacht in Miami to find her own way back to her husband in New York. Although her privileged past has ingrained in her certain social expectations, she does not exhibit the pretensions that could inhibit her from mingling with the lower classes and falling in love with someone below her station. Her feistiness and determination make her a capable combatant in her battle of the sexes with Peter Warne. In 1934's *Twentieth Century*, Mildred Plotka (Carole Lombard) arrives in New York as a neophyte to the stage, but under the tutelage of the great Oscar Jaffe (John Barrymore), she is reborn as Lily Garland and becomes a popular Broadway star. After a schism with her mentor, she travels to Hollywood where, on her own, she makes a successful transition to film acting. Oscar's career plummets while his starlet triumphs professionally and financially (perhaps a comical inversion of George Cukor's melodramatic *What Price Hollywood?* that appeared two years earlier and a humorous precursor to William Wellman's more serious *A Star is Born* that arrives three years later). With Lily's fame and fortune now surpassing that of the man who discovered her, Oscar, frantic and desperate and knowing that her name can guarantee a hit for his next Broadway play, humiliates himself by becoming what he despises most, an actor—he resorts to emoting in his grandest style to deceive her into signing a stage contract. *The Thin Man* introduces Nick and Nora Charles (William Powell and Myrna Loy) as a slightly eccentric couple. Nora has inherited several businesses, which make her independently wealthy, and although Nick claims to supervise their operation, they are technically owned by the heiress. Nora is not a retiring wife; she stands toe-to-toe with her husband on drinking sprees—in their first scene together, she finds him in a bar where she immediately orders six drinks to catch up to him—and she shows herself adept at trading quips and playing along with his childish whims.

These three women, Ellie Andrews, Lily Garland, and Nora Charles—intelligent, witty, strong-willed, capable, independent, resourceful—set a standard for the screwball female who must match her male foil so that, after the dust of battle clears, they both are left standing, knowing they truly deserve each other.

Among its central characters, noir contains two general female types, the femme fatale (also termed the femme noire or Spider Woman) and the femme blanche (the good woman or nurturing female). Either may appear as a main or minor character, and each has some effect, profound or tangential, on the male protagonist. The femme fatale, evil by nature, always works from selfish motives, whether her goal is to gain power, wealth, or revenge, or solely to possess some man on whom she has a fixation. She is irrepressible, determined to compete with any man until she gets what she wants, even if it means destroying him and herself. She is implicitly aware that sex is power, that sex is the catalyst in the chemical reaction between a man and a woman, and she uses her beauty like bait to lure her man and achieve her objective. Brigid O'Shaughnessy in *The Maltese Falcon* (1941) is one of the earliest of noir's duplicitous femmes fatales, dangerous to the man (having killed her ally Thursby and posing a latent threat to Spade) and obsessed with acquiring the black bird that can bring her immense wealth. In *The Shanghai Gesture* (1941), Mother Gin Sling (Ona Munson) flashes her stiletto-nails and wears the robes, make-up, and hairstyles that code her as a dragon lady, grasping, cunning, and mysterious. She avenges herself on her former husband (Walter Huston) by seducing his daughter (Gene Tierney) into a life of gambling and dissipation, never realizing—in one of noir's most incredible and ironically fateful complications—that Poppy is her daughter, too. And Ruth Dillon (Claire Trevor) in *Street of Chance* (1942) appears to be a guardian angel to amnesia victim Frank Thompson (Burgess Meredith), when all the time she is concerned with her own self-preservation. These earliest noirs establish the image of the femme fatale, and some of her successors become even more notorious for their inherent wickedness: Phyllis Dietrichson (*Double Indemnity*), Kathie Moffat (*Out of the Past*), Helen Grayle (*Murder, My Sweet*), Diane Tremayne (*Angel Face*), Kitty Collins (*The Killers*), Martha Ivers (*The Strange Love of Martha Ivers*), and Elsa Bannister (*The Lady from Shanghai*).

If the femme fatale fulfills the male's darkest sexual fantasies, the femme blanche represents his ideal of the pure and virtuous female. The antithesis of the femme fatale, the femme blanche is essentially good, resolutely loyal and nurturing. Because of her basic decency, she is usually less complex than the femme fatale, yet that simplicity is countered by her varied incarnations and especially by her link to the unpredictable nature of fate. The femme blanche, despite her thoughtful and well-meaning actions, may ironically cause the downfall, and even the death, of the male protagonist. It is as if this idealized woman, whether wife or lover, cannot rescue the man from his grim, inevitable destiny. Stella Bergen (Ingrid Bergman) in *Rage in Heaven* (1941) is one early prototype of this character. She forsakes a romance with Wade Andrews (George Sanders) to marry Phillip Monrell (Robert Montgomery), but her husband's paranoia makes him think the worst of her, despite her efforts to convince him of her love and faithfulness. Monrell's distrust of her and envy of his friend lead him to commit suicide, in which he frames Andrews for his murder. In another 1941 noir, *I Wake Up Screaming*, Vicky Lynn (Carole Landis) stands innocently between two men, Frankie Christopher (Victor Mature), a promoter working to further her career as a model, and Inspector Ed Cornell (Laird

Cregar), a burly, repulsive, unlikable creature who admires her from afar. When Vicky is murdered, her death affects the fate of both men: Christopher becomes the prime suspect, and Cornell, jealous of Christopher and his relationship with her, amasses evidence against him, regardless of whether it is valid or not.

In the early noirs *High Sierra* (1941) and *This Gun for Hire* (1942), the femme blanche (Ida Lupino as Marie, and Veronica Lake as Ellen Graham, respectively) develops a friendly relationship with the man (both of whom happen to be criminals). Ultimately, that relationship is responsible for putting the man in jeopardy: Roy "Mad Dog" Earle (Humphrey Bogart), hiding in the craggy Sierras from the police, sees Marie's dog, Pard, running toward him and he makes himself known just long enough to get shot by a police sharpshooter; hired assassin Philip Raven (Alan Ladd), softened by Ellen's kindness to him, sacrifices his life to secure information for her that proves a traitorous industrialist is selling chemical weaponry to the Germans. Some later noirs in which the femme blanche is inadvertently responsible for the demise of a male (not always a protagonist) are *Shadow of a Doubt, Laura, The Unsuspected, Road House,* and *He Ran All the Way.*

Some noirs feature both the femme fatale and the femme blanche with the male protagonist struggling between them. Symbolically, the two women represent the male's two alternate destinies. The femme blanche represents a conventional life, decent and upright, with a family and a home, if the man does not already possess them. However, this kind of life suffers from predictability, laden as it is with mundane routine and unfulfilled sexual desire. Life with the femme fatale, on the other hand, promises an exciting alternate existence. She may lead the man into a world of vice and depravity, but she is too fascinating to resist and her sexual allure compensates for any pesky doubts. (As Markham says when Kathie Moffat warns him about getting involved with her: "Baby, I don't care.") Even though the male may for a time balance the triangle successfully, his violation of the trust of the femme blanche eventually demands harsh retribution. He may commit outright adultery, as in *Pitfall* and *Nora Prentiss,* or he may entertain thoughts of an affair, as in *The Two Mrs. Carrolls,* or he may cheat on a loyal lover, as in *Angel Face* and *Where Danger Lives.* Unfortunately for the male, though, no matter which ideal he chooses, the wholesome, lackluster helpmate or the sexually charged wicked woman, he faces unpleasant consequences.

While the particular reason for screwball's battle of the sexes may vary among films, the fundamental nature of the conflict in the comedies depends on the man and woman working at cross-purposes to each other: the man's goal interferes with the woman's, and vice versa. This occurs either at the outset because of some immediate contentious situation, such as in *Take a Letter, Darling* and *The Doctor Takes a Wife,* or shortly after the start of the story due to some sudden and unexpected change in the status quo, such as in *Ball of Fire* and *The Awful Truth*. The resolution of the conflict, while it means smoothing over the obvious source of the antagonism—jealousy, professional rivalry, class differences, disparity in wealth, and so on—it also suggests an acceptance of equality between the sexes, the ignoring of any sexist barriers to the relationship. Thus, at the end of *His Girl Friday*, Walter Burns may appear cruel and inconsiderate because he lets Hildy carry her own bag, but there is no need for him to show her this courtesy since, in their modern estate, they are equals, and carrying her own bags signifies this equality. In *Adam's Rib*, the visual sex reversals of Doris and Warren Attinger (Judy Holliday and Tom Ewell) in one of the courtroom scenes, along with Beryl Caighn's (Jean Hagen) transfor-

Adam's Rib (1949, MGM; George Cukor, director)—Adam Bonner (Spencer Tracy) wears that perplexed look for most of the film, wondering why his wife Amanda (Katharine Hepburn, right) should defend Doris Attinger (Judy Holliday, sporting the hat that Adam originally bought for Amanda), a woman obviously guilty of attempted murder. Over Adam's left shoulder is Kip Lurie (David Wayne), who watches the proceedings with interest since, as the third corner of the romantic triangle, he awaits his opportunity to win Amanda for himself.

mation into a male home-wrecker, and the female role-playing by Adam Bonner (Spencer Tracy) in the accountant's office suggest a simple interchangeability between the sexes that makes them essentially little different from one another—although as Adam declares to his wife (Katharine Hepburn) before he closes the final curtain on their canopied four-poster bed, "Vive la différence!"

Screwball comedy begins with the screwball couple in the throes of a contentious relationship and moves gradually toward a truce and compromise, whereas film noir more often adopts the opposite tack and leads the lovers from unity to dissension. Examples of the former are the comedies of remarriage, such as *Mr. & Mrs. Smith, His Girl Friday,* and *The Awful Truth,* and those stories where potential lovers meet and have to purge their relationship of all barriers that thwart their union, films such as *Nothing Sacred, Merrily We Live,* and *Bringing Up Baby.* Examples of the latter are replete throughout film noir: *Angel Face, Double Indemnity, Criss Cross,* and *Scarlet Street,* to name a few.

Noir discourages any compromise between the sexes and highlights the unbalanced relationship between the vulnerable male protagonist and the duplicitous femme fatale. The common purpose that brought them together in the first place becomes strained and muddled, and the relationship, once poisoned, becomes deadly for one or both of the parties. They may bond for a noble objective, such as in *Black Angel,* where composer Marty Blair (Dan Duryea) teams up with Cathy Bennett (June Vincent) to prove that her husband is innocent of murder, and for his gallant effort, Blair discovers something about himself that proves detrimental. Or more frequently, the pair may make a pact for some illicit end, such as in *The Postman Always Rings Twice,* in which Frank Chambers (John Garfield) plots with Cora Smith (Lana Turner) to kill her husband (Cecil Kellaway), a conspiracy that produces disastrous consequences. Conversely, screwball rectifies a couple's hostile rivalries by salvaging their relationship with marriage. In the wartime *The Impatient Years* (1944, and a more serious version that appeared in 1952, *The Marrying Kind*), a couple on the verge of divorce have to look back on their past to discover what caused them to fall in love in the first place. Their ability to reclaim their forsaken ideals is an inversion of the outcome of most noirs, which seldom allow two lovers to redeem their troubled relationship. (There are exceptions, of course, such as *Nightmare Alley* and *Body and Soul.*)

Male-Female Competition Related to Social and Professional Status

In those screwball comedies that open with the man and woman already sharing equal social status, the couple is often from the upper middle

Black Angel (1946, Universal; Roy William Neill, director)—With her husband falsely convicted of murder and sitting on death row, Catherine Bennett (June Vincent) assumes one corner of an odd romantic triangle with Martin Blair (Dan Duryea, left) who is trying to help her prove that Marko (Peter Lorre) is the guilty party.

or wealthy class rather than a lower class, in part to demythologize the rich by showing that their behaviors and their problems are little different from those of the ordinary masses, and in part because humor and irony are automatically inherent in situations in which the supposedly sophisticated and privileged elite are reduced to conducting themselves in incongruously childish and mundane ways. The audience must feel gratified when, in *Easy Living*, they see wealthy Edward Arnold trip and roll down his carpeted staircase, and then, like a silly, belligerent child, chase his wife (Mary Nash) around their richly furnished suite, trying to wrest from her the fur coat she bought. Or they must snicker at the idea that Charles Coburn, as wealthy Mr. John P. Merrick in *The Devil and Miss Jones*, is forced to eat crackers and milk—that is, a baby's pabulum—to soothe the ulcers brought on by his capital gains. In films where the protagonists are social equals, the romantic pair begins either as a married couple, a newly divorced (or separated) couple, or two people bound by some fateful circumstance. Like one of Shakespeare's comedies, the story starts with the world in balance, the two people accepting their present arrangement, such as in *The Awful Truth* and *Mr. & Mrs. Smith* (the latter in the throes of an argument, but one that is part of their normal routine). Other films, such as *Topper, My Favorite Wife,* and *The Philadelphia Story,* suggest that, at some time before the story starts, the world of the screwball couple was in equilibrium, but now, something has happened to upset that status quo. In either of the two cases, the peaceful coexistence quickly deteriorates (or has already deteriorated) into a combat zone through which the couple must tread their way toward some state of stability and mutual acceptance.

A few screwball films place the male and female in the same profession wherein they can act as rivals, the woman transgressing on the once-exclusive male turf and able to demonstrate her capabilities and her mastery of the job requirements. In *Adam's Rib,* a virtual parable on sexism, the husband and wife are both lawyers. Defense lawyer Amanda Bonner competes against her husband, assistant district attorney Adam Bonner, she using theatrics and outlandish demonstrations to defend her client Doris Attinger, he striving to use reason and persuasion within the context of the law to convince the jury of the defendant's guilt. She proves more imaginative and inventive than he and wins the case, but he counters by playing a trick on her to prove, if only to themselves, that even though he lost the case, his position was the correct one.

Director Howard Hawks plays with this professional parity when he takes the 1931 comedy *The Front Page,* incorporates a number of screwball elements, and reshapes it into *His Girl Friday.* Whereas the two warring factions in the original film were men, Hawks transforms the star reporter into a female who duels with her managing editor, a man. Hildy Johnson (Rosalind Russell) is a crack journalist who out-scoops and out-writes all the male reporters. Her abilities make her invaluable to her boss, Walter Burns (Cary Grant), who fears he may lose her because she plans to marry an insurance salesman from Albany (Ralph Bellamy). Burns contrives different ways to break up their engagement, but she is already familiar with his tricks and is able, for a time, to counter most of his attempts, proving herself his worthy adversary.

While professional status can give the screwball female equality with the screwball male, it occasionally places her in a dominant position over him, a situation that automatically justifies the battle of the sexes by provoking the male to take action to subdue the female and place her once again on equal footing with him. Some examples: Rosalind Russell as an upright judge in *Design for Scandal* (and being manipulated into a compromising situation by newsman Walter Pidgeon); Rosalind Russell as an attorney aspiring to a judgeship in *Tell It to the Judge* (yet conflicted in her relationship with ex-hubby, lawyer Robert Cummings); Myrna Loy as a

His Girl Friday (1940, Columbia; Howard Hawks, director)—The screwball combatants try to stare each other down, both determined to gain the upper hand in their battle of the sexes. Walter Burns (Cary Grant) wears a stylishly conservative suit, denoting quiet confidence, while Hildy Johnson (Rosalind Russell) sports a blatant array of clashing diagonal, vertical, and horizontal lines, suggesting a conflict not only between her and her ex-husband but within herself as she decides between two men and two careers.

judge in *The Bachelor and the Bobby-Soxer* (who becomes legally entangled with artist Cary Grant); both Loretta Young in *The Doctor Takes a Wife* and Irene Dunne in *Theodora Goes Wild* as best-selling authors (who have the confidence to make demands on their romantic male foils, medical professor Ray Milland and artist Melvyn Douglas, respectively); Ann Sheridan as an army officer in *I Was a Male War Bride* (who has greater status than her civilian husband, Cary Grant).

Deliberately countering these attempts to equalize women with men, Preston Sturges writes and directs *The Palm Beach Story* (1941), a subtle parody of *It Happened One Night* in that it inverts the trajectory of Capra's original film: the wife runs away from her husband, not to him, and travels from New York to Palm Beach, Florida, instead of from Miami to Long Island. (The film also borrows from *The Girl from Missouri* in that the gold digger heads to Palm Beach to find a millionaire.) Instead of championing women's equal rights with men, Sturges postulates the notion that female allure is a unique and valuable commodity that should never be underrated or depreciated. Gerry Jeffers (Claudette Colbert, in both films) has no homely skills, but she is winsome and charming. She and her husband, Tom (Joel McCrea), are in financial straits. By chance, a wealthy old man, the self-proclaimed Wienie King (Robert Dudley), walks into her apartment, takes a liking to her, and gives her money just because she is beautiful. Tom jealously argues, "And sex didn't even enter into it, I suppose." She surprisingly answers, "Oh, but of course, it did…. Sex always has something to do with it, dear." Gerry believes Tom can become successful if he is on his own, so she runs away. Without money, she relies on her womanly charms to secure help from the zany millionaires on the train and to seduce wealthy John D. Hackensacker III (Rudy Vallee). When the double wedding takes place at the end of the film, Hackensacker and his sister Princess Centimillia (Mary Astor) marry the twin siblings of Tom and Gerry purely on the basis of their being attracted to their good looks. Sturges mocks the sanctimonious posture of the Motion Picture Production Code by highlighting the sexual ingredient in romantic relationships and emphasizing everyone's awareness of its existence and importance.

Unlike screwball comedy, film noir, with few exceptions, starts with the man and woman sharing equal or nearly equal status rather than one holding a higher social or professional position over the other. More likely, the superiority of the femme fatale stems from her superficial beauty and domineering personality coupled with the male's intense sexual obsession and gullibility which cause him to submit willingly to her directives. Their alliance usually flames a torrid passion that soon cools into a contentious coexistence aggravated by issues of greed, jealousy, and power, a formula apparent in many noirs: *The Maltese Falcon, Double Indemnity, Out of the Past, The Killers, Criss Cross, Scarlet Street, Mildred Pierce, The Lady from Shanghai,* and so on.

In contrast to those situations where equality exists between the male and female are those exceptions where the female stands a rung or two above the male: *The Strange Love of Martha Ivers, Sunset Boulevard, Nightmare Alley, Angel Face,* and a number of hardboiled detective films (*The Big Sleep* and *Murder, My Sweet,* for instance). Yet here, that social gulf is quickly bridged and hardly treated as an issue other than to call attention to the corruption that exists even in those gilded mansions.

Empathizing with the Assertive Female

There are those screwball comedies and films noirs where the female protagonist rebels against the male's expectation that she submit humbly and quietly to traditional stereotypes. Both the femme noire and her screwball counterpart appear as radical symbols of the new female who has upset the balance of power between genders by usurping some of the male's status, power, and prominence. However, while the femme noire is abhorred and punished for her effrontery, the screwball female is not. One reason for the different treatment is that, in the comedies, the female protagonist may display ambition, self-sufficiency, and pretentiousness, but ultimately she includes the male in her designs, and the outcome—marriage or some form of reconciliation—is a conventional solution that culminates in benefits and a happy ending for both parties. *It Happened One Night, Twentieth Century, The Doctor Takes a Wife, Tell it to the Judge, Design for Scandal, The Awful Truth,* and *The Footloose Heiress* are examples wherein the self-confident woman claims her right to an equal position with the male, and she is willing to compromise for the sake of their (re)union.

Not so with noir's femme fatale. As a symbol, the femme fatale is a paradoxical figure. To women, she can represent a bastion of strength, an ambitious go-getter, an avenging angel, and a model of determination and resourcefulness; to men, she can stand for something aggressive and dangerous, a threat to their masculinity and their dominant position in society. For the femme fatale, men are expendable. She wields them like workbench tools, seducing them for their utilitarian value, and then discarding them once her selfish ends are attained. Her self-centered and uncompromising position becomes a cause of her downfall.

Placed in comparable situations, the screwball female and femme noire have the potential to become either an amorous partner or an agent of destruction. The personality each finally adopts reflects the nature of her respective genre. In the comedy *Take a Letter, Darling,* Tom Verney (Fred MacMurray) finds himself in a similar quandary as *Sunset Boulevard's* Joe Gillis (William Holden)—each man is an artist (Verney, a painter; Gillis, a screenwriter) who takes a humiliating position as minion to a woman in order to earn money that will enable him to pursue his primary goal. In Verney's case, the woman (Rosalind Russell as "Mac" MacGregor) eventually appreciates his aspirations and supports him. The woman financing Gillis, Norma Desmond (Gloria Swanson), discounts his ambitions, believing he should be satisfied that she can support the two of them, and places her career (her unrealistic comeback) ahead of his. Although Norma claims she loves Joe, she is too grasping and possessive, so that when he tries to leave her, she declares with dreadful self-righteousness, "No one ever leaves a star. That's what makes one a star," and shoots him dead.

In screwball comedy, the female can be conniving, devious, manipulative, and self-serving, and yet her behavior is perceived as amusing and acceptable. After all, her goal is marriage, and even though this is something the male protagonist may fear and try to avoid, it is the social norm, the conventional expectation for most individuals in the community. As if driven by some natural law, the woman maneuvers the male toward marriage, not with malicious intent, but with the altruistic belief that, whether the man realizes it or not, he will benefit from the union. Susan Vance (Katharine Hepburn in *Bringing Up Baby*) knows implicitly, long before David Huxley (Cary Grant), that she is destined to marry him. She uses decoys and deceptions to keep him near her and away from his fiancée, succeeding in winning him in the end. The same is true of Irene Bullock (Carole Lombard in *My Man Godfrey*) who plots to marry the tramp-turned-butler (William Powell) from the very first time she encounters him. Ellen Arden (Irene Dunne in *My Favorite Wife*) finagles her vacillating husband (Cary Grant) into a compromising situation in which he is finally forced to make up his mind by choosing her and abandoning his recent infatuation with an unworthy woman. Paula Bradford (Jean Arthur in *The Ex-Mrs. Bradford*) tries to prod her ex-husband (William Powell) toward remarriage by moving into his apartment under the pretense that she is helping him solve a murder mystery.

The screwball female may not always pursue the male deliberately for the purpose of marriage or remarriage (as Katharine Hepburn does in *Bringing Up Baby*). She may deny her subconscious intentions (to him and herself) and play hard-to-get. Such a situation is found in the first screwballs, *It Happened One Night* and *Twentieth Century*, and recur frequently in later films, such as *I Love You Again*, *His Girl Friday*, and *Love Crazy*. In *Mr. & Mrs. Smith*, Carole Lombard at first shows only contempt for Robert Montgomery's fawning overtures and offers no hope for reconciliation, but her cavalier treatment of suitor Gene Raymond suggests where her deeper, unacknowledged feelings lie.

If the female is a strict and stuffy authoritarian, she may have to learn flexibility and humility before she can be worthy of her destined soul mate. When Cosmo Topper's wife (Billie Burke in *Topper*) finally dons the sexy lingerie she previously spurned, she shows she can learn to be more considerate of her husband (Roland Young) and less wrapped up in her petty social ambitions. In *Libeled Lady*, rich, aloof Connie Allenbury (Myrna Loy) needs to have a number of attitudinal barriers leveled before she becomes warm toward Bill Chandler (William Powell). In *Double Wedding*, Charlie Lodge (William Powell) has to convince Margit Agnew (Myrna Loy) that the simple life has advantages over a staid life filled with dreary routine and excessive amenities. And in *The Footloose Heiress*, essentially an adaptation of *The Taming of the Shrew*, a wealthy man recruits a confident tramp (Craig Reynolds) to wean the hubris and stubbornness out of his recalcitrant daughter (Ann Sheridan), who eventually—albeit predictably—surrenders herself to her suitor.

On the other hand, if the screwball woman is unconventional and carefree (whether she comes from wealth or not), she may already merit the screwball male's love—yet he may have to change to merit hers. *Bringing Up Baby* is one example. Susan Vance, a rich but daffy female, does not let her wealth hinder her enjoyment of life. She is more uninhibited than paleontologist David, but she wants him anyway, probably under the impression that she can rescue him from his musty thinking and rigid behavior—as symbolized by her causing the collapse of the museum's dinosaur skeleton. In *The Lady Eve*, Jean Harrington (Barbara Stanwyck) knows that her unorthodox past as a con artist can endanger her relationship with naïve, idealistic Charles "Hopsie" Pike (Henry Fonda), but she trusts that his love will overcome his distaste for her failings. She is wrong, however, and has to invent an elaborate scheme involving false identity to avenge herself while winning him back. In *It's a Wonderful World*, Edwina Corday (Claudette Colbert) finagles ways to stay close to single-minded detective Guy Johnson (James Stewart) to convince him that they are destined to spend their lives together.

Noir's femme fatale shares similar traits with her screwball sister, but she is too selfish and self-serving to win audience sympathy. Her objective achieved, she no longer needs the male, and if he is around at the end, he is there on her terms.

The screwball heroine makes us laugh, and so her outrageous antics earn acceptability. She can punch the male on the jaw (*Nothing Sacred, Breakfast for Two*), close the door on his nose (*Mr. & Mrs. Smith*), drop an apple on his head (*The Lady Eve*), and humiliate him in public (*Adam's Rib*), and yet we make an allowance: she is justified either because the male is doing some of the same things to her or because he has done something that invites such treatment. Also, we recognize these assaults as childish pranks that disguise the true feelings of an innocent boy and girl who like each other.

Such an interpretation is not possible in noir, where the femme fatale is icy to the bone and the noir protagonist is guilty of some indiscretion that makes him undeserving of complete absolution and redemption. The Spider Woman commits acts of violence that are meant to hurt and destroy. In films such as *Out of the Past, Double Indemnity, Angel Face, Detour, Where Danger Lives, The Killers, Criss Cross, The Lady from Shanghai,* and *Kiss Me Deadly*, when she comes to a bad end, we have little pity or compassion for her.

Ambivalence Toward the Professional Female

Even while women were struggling in reality to make inroads into male-dominated professions, some films were reflecting social ambivalence toward this revolution. Two Barbara Stanwyck films exemplify these mixed attitudes. In *The Bride Walks Out* (1936), Michael Martin (Gene Raymond) marries Carolyn (Stanwyck), expecting to support her on his income alone.

Against her protests, he orders her to quit her job as a store model, which pays more than his position as a surveyor. (The fact that his college degree entitles him to this low-paying job purposely shatters the myth about the correlation between higher education and high-income opportunities.) Carolyn tries to be honest with Michael and insists that, although certain luxuries are "unimportant," she does not want to live without them. Without telling him, she goes back to work, and when he finds out, his pride causes their breakup. The central conflict lies between stubborn tradition, the man's insistence that he be the sole breadwinner while the woman remains the homely wife (also seen in *Million Dollar Baby*), and the new progressive order, the woman's defining herself in the workplace and competing against men, if not for a specific job, then for the status that a lucrative income can signify (also seen in *Take a Letter, Darling*). The film ends with an abrupt and not wholly satisfying reconciliation: Carolyn forsakes her dream and conforms to hubby's chauvinistic standards because it will restore harmony to their happy home.

In the second example, *You Belong to Me* (1941), Stanwyck plays Helen Hunt, a medical doctor who marries rich playboy Peter Kirk (Henry Fonda), whose money gives him the option not to work. Peter would like Helen to quit her career—he is intensely jealous of her male patients—but Helen argues that she loves her job and cherishes her ability to help people. She convinces Peter to do something with his life, and he gets a job selling ties in a department store. His effort impresses Helen, and she decides to forfeit her career because she has learned the importance of sacrifice in a relationship. In the end, Peter uses his money to buy a hospital where he can work as an administrator and his wife can continue to tend to patients as a doctor. The message appears to be that mutual give-and-take is the key to maintaining a viable marriage—Helen was willing to make a sacrifice for Peter, as he had made a sacrifice for her, and as a result, not only does their relationship blossom, but both partners get what they want.

This supposed solution to finding marital bliss is conventional sexist propaganda. The man has not really made much of a sacrifice. As owner of the hospital, he places his wife where he wants her, under his authority where he can monitor her activities. Although Helen can continue in the medical practice she claims she loves, she does so because the male sanctions it. Her career had made her an independent, self-confident individual, and now she is ready to fall into the same traditional trap that women had fallen into for years, forfeiting her dreams and talents for the sake of her husband and home. Marriage (and all it entails, such as sacrifice and love) is touted as the higher good, the union taking priority over the individual, and although there is truth to this, we must return to the feminists' question: If the man can honor the marriage while pursuing his personal career, why not the woman?

World War II: Threats of New International Conflicts and the Outbreak of Global Warfare

The international unrest of the 1930s was another factor contributing to the satirical cynicism in screwball and the cynical fatalism in noir. Hardly 20 years after World War I, with that debacle still strong in memory, Europe was already setting the stage politically, economically, and industrially for another major conflict. These uncertainties and tensions, coupled with the Depression, must have made it seem that God had deserted humanity—or if one preferred to think in more secular terms, that some irrepressible evil had unleashed itself on the world and no power was capable of opposing it.

For the most part, screwball comedy focuses on the immediate, microcosmic conflict between the male and female protagonists and avoids direct references to events on the world's stage. However, once in a while an allusion appears, such as in Sturges's *The Lady Eve* (1941), when Muggsy (William Demarest) tells Hopsie that anyone can do an imitation to fool the people, and without mentioning names, he holds a clothes brush across his upper lip to mimic Adolf Hitler. Muggsy himself exemplifies to what extent cynicism has overtaken society. After playing cards with the cardsharp Gerald (Melville Cooper) and losing money to him, Muggsy suspects that he was cheated. At the same time, although Hopsie says that he played cards with Jean and her father and *won* money, Muggsy surmises (correctly) that something is odd and that they must have cheated him in order to set him up for a bigger fall later. Winning or losing, success or failure, is no proof either way that the world is or is not corrupt. The most that anyone can do to protect him- or herself is to heed the warning, "Caveat emptor." Cynicism, doubt, and suspicion hover around us like pesky insects in a world subject to Darwinian law and the arbitrary workings of Fate.

In noir, this cynicism is not integrated with comical situations as it is in screwball where it is diluted and even laughed at. World War II erupts in 1939 and the United States enters the war in 1941, the same year that sees the release of *The Maltese Falcon, I Wake Up Screaming,* and *The Shanghai Gesture,* and initiates the classical cycle of film noir. (*Citizen Kane* may also be included. Debatable as a true noir, it lacks a violent crime, but the central story is concerned with solving a mystery and the film is replete with technical and visual elements that are wholly noir—and no wonder, with premier cinematographer Gregg Toland applying chiaroscuro techniques to the production and mentoring callow director Welles for his induction into filmmaking.) Sam Spade, as a hardboiled detective, epitomizes the cynicism of his profession. He must be skeptical, he must be wary, if he is to survive in the urban jungle. It means wearing a suit of armor over some of his emotions, hiding his humanity under a hard crust.

If he did not, he would be easy prey for all predators. *I Wake Up Screaming* concerns a detective (Laird Cregar) who, repugnant to look at, is forced to feign indifference toward emotional sensitivity. And yet, he has emotions like anyone else, and longs for companionship and love. However, he could never get what he wants, never be part of that other soft and delicate world with the woman of his dreams, Vicky Lynn (Carole Landis). The dream is out of reach for him—and so he becomes cruel, vindictive, and unjust to avenge himself on an unfair world. He is willing to disregard law and justice and frame handsome Frankie Christopher (Victor Mature) for Vicky's murder in order to satisfy both his jealousy and his pain.

World War II may appear to have affected film noir more than the screwball comedy because the serious nature of the international conflict invited sober treatment and did not lend itself to many humorous situations. However, a number of screwball films, before, during, and after American involvement, reflected issues related to what was going on in both Europe and the United States. The screwball comedy *The More the Merrier* (1943) depended for its comic tension on the wartime housing shortage in Washington, D.C., and *The Impatient Years* (1944) put a comic spin on the relationship of a husband and wife who barely got to know each other before he went off to war. *To Be or Not to Be* (1942), if not outright screwball, is a comedy that contains screwball elements (as do a number of director Ernst Lubitsch's romantic comedies), especially in the romantic triangle of Joseph Tura (Jack Benny), his wife Maria Tura (Carole Lombard), and Lt. Stanislav Sobinski (Robert Stack), a young military pilot smitten with Maria. The Turas are members of an acting troupe who learn that a German spy has information damaging to the Polish resistance. The troupe uses its acting talents to short-circuit the transference of that information.

Noirs like *Casablanca* (1942, arguably noir, and with enough noir elements to share a kinship) and *The Fallen Sparrow* (1943) serve as propaganda disguised as story, shoring up Allied patriotism while exposing the evil inhuman side of the Nazis. Hitchcock's *Shadow of a Doubt* (1943) contains an implicit reference to the war through the symbolism of psychotic Uncle Charles (Joseph Cotten) invading innocent small-town America. As government agent Jack Graham (Macdonald Carey) explains in a final comment to young "Charlie" Newton (Teresa Wright), the world "seems to go crazy every now and then, like your Uncle Charlie." *Crossfire* (1947) deals with anti–Semitism, raising questions about a kind of patriotism that, if too overzealous, can be perverted into xenophobia.

Film noir thrives during the war and postwar years primarily because its themes, tonal shadings, and subject matter so accurately reflect the very despair, cynicism, and fatalism pervading the real world. In films such as *Out of the Past, Detour, They Won't Believe Me, Black Angel, Body and Soul, The Set-up,* and *The Asphalt Jungle*, protagonists struggle to gain some end that they know is not only difficult to attain but perhaps impossible. Or if the undertaking is feasible, they realize that attached to the outcome are dire consequences that can maim or even destroy them. Yet human determination discounts the fear of failure, and so they make extraordinary efforts against the odds and accept whatever fate awaits them.

Conversely, screwball comedies flourish in the mid- to late-1930s and enjoy their peak output in 1941, before production sharply tapers off. It is as if their overt humor served a useful purpose in fending off the economic woes of the Great Depression, but could not sustain people's cynical optimism when they were confronted with the horrors of the Great War. Films such as *Lady of Burlesque* (1943), *Arsenic and Old Lace* (1944), and *Unfaithfully Yours* (1948) exemplify the deterioration of the screwball formula by including darker elements that shock and horrify even while they divert and entertain.

Pre-Code Melodramas and Their Relation to Screwball and Noir

In his comprehensive study of the screwball comedy, Wes D. Gehring singles out the comic antihero, a modified reincarnation of the cracker-barrel hero of earlier literature, as the primary factor giving the genre its identity (see the discussion under "Part 3: Genre Analysis"). He shows how the attributes of this one character can, by extension, infuse the genre with its main features. His analysis is convincing in respect to defining the genre. However, we can also look at the evolution of the screwball comedy within the context of film history. Looking at certain melodramas of the pre–Code era, those earliest talkies produced between 1929 and 1934, we can see how their storylines prefigured the content of both screwball comedy and film noir.

When sound arrived in 1927, the two most important genres for exploiting this new technology were musicals and gangster films. Both of these genres thrived on sound, musicals for their grand orchestral arrangements, vocalized melodies, and cleat-clicking dance numbers; gangster films for their wisecracking dialogue, noisy fusillades from gats and Tommy guns, and screeching tires from automobile chase sequences. Another type of film that emerged, not so much because of the development of sound but as a response to the current social climate, was a particular melodrama that focused on social ills and corruption of the individual, especially of women. Despite the sordid nature of many of these films, they were condoned because they supposedly performed a beneficial service by calling attention to those evils that needed eradication, even if they tended to titillate and pique curiosity because of their pre–Code titles: *Illicit, Forbidden, Shopworn, Baby Face, Transgression, Virtue, Female.*

One of the silver screen's first indelible sex symbols, Jean Harlow had a natural flair for portraying the lusty siren whose street smarts made her a not-so-dumb blonde. In *Hold Your Man* (Sam Wood, uncredited, 1933), Eddie Hall (Clark Gable) has to learn the hard way to realize and appreciate her attributes.

The central character in these particular melodramas was often a woman, either herself a victim of circumstance or an already corrupt and ambitious individual, who, fatefully or willingly, became the bane of the men she influenced, disrupting their lives in some way and bringing scandal, alienation, and disaster to them and to herself. Jean Harlow, Barbara Stanwyck, Carole Lombard, Kay Francis, and Norma Shearer were among the most prominent of these actresses who portrayed this fallen or ill-fated woman and embodied traits that made her the forerunner of both the female screwball protagonist and the noir Spider Woman.

The characters portrayed by these actresses were known for their sassiness, brassiness, and self-confidence in dealing with men. Harlow flaunted her salty sensuality in *Platinum Blonde* (1931), *Red-Headed Woman* (1932), *Red Dust* (1932), *Hold Your Man* (1933), *Bombshell* (1933), and *Reckless* (1935). Stanwyck, gritty as gravel, experimented with a variety of relationships in *Illicit* (1931), *Ten Cents a Dance* (1931), *Forbidden* (1932), *Shopworn* (1932), *Ladies They Talk About* (1933), *Baby Face* (1933), *Gambling Lady* (1934), and *A Lost Lady* (1934). Shearer exuded her lustrous independent air in *Their Own Desire* (1929), *The Divorcee* (1930), *Let Us Be Gay* (1930), *A Free Soul* (1931), *Strange Interlude* (1932), and *Riptide* (1934). Elegant Kay Francis was in and out of scandalous situations in *A Notorious Affair* (1930), *The Virtuous Sin* (1930), *Passion Flower* (1930), *Scandal Sheet* (1931), *Ladies' Man* (1931), *Transgression* (1931), *Guilty Hands* (1931), *The False Madonna* (1931), *Mary Stevens, M.D.* (1933), *I Loved a Woman* (1933), and *Wonder Bar* (1934).

Screwball comedy can be perceived as a reaction to these earlier melodramas, taking their serious tonal quality and heavy-handed social message and converting them into comic situations with less ponderous implications. Author Balio comments on this connection between the pre–Code melodramas and the first screwball comedies: "*The Thin Man* was a comic variation on a dramatic genre, as was *It Happened One Night*" (270). In 1930's *The Divorcee,* for instance, Jerry Martin (Shearer) breaks with husband Ted (Chester Morris) over his unfaithfulness and she descends into a life of promiscuous frivolity. In time, their social circles overlap, they reconnect, and they rediscover their love. In 1931's *Transgression,* Elsie Maury (Kay Francis) has an adulterous affair with Latin gigolo Don Arturo de Borgus (Ricardo Cortez). She writes a letter to her husband, intending to divorce him, and minutes after she sends it, Don Arturo is killed by the father of a young girl he had defiled. Elsie is forced to return home, where she agonizingly tries to intercept the letter before her husband sees it. However, he knows about her indiscretion and forgives her, and she suddenly appreciates the true love she almost lost.

These particular scenarios foreshadow a recurring plot in screwball comedies of remarriage where the screwball couple undergoes a schism and

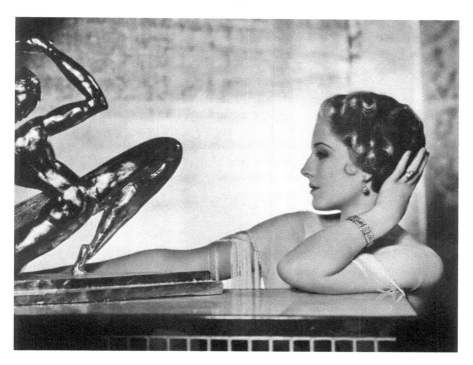

This classical pose suits Norma Shearer, who often graced her roles with a refined and dignified stature.

one or both of them ally with an alternate love interest until they realize their mistake and resolve their differences. Among the many films that adopt this pattern are *The Awful Truth, My Favorite Wife, His Girl Friday,* and *The Philadelphia Story*. Related to this storyline are those situations where the male or female is paired initially with the wrong mate, and only after a series of farcical ordeals do the two destined lovers realize that they are the ones best suited for each other. Capra's *It Happened One Night* is screwball's prototype for this formula. Later examples are *Ever Since Eve, Next Time I Marry, Midnight, Ball of Fire,* and *The Bachelor and the Bobby-Soxer*.

Ironically, as screwball had inverted the tonality of the melodrama, noir inverted the tonality of screwball, returning to the more serious and cynical treatment of these themes and situations. Unlike screwball comedy, where everything turns out favorably for the man or woman who struggled between the two choices, noir is not so generously forgiving. The noir male seldom finds redemption after his mistake of flirting with the wrong woman, even if the flirtation is brief or innocent. Once he acts on his fantasy and associates with the seductive femme fatale, it is too late—he has betrayed the compassionate woman and set foot on the path to perdition. He can only come to a bad end as a result of his lapse. Robert Mitchum never seems to learn this, for he squanders his chances with the right woman in several films: *Out of the Past* (1947), *Where Danger Lives* (1950), and *Angel Face* (1952). In Edgar G. Ulmer's *Detour* (1945), Al Roberts (Tom Neal) lets Vera (Ann Savage) temporarily "detour" him from his direct route to his girlfriend and he ends up stranded on the highway of life. Similarly, in *Pitfall* (1948), John Forbes (Dick Powell) forsakes ideal wife, Sue, (Jane Wyatt) for an affair with enticing Mona Stevens (Lizabeth Scott), a momentary fling that leads to irrevocable complications for the man's marriage.

In a Lonely Place (1950) has Humphrey Bogart caught between two women in a different way. He plays Dixon Steele, a temperamental screenwriter, who meets a truly loving lady Laurel Gray (Gloria Grahame) at the same time that he is the prime suspect in the murder of a young woman who had visited his room shortly before she was killed. The investigation and inconclusive evidence place a strain on the lovers' relationship, bringing it to a breaking point. For his brief—and innocent—encounter with the wrong woman, Steele must suffer fateful consequences.

In another pre–Code talkie, *Shopworn* (1932), Stanwyck plays kindhearted waitress Kitty Lane who falls in love with one of her customers, David Livingston (Regis Toomey), a young college student with a pedigree. They plan to marry, but Ma Livingston (Clara Blandick) disapproves and her lawyer frames Kitty for soliciting sexual favors. After several months on a prison farm she is released. Her fortunes change when she enters show business and soars to instant fame. David tries to renew their romance, but Ma Livingston visits Kitty privately and protests the marriage. Kitty honors the old woman's wishes and tells David to stop seeing her. His mother, however, overhears Kitty's speech and, moved by the deferent sincerity of her words, changes her mind and grants the lovers her blessing.

This formula of "unacceptable" love between a man and woman of different classes, treated seriously in the melodramas, gets comedic handling in screwball. There are those screwball comedies where the gap between the wealthy and lower classes is overcome without making a major issue of their radically different financial positions, such as *It Happened One Night* and *The Palm Beach Story*. These films contain the implicit understanding that individuals from upper and lower classes are not so dissimilar in their values and can find ways to compromise and exist harmoniously. However, there are also those films where class difference presents a more imposing obstacle, such as *The Devil and Miss Jones, Next Time I Marry, Bachelor Mother, Vivacious Lady,* and *5th Ave Girl*. In these films, the wealthy protest more vociferously against any consorting with the lower classes, and it takes

The Chase (1946, United Artists; Arthur Ripley, director)—Chuck Scott (Robert Cummings) and Lorna Roman (Michèle Morgan) make their escape from her sadistic husband (played by Steve Cochran).

a more deliberate effort to show that love can cross boundaries and equalize the distinctions between discrete social strata.

Noir occasionally incorporates the division between classes as a source of conflict, but this conflict is not so easily resolvable and will most often culminate in tragedy. When Philip Marlowe (Dick Powell) of *Murder, My Sweet* finally locates the missing ex-girlfriend of Moose Malloy (Mike Mazurki), he uncovers the mystery of a dance-hall hostess (Claire Trevor) who married an elderly millionaire (Miles Mander) to improve her status while changing her identity. In the end, the skid-row gold digger and her upper-class husband are both killed. *Sunset Boulevard* establishes a contrast of lifestyles by comparing Joe Gillis's (William Holden) constricted apartment with Norma Desmond's (Gloria Swanson) sprawling, albeit outmoded, mansion. The issue of money—his dearth of it and her extravagance with her fortune—bonds the two at the outset, but the bargain grows into something more complicated and deadly for them both.

In *The Chase* (1946), Chuck Scott (Robert Cummings) is a down-on-his-luck drifter when he is hired as a chauffeur by wealthy crime boss Eddie

Roman (Steve Cochran). Scott is attracted to Roman's wife Lorna (Michèle Morgan), but maintains the respectable distance of a servant until she asks him to help her escape her cruel husband. Their union and attempted flight place them in jeopardy, but the outcome is blurred by an ambiguous double ending: the first suggests that Roman manages to get his revenge on them both, while the second suggests that they successfully escape.

Another example of a melodrama that contains source material for screwball and noir is *Virtue* (1932). A prostitute (Carole Lombard) marries a naïve misogynistic cab driver (Pat O'Brien) who, when he learns of her past, first rejects her, but then resigns himself to his fate and gives the marriage a trial run. In time, he accepts her as a loyal, loving wife. A jarring complication occurs later when she loans a friend money she was saving for her husband to buy a gas station. When she tries to recover the money, her husband misconstrues her unusual behavior as a return to her former occupation. She gets implicated in a murder and he has to decide whether he wants to abandon her or stand by her.

A number of screwball comedies borrow this particular motif where, for the sake of love, the man avoids making an issue of the woman's lost chastity, either because he minimizes its importance, or because he is too naïve to consider it. Examples of the former situation occur in *The Miracle of Morgan's Creek* and *People Will Talk*. In both films, a woman (Betty Hutton and Jeanne Crain, respectively) is pregnant with another man's child. She never grovels before society's strict proprieties, and she marries a man (Eddie Bracken, Cary Grant) without feeling the need for compromise. An example of the latter is *Ball of Fire*. Barbara Stanwyck as Sugarpuss O'Shea replaces Lombard's socially shameful character and seduces the naïve encyclopedia researcher (Gary Cooper) who deliberately overlooks her past and accepts her for herself.

In a variation of the lost chastity theme, David (Robert Montgomery), the lesser half of *Mr. & Mrs. Smith,* learns that, because of a mix-up in the laws of jurisdiction at the time of his marriage, he is not legally married to his wife, Ann (Carole Lombard). He becomes excited at the prospect of having illicit sex with his "mistress," as he privately dubs her, but unfortunately for him, Ann also learns about the mix-up and staves off his advances until they can rectify the situation. Ironically, after she has rejected David's many pleas to remarry him, the film ends with the suggestion that she surrenders herself to him without benefit of clergy. The significance of this is, of course, that it flouts the Code, which forbids talk of "virginity." Yet these films constantly remind the audience, sometimes discreetly, sometimes not so delicately, that a sexual intrigue is always at issue.

Noir also has its host of gullible males who fall under the spell of an experienced, worldly femme fatale. She makes no secret of her lost virginity, and the men make whatever excuses they can to allow them to get involved with her. As in screwball, this opens an unpredictable Pandora's Box, but unlike screwball, this generally leads to tragic consequences. In *Criss Cross* and *The Killers,* the protagonist (Burt Lancaster in both) knows that the object of his desire (Yvonne DeCarlo and Ava Gardner, respectively) belongs to another man, but his obsessive love (lust?) blinds him to her failings, and his grandiose designs crumble into dust.

Brigid O'Shaughnessy (*The Maltese Falcon*), Kathie Moffat (*Out of the Past*), and Gabrielle (*Kiss Me Deadly*) are obviously women of loose morals, yet clever detectives Sam Spade, Jeff Markham, and Mike Hammer entertain private fantasies about the seductress, fooling themselves that they are in control, that they can flirt with the Black Widow and come away intact. If they are lucky to escape death in the end, they do so with physical and emotional scars.

In *Scarlet Street* (1945), Chris Cross (Edward G. Robinson) knows that Kitty (Joan Bennett) is friends with street hustler Johnny Prince (Dan Duryea), yet he is too naive and gullible to recognize the kind of woman she truly is. When Cross learns of her actual feelings for him, that she finds him repulsive and pathetic, his adoration turns to vicious hate, and he kills her. Walter Neff in *Double Indemnity* (1944) flirts with the married Phyllis Dietrichson, yet he has to know that, being the type of woman she is, she must have a history of promiscuity.

There are, however, occasional exceptions where the noir male associates with the wanton woman, yet escapes the inevitable bleak outcome. In *The Strange Love of Martha Ivers,* Sam Masterson (Van Heflin) is caught between two such women, Martha Ivers (Barbara Stanwyck) and Toni Marachek (Lizabeth Scott). He sees one destroyed and rides off into the sunrise with the other. In *Road House,* the opposite situation occurs where the world-wise woman Lily Stevens (Ida Lupino) is caught between two men, maniacal Jefty Robbins (Richard Widmark) and sober Pete Morgan (Cornel Wilde). In *Deadline at Dawn,* a story based on a Cornell Woolrich novel, the clock works against the male protagonist. A young sailor (Bill Williams), on liberty, fears he murdered a woman and has to solve the mystery in time to get back to his ship. To help him, he recruits a taxi dancer (Susan Hayward). Her street savvy contrasts his boyish innocence, and her profession suggests how she acquired her cynicism and experience. She proves a valuable asset to the troubled protagonist, and together, they manage to surmount fate's formidable barriers.

One of the most famous noirs dealing with a woman notorious for her lost innocence is *Gilda.* The film, however, is filled with ironies that raise questions about Gilda's (Rita Hayworth) real history, whether it was, in fact, as racy and risqué as she lets everyone believe. She marries Ballin Mundson (George Macready), then goes out regularly with other men, all the time teasing Johnny Farrell (Glenn Ford) for his prudish efforts to enforce her marital faithfulness to his boss. Yet it appears that her adulterous behavior is merely for show, to create a bad-girl image that rankles Johnny, who is her real love. She is, in effect, a false flirt, a sham temptress. The film is incidentally laden with implications that Ballin is homosexual, suggesting that he never consummated his marriage to Gilda and that she is still chaste or at least untouched by him. Gilda shares many parallels with Jean Harrington (Barbara Stanwyck) of Preston Sturges's 1941 *The Lady Eve,* where the worldly attitude and seductive behavior of the woman belie the true nature of her sexual prowess with men.

These general comparisons attempt to show that the pre–Code melodramas contain plots and characters that prefigure the plots and characters of screwball and noir. One could argue that the pre–Code melodramas contain basic storylines that are easily adaptable to any genre, so that any parallels with screwball and noir are merely coincidental. However, because screwball comedies and films noirs emerge so soon after these pre–Code melodramas, it seems more likely that many of the earlier premises found their way into the two successive genres as a natural evolution in the history of film. The melodramas treat their stories as serious social commentary; screwball reacts to the seriousness by parodying the same stories in a kind of comic burlesque; noir returns to the frank treatment, but adds additional motifs (the role of fate, the image of the labyrinth, overwhelming guilt, and so on) to offer a fresh perspective on the human condition.

Basic conventions remain strikingly similar in the transition from the pre–Code melodramas to screwballs and noirs. All of these stories are generally set in the modern day (relative to when the films were produced) and most action occurs in the city, the time and place being a critical influence on character behavior. Women play pivotal roles in all of these films; whether main or secondary characters, they exercise powerful sway over the male and serve as important factors in determining his fate. Cynicism pervades many of these films—including the screwball comedies, which manifest their cynical tone through sarcasm and satire.

3

Genre Analysis: Classifying Noir and Screwball as Genres

Besides sharing coincidental historical origins, both screwball comedy and film noir are debatable as independent genres. Screwball comedy is sometimes tucked under the general heading of romantic comedy, while film noir, once classified simply as crime film, is open to critical argument as to whether it can be called a genre, a cinematic movement, or a style.

In his 1972 seminal article "Notes on Film Noir," writer-director Paul Schrader argues that noir deserves to be considered a movement, like German Expressionism and Italian neo-realism, rather than a genre like the western or musical. The basis for his rationale is that this body of crime films, produced during the 1940s and 1950s, was born out of a unique period in American history: the films were made to reflect the explicit social, economic, and political circumstances—the Great Depression, World War II, and so on—that intersected and influenced each other at a specific time in the United States. The films noirs of this phase in American history, what we call noir's classical period, could have been made only at this time because of these converging conditions, and although filmmakers may continue to imitate the style and themes of these films, the dynamic cultural forces that motivated their original plots and ideas can never be genuinely duplicated.

Schrader's argument is unquestionably valid. For one thing, noir *is* a style, regardless of whether we also wish to call it a genre. For another thing, historical contexts influence not only the content of particular films, but also the way those films are made and how they are perceived by the audience. And so post-period and modern noirs (and post-period and modern screwball comedies, for that matter, since Schrader's arguments have indirect application to that other genre as well) cannot be produced in the same way and with the same implications as those films made in their classical periods because the exact coincidental set of socio-political events from those eras are forever gone.

Film historian and critic Thomas Schatz concurs with Schrader. In his comprehensive analysis of film genres, Schatz concludes that "*film noir* was itself a system of visual and thematic conventions which were not associated with any specific genre or story formula, but rather with a distinctive cinematic style and a particular historical period" (112). To justify his position, Schatz offers an ingenious yet practical argument: he asserts that the hardboiled-detective film is a genre in its own right and that noir is a style that, although closely identified with it, is distinct from it—that is, the term "noir" refers not to the hardboiled-detective genre itself but to its style, a particular system of techniques and tonal qualities that can be imposed on any film, regardless of genre. As a style, noir is associated primarily with the World War II and post–World War II era, which Schatz labels American Expressionism (suggesting a kinship with German Expressionism of the 1920s and reinforcing Schrader's assertion that it is both a style and a movement). The hardboiled-detective film that coincidentally originates in this era relies heavily on noir stylistics—films such as *The Maltese Falcon*, *Murder My Sweet*, *Out of the Past*, and *The Big Sleep*—and has its own unique conventions that give it a classification distinct from other crime films and genres. Although noir techniques are inherent in the hardboiled-detective film, they in themselves are not the reason that these films should be categorized as noir. Melodramas, westerns, gangster films, psychological thrillers, and even comedies may incorporate noir stylistics, but this is merely incidental to their production; they still retain their fundamental genre classification. Noir, then, is not a genre but a style that can be imprinted on virtually any genre.

Yet as convincing as Schrader's and Schatz's rationales may be for classifying noir as a stylistic movement, the counterargument that defines noir as a genre still persists and can be equally persuasive. In his same text, Schatz asserts that successful producers, even those cursed with the artistic temperament of a toad, are skilled in the ways of commercialism and know how to keep churning out a successful product (4). This is to say that genres are born when filmmakers recognize the popularity of a type of film and they reproduce the formula again and again for the purpose of financial profit. In the noir-as-genre argument, despite the fact that noir refers to the tonal and stylistic qualities of these films, such films are a specific type of crime drama with certain plots, themes, characters, iconography, and tonalities that can be reproduced again and again, which suggests implicitly that they belong to a distinct genre. Even if we confine "classical" noir to a specific era, it is difficult to argue that noirs cannot still be made. Neonoirs such as Roman Polanski's 1974 *Chinatown*, Carl Franklin's 1995 *Devil*

The Maltese Falcon (1941, Warner Bros.; John Huston, director)—Detective Sam Spade (Humphrey Bogart) considers the true worth of the black bird, symbol of "the stuff that dreams are made of."

in a Blue Dress, and Christopher Nolan's 2000 *Memento* contain reincarnations of the hardboiled detective, which may simply reinforce Schatz's claim that the hardboiled-detective film is a genre and so of course it can be recreated. However, films without the hardboiled detective, such as John Schlesinger's 1969 *Midnight Cowboy*, Lawrence Kasdan's 1981 *Body Heat*, and Sam Mendes's 1999 *American Beauty*, are examples of neo-noirs that, unburdened by the obsolete stringencies of the 1934 Code, capitalize on modern mores and tolerances while managing to instill the visual and thematic elements of classical noir. The irony of all these arguments that would classify noir as a style or movement or genre or period is that noir, its dark, shadowy stories filled with all sorts of ambiguities, is itself an ambiguous entity that defies an incontrovertible classification.

Andrew Dickos in *Street with No Name* makes a case for treating noir as genre. He poses the question,

> Why must we resist recognizing the development of a *kind* of film during World War II that later increasingly embodied in its narrative concerns the disruptive, dark forces that drive and deplete modern urban man? The growth of such a cinema cannot be regarded only as a historical development, although it surely is that. Rather, it must be seen as a specific aesthetic response to the way we have come to see our human condition, shaped by the world and the movies expressing it [4].

Dickos goes on to list the many iconographic and structural elements and conventions that appear and reappear throughout the vast noir filmography and define noir as a genre. To validate his conclusion that noir is a genre, he quotes Sylvia Harvey, who, he believes, gives "one of the best definitions of the film noir: '[I]n *film noir* these strained compositions and angles are not merely embellishments or rhetorical flourishes, but form the semantic substance of the film. The visual dissonances that are characteristic of these films are the mark of those ideological contradictions that form the historical context out of which the films are produced'" ("Woman's Place" in Kaplan's *Women in Film Noir* 9).

Foster Hirsch addresses the genre controversy in his book *The Dark Side of the Screen: Film Noir*, and reaches a similar conclusion for similar reasons: "A genre, after all, is determined by conventions of narrative structure, characterization, theme, and visual design, of just the sort that *noir* offers in abundance.... Unified by a dominant tone and sensibility, the noir canon constitutes a distinct style of film-making; but it also conforms to genre requirements since it operates within a set of narrative and visual conventions" (72).

In the introduction to their book *Film Noir: An Encyclopedic Reference to the American Style*, Silver and Ward lean more toward classifying noir as a style, as implied in their title. Even though they insist that noir is devoid of established "icons," they list the numerous elements that define noir, the same ones identified by Hirsch, Schatz, and others, thereby suggesting how the noir style depends on so many conventions that it becomes recognizable as a "type" of film—that is, it has the earmarks of a genre. What's more, they admit that if there is one staple in noir, it is the protagonist who is haunted and motivated by one or both of two primary factors, alienation and obsession. By placing at noir's core a main character with consistently identifiable traits, Silver and Ward in effect emphasize one of noir's primary generic qualities, echoing Schatz's claim that central to a genre are the recognizable characters facing specific kinds of conflicts (see p. 80). Foster Hirsch makes a similar claim about the importance of the central character in defining a genre (see p. 80).

In my earlier book on noir, *Cornell Woolrich from Pulp Noir to Film Noir*, I argue for considering noir a genre:

> What makes *film noir* such a slippery beast is its chimerical qualities: it is made up of all these features, so that, while it may be a series or a style or a genre, it may also be a series and a style and a genre....
> If the term "cycle" or "series" presupposes some common denominator linking these films, and if, as is apparent, crime alone is not enough to connect them, we should be able to identify a number of shared characteristics. Once we start to enumerate these shared characteristics, we begin to move toward the area of genre [19–20].

Because noir exhibits traits that qualify it for all of these classifications, perhaps we have to admit another option: its concurrent properties challenge our attempt to lodge it under one label. We might compare this to the ambiguous nature of light. Scientists recognize light as both energy and particle and will treat it as one or the other, depending on the specific circumstances under which it is analyzed. Noir is like that; it has an amorphous quality that enables us to discuss it in several categories. If tonal quality alone defined noir, the arguments would hold up that noir is exclusively a style. But besides the mix of unusual camera angles, chiaroscuro patterns, and cynical themes, noir contains many recurring features—the noir protagonist, femme fatale, urban setting with rain-drenched streets and nighttime scenes, encroaching shadows, winding labyrinths, bar imagery, ubiquitous mirrors that produce reflections to indicate duplicity, intervention of fate or chance, corruption of the American Dream, and so on. When these specific iconographic, stylistic, and thematic elements are reproduced in a series of films, we can justifiably place them in that generic category called noir.

Schrader's position, though debatable, is important to our present study because what it says about noir is in some ways applicable to screwball comedy. First, both have an initial classical period confined to a definite span of years (14 of which overlap), screwball from 1934 to 1954 (see Chapter 1, pp. 11–13, for a discussion on the limits of the classical screwball period) and noir from 1941 to 1960 (also with a disputed end date). Second, both contain ambiguities that defy absolute, restrictive definitions. Noir is a type of crime drama that has features in common with gangster, police procedural, and mystery films, yet its peculiarities earn it a classification distinct from those other crime films; screwball is comedy that synthesizes facets of other genres, including romantic comedy, farce, slapstick, and even drama, yet this conglomeration is what places it in a niche apart from any of these other types of comedy. As Belton aptly puts it, screwball is a "hybrid form" (180).

Schatz offers an overview of genre that applies equally to noir and screwball:

> The determining, identifying feature of a film genre is its cultural context, its community of interrelated character types whose attitudes, values, and actions flesh out dramatic conflicts inherent within that community [21–22].

Schatz, then, sees a genre determined primarily by specific conflicts that involve specific characters who appear again and again in a specific type of film. Time and place and iconography may have significance in defining a genre, but at the core of each genre are particular types of characters engaged in particular types of conflicts. Foster Hirsch would probably agree with Schatz, at least in part. In *The Dark Side of the Screen*, he notes that noir is dependent on the interaction of three main character types: the noir protagonist (whether hero, villain, or victim), the femme fatale (whether wicked or well-intentioned), and the psychopath (whether a third separate character or one simultaneously merged with one of the other two).

Just as film noir so often places the noir protagonist and the femme fatale (or femme blanche) at the heart of its conflict, screwball comedy always places the romantically paired couple at the center of its story. In both genres, we can see "dramatic conflicts that we associate with specific patterns of action and character relationships." With screwball, it is the battle of the sexes and discrepancies in the roles of men and women in society. Circumstances may vary, but the two warring lovers always find a reason to take opposite sides on an issue, be it domestic (*Mr. & Mrs. Smith, Turnabout*), professional (*His Girl Friday, Adam's Rib*), or idealistic (*The Devil and Miss Jones, You Can't Take It with You*). With noir, it is the dangerous flirtation between the femme fatale and noir protagonist, their warped obsession with each other and with some elusive goal (*Double Indemnity, Angel Face, This Gun for Hire, The Chase*, and so on). Out of these behaviors, we can recognize a "community of interrelated character types whose attitudes, values, and actions flesh out dramatic conflicts inherent within that community."

Schatz elaborates on how genres are determined by the relationship between the story's central conflict and the characters caught in that conflict that jeopardizes the social order:

> Certain genres (Western, detective, gangster, war, et al.) have conflicts that, indigenous to the environment, reflect the physical and ideological struggle for its control.... Other genres have conflicts that are not indigenous to the locale but are the result of the conflict between the values, attitudes, and actions of its principal characters and the "civilized" setting they inhabit. Conflicts in these genres (musical, screwball comedy, family

melodrama) generally are animated by a "doubled" hero—usually a romantic couple whose courtship is complicated and eventually ideologically resolved [26].

When it comes to noir and screwball, these generalizations, valid as they are, do not fit all the films so neatly. Noirs are of two main types, each of which matches one of the categories Schatz outlines above. Those noirs concerned with the hardboiled detective clearly belong to the first type of conflict in which the detective, from Bogart's Spade to Welles's Quinlan, is a law enforcer defending and protecting the social order. The detective usually faces a dual conflict: on the one hand is a personal conflict that usually concerns a woman, such as Spade with Brigid O'Shaughnessy and Marlowe with Helen Grayle, or a private matter, such as Hammer avenging the death of Christina Bailey; and on the other is a professional conflict (a client's problem, a mystery). At the same time, there is the non-detective noir, what is often called the "domestic" noir (*In a Lonely Place, Angel Face, The Two Mrs. Carrolls, Scarlet Street, Detour,* and so on), where the emphasis is on the melodrama. Although a murder occurs and has bearing on the couple, its treatment and solution are secondary to the story. Interest is centered more on the intimate contention between the male and female (married or not) than with the solution of that particular crime.

Ironically, there happen to be two types of screwball films that correspond conveniently to the domestic and detective types of noirs. "Screwball comedy" generally refers to the main body of screwball films that, like the domestic noirs, emphasize the "conflict between the values, attitudes, and actions of its principal characters and the 'civilized' setting they inhabit." The other type of screwball film, referred to as the "screwball mystery," corresponds to the hardboiled-detective noir. The mystery adds a dimension to the story that prevents exclusive focus on the screwball couple, diverting some of the attention to the whodunit in much the same way that the hardboiled detective's professional quest diverts attention from his private intrigue. However, the relationship between the screwball detective and his mate differs considerably from that of the noir detective and the femme fatale in that it is less a contentious cat-and-mouse game than it is a playful battle of the sexes, a husband and wife acting as a detective team (*A Night to Remember, Remember Last Night?, Fast and Furious, The Thin Man* series) or unmarried partners bonding while trying to solve a mystery, such as in *The Mad Miss Manton* and *Adventure in Manhattan.*

Recognizing this difference between the two types of noirs and screwballs becomes important in respect to Schatz's discussion of two features of genres that he calls "determinate" and "indeterminate space." Although he had de-emphasized setting when he talked of character conflict as central to a genre, he brings setting back into the discussion when he mentions these two terms:

In a genre of determinate space (Western, gangster, detective, et al.), we have a symbolic arena of action.... A specific social conflict is violently enacted within a familiar locale according to a prescribed system of rules and behavioral codes....

In contrast, genres of indeterminate space generally involve a doubled (and thus dynamic) hero in the guise of a romantic couple who inhabit a "civilized" setting, as in the musical, screwball comedy, and social melodrama.... Here, conflicts derive not from a struggle over control of the environment, but rather from the struggle of the principal characters to bring their own views in line either with one another's or, more often, with that of the larger community....

[Genres of indeterminate space] tend to celebrate the values of *social integration*, whereas [genres of determinate space] uphold the values of *social order* [27–29].

Contradictions arise when we attempt to apply this theory of determinate and indeterminate space to all films noirs or all screwball comedies. Genres of determinate space use a preconceived conventional setting where the protagonist upholds and preserves the social order against some destructive, anarchic force. The hardboiled-detective film, for instance, set in the city and pitting a detective-hero against some sinister foe, fits this category—and so does the screwball mystery. Protagonists in a screwball mystery, engaged in solving a murder case, carry on antics similar to those of the mainstream screwball couple, but their ultimate goal, not marriage but the solution of the crime, takes precedence in the story, and so they, too, are responsible for preserving the social order. Genres of indeterminate space, on the other hand, do not depend on any single conventional setting, yet the screwball comedy (whether of the mystery or mainstream variety) centers most of its action in the city, suggesting that this particular venue has an important, undeniable impact on the characters, their lifestyle, and their circumstances. Even in those films where a small town or rustic locale has a prominent purpose in the story (screwball's *Theodora Goes Wild*, *The Bride Came C.O.D.*, and *Bringing Up Baby*; noir's *Fallen Angel*, *Ace in the Hole*, and *The Hitch-Hiker*), the city still lingers subliminally as an influence on the characters and their actions.

Screwball lovers, rather than working to preserve the social order, are more concerned with resolving their private conflict and integrating (or reintegrating) themselves into society as a traditional married couple. This would seem, at least in part, to apply to domestic noirs as well. Where the social order is upset by the noir protagonist (*Ace in the Hole*), femme fatale (*The File on Thelma Jordan*), or noir couple (*Gun Crazy*), the films relate to genres of determinate space. At the same time, however, because the noir couple frequently struggles with a private concern, whether legitimate or illegal, they often face issues of social dis-integration, or alienation, which links them inversely to the screwball couple and to genres of indeterminate space.

In films of indeterminate space, conflict is less about controlling one's external environment than about the conflicted pair reaching a resolution or compromise. Interest in the conflict is often sustained because both sides offer valid and logical arguments, although, as Schatz points out, one value appears more convincing than the other, and the less attractive position finally falls in line with the more universally accepted one. It is obvious in *Topper*, for instance, that while the Kerbys are immersed in a life of incessant revelry, Topper, restrained by his wife's demand for strict routine, secretly longs to adopt their profligate habits. Yet both positions can be defended and refuted: the Kerbys may enjoy their active, exciting, fun-filled existence, but their lives are also prodigal and unproductive. The Toppers may follow a structured lifestyle that is practical and lucrative, but it is also stilted and joyless. The advantages to both lifestyles are debatable, and in the end, Clara Topper's consent to wear the sexy lingerie symbolizes a "modest" concession to a more flexible routine, a compromise embracing the more appealing outlook.

Schatz places the "detective" genre under films of determinate space, and although when discussing films of indeterminate space he does not use the term "noir," he refers to a genre called "social melodrama." This latter term may encompass a broad range of films (*Inherit the Wind, Executive Suite, Written on the Wind, Rebel Without a Cause*), but it also could easily include the domestic noirs, those noirs in which a detective is not a mandatory figure in the story and, if present at all, is merely an incidental element. Examples of these noirs are *The Spiral Staircase, Road House, Clash by Night, The File on Thelma Jordan*, and *Beware, My Lovely*. If we accept domestic noirs as a type of social melodrama, then, like screwball comedy, they would fall into that category of films associated with indeterminate space. Their primary conflict occurs between the paired main characters, noir's protagonist and femme fatale, who represent the dark side of screwball's embattled romantic couple. A primary contrast, however, is that while the embattled screwball couple finally integrates with society, the noir couple (one or both of them) often faces social alienation (if not that ultimate sign of rejection, death). In *Angel Face* and *Where Danger Lives*, the Robert Mitchum character surrenders to the femme fatale who either takes his life or mars his reputation. In *Detour*, the hapless traveler (Tom Neal), on a quest to reunite with his girlfriend, becomes culpable for two bizarre deaths and he is ultimately arrested (or as symbolized in the ambiguous ending, left to wander interminably on the highway of life).

In discussing the evolution of a genre, Schatz indirectly reinforces Schrader's argument that noirs can no longer be made because of evolution in the social and political environments. Schatz discusses a "static nucleus" (the standard problem or conflict) and a "dynamic surface structure" (varied approaches to a solution of the problem) as being critical to sustaining interest in a genre. That is, a genre has a limited number of conflicts or problems, but may introduce numerous ways to solve them. If, in time, the audience's attitude changes or cultural perspectives change on how to deal with those problems, it could spell the end of a genre as it was originally known—which seems to be the case for both screwball and noir as they moved from their classical periods in the mid–20th century to mutated forms later on. The eventual easing of the strictures imposed by the MPPC of 1934 and the passage of time after World War II and the Great Depression (which had accentuated the demarcation between the classes of haves and have-nots) affected approaches to screwball—consider the emphasis placed on sexual themes in the Doris Day-Rock Hudson/James Garner/Cary Grant collaborations of the 1960s or in the films written or directed by Nora Ephron after 1989. Distance from the Depression and World War II also changed the outlook in noir, as reflected in films like those made by the Coen brothers, *Blood Simple* and *Fargo*. Both the noir and screwball genres emerged in response to certain cultural and sociopolitical events, and when conditions for those events changed or faded, these genres had to adapt to new conditions in order to survive in a revised form.

Gehring's Approaches to Genre-lizing Screwball and Their Applications to Noir

Wes D. Gehring iterates Schatz's theories about determinate and indeterminate space and agrees that screwball belongs in the latter category. He also categorizes screwball as a genre by examining it in two different ways: first, by identifying screwball with five traits that define the screwball antihero; and second, by looking at screwball through the filter of comic theory.

First, Gehring notes how the comic antihero is associated with five specific features that become, in a larger sense, five basic conventions earmarking the screwball genre.

Leisure time. The male antihero somehow finds ample time to interact with his female partner. David Huxley gets away from his museum for an extended time to interact with Susan Vance (*Bringing Up Baby*) and Norval Jones is constantly in the company of Trudy Kockenlocker (*The Miracle of Morgan's Creek*). Or somehow the antihero is thrown into a situation that gives him extra opportunities to socialize with the female. In *My Man Godfrey,* derelict Godfrey is hired as a butler for the Bullock family, keeping him in close proximity with daughter Irene. In *Take a Letter, Darling,* Tom Verney assumes unusual after-hour duties as secretary for female boss Mac MacGregor.

Childlike attitude. The male protagonist often exhibits behavior reflecting his immaturity, irresponsibility, and playfulness. In *Mr. & Mrs. Smith,*

David Smith acts like a capricious teenager when he fantasizes that his wife is his mistress, he runs after her like a jealous lover, and then he tries to win her sympathy by feigning overexposure in the wild. In *The Thin Man*, Nick Charles is thrilled to get an air-gun for Christmas, then proceeds to shoot balloons on the tree and eventually knocks out a window pane. Game-playing is an important part of this unconventional courtship—like silly juvenile lovers, the combatants play different kinds of "games," from the first screwballs of the classical period (along with *The Thin Man* are *Twentieth Century* and *It Happened One Night*) to the later ones (*Unfaithfully Yours* and Hawks's *Monkey Business*).

Urban lifestyle. The city contributes implicitly or explicitly to the kind of life the male and female protagonist lead and may be a factor in their dissension. In *The Palm Beach Story*, the city gives Tom the inspiration for his invention (a landing net for airplanes that is strung over the roofs of skyscrapers), but Tom and wife Jerry have to flee New York before they can

Twentieth Century (1934, Columbia; Howard Hawks, director)—Lily Garland (Carole Lombard) demonstrates how, in screwball's battle of the sexes, the female makes her male counterpart—in this case, ex-lover Oscar Jaffe (John Barrymore)—the brunt of her physical abuse.

rediscover their love in Palm Beach. Topper lives a sedate, reclusive lifestyle in a countrified setting, but he prefers the life of the party-going Kerbys, whose habits include frequent bar-hopping through the city's nightclubs. In *Twentieth Century*, the city is kind to Lily Garland, who gains fame as a leading stage actress, while it proves a disastrous backdrop for Oscar Jaffe, who watches his career collapse in ruins.

Apolitical viewpoint. Politics are of no concern to the comic antihero who is more absorbed in a personal matter, particularly the quest to win or reclaim the woman he loves. This attribute reinforces Schatz's theory on genres of indeterminate space in that the protagonist focuses on private affairs rather than on issues related to the larger community. In *Vivacious Lady*, Peter Morgan, Jr., (James Stewart) is less interested in observing the proprieties of his position as college professor than he is in finally consummating his marriage with new wife Francey (Ginger Rogers). In *The More the Merrier*, Joe Carter (Joel McCrea) ignores his military obligations momentarily while he pursues Connie Milligan (Jean Arthur). In *Holiday*, Johnny Case intends to go on an extended freewheeling hiatus, a plan directly at odds with the straitlaced, practical-minded father of his fiancée.

Frustrated ambitions, especially sexual frustration with women. The screwball male may pursue the female exclusively (such as in *Mr. & Mrs. Smith*), but more often this romantic pursuit is entwined with the pursuit of some personal goal. The delay in his attaining his dual objectives is central to the story's conflict. The frustration he endures contributes to the suspense as he and the female move gradually toward harmonious compromise. In *Bringing Up Baby*, David Huxley needs grant money to sustain his archeological work, and so he continuously accosts Mr. Peabody, lawyer for an elderly female philanthropist. Into his life comes Susan Vance with whom he is totally incompatible, yet his resignation to the fact that they are fated for each other solves both his money problems and his conflict with her. In *My Favorite Wife*, Nick gets caught between two women, Bianca, his recent bride, and Ellen, his wife who was declared dead. His frustration comes from trying to break the news delicately to Bianca while appeasing Ellen. He can find no solution to satisfy everyone, and so he becomes paralyzed by indecision.

When these five traits of the comic antihero are expanded to include larger elements of the story, they actually define screwball comedy. Leisure time applies to both the male and female protagonists who must find time to wage and resolve their conflict. Eccentric behavior is often demonstrated as much by the woman as the man, and by extension, occurs in many supporting characters who populate these stories. The city is always a prominent setting in screwball. Private concerns, not political issues, take precedence for all the characters, not only for the male protagonist. And personal frustration with the opposite sex is not limited to the male.

Ironically, these same five traits, with some modification, also define both the noir protagonist and the general qualities of film noir.

Leisure time. The characters manage to finagle their schedules so they have time to interact and stoke the fires of their obsessive liaison. In *Double Indemnity*, Walter Neff and Phyllis Dietrichson hold several trysts, fueling their illicit affair while sealing their pact to commit murder. Jeff Bailey, in *Out of the Past*, is able to forego his detective career while he and Kathie Moffat enjoy each other's company in their idyllic romantic retreat. Like screwball comedy, noir manipulates time to allow more complications to develop in the couple's relationship, producing greater friction, discontent, and alienation.

Childlike attitude. In screwball, a childlike attitude fosters the eccentric, sometimes infantile behavior exhibited by the male protagonist and his romantic counterpart. In noir, this childlike attitude manifests itself in the protagonist's naiveté and gullibility that predispose him to being duped by the femme fatale. Obsessed with a woman in *Criss Cross* and *The Killers*, Burt Lancaster displays the rationality of a hormone-driven teenager too blinded by desire to see how the femmes fatales (Yvonne DeCarlo and Ava Gardner, respectively) are manipulating him. In *The Lady from Shanghai*, protagonist O'Hara is so smitten with the femme fatale that he becomes enmeshed in a murder intrigue that he could have avoided with a little mature common sense. *Fear in the Night* and its remake *Nightmare* (both adapted and directed by Maxwell Shane) signify the male's childlike quality in a different way: the weak-minded protagonist is susceptible to hypnotic suggestion, placing him under control of a devious villain who prompts him to commit murder by proxy.

Urban lifestyle. Like screwball, film noir tends to depend on the influence of a modern urban milieu. The concrete (or asphalt) jungle suits stories that plumb the baser instincts of the human animal living a fast paced, dog-eat-dog lifestyle. The city, a man-made citadel of creativity and corruption, rouses a basic instinct of survival of the fittest that replaces human consideration and communal ethics.

Apolitical viewpoint. Just as screwball protagonists are more concerned with their private interests and personal goals than they are with public and political causes, the noir protagonist and femme fatale are more occupied with their intimate desires and ambitions than they are with larger community matters. Guy Haines (Farley Granger) of *Strangers on a Train*, engaged to Anne Morton (Ruth Roman), daughter of Senator Morton (Leo G. Carroll), devotes his time trying to prevent Bruno Antony (Robert Walker) from framing him for murder, giving the impression that he is protecting his future father-in-law from a scandal, when in actuality he is protecting himself because of his own political ambitions. In *Touch of Evil*, the story revolves more around the private rivalry between the upright Mike

Vargas (Charlton Heston) and the corrupt Hank Quinlan (Orson Welles) than around the crooked politics that keep Quinlan's border town operating smoothly.

Frustrated ambitions, especially sexual frustration with women. This is evident in that much of the central conflict in noir, as in screwball, concerns the frustration the protagonist feels in his relationship with the femme fatale or femme blanche. *I Wake Up Screaming, Double Indemnity, Angel Face, Scarlet Street, Gun Crazy,* and *Gilda* are but a few examples of the many noirs in which the male protagonist (or male antagonist in the case of *I Wake Up Screaming* and *The Chase*) is driven to extreme, and sometimes desperate, behavior because of how he is treated by his female love interest.

In addition to defining screwball as a genre in terms of these five central traits, Gehring uses a second approach, showing how the genre is linked to comedy theory, particularly to that aspect concerned with the viewer's feeling of superiority.

He begins by pointing out observations from philosophers such as Aristotle, who in his *Poetics* defined comedy as works which thrived on the "imitation of baser men," and Thomas Hobbs, who in his *Leviathan* asserted that laughter depended on "the apprehension of some deformed thing in another, by comparison whereof [viewers] suddenly applaud themselves" (153). Gehring then refers to conjectures contained in one of the cornerstone treatises on comedy, "Laughter," by Henri Bergson:

> Laughter is, above all, a corrective. Being intended to humiliate, it must make a painful impression on the person against whom it is directed. By laughter, society avenges itself for the liberties taken with it.... [Laughter] ... must have social signification [154].

Gehring goes on to postulate "three key barometers" for measuring what he calls "the conservative nature of this approach to comedy theory": "the concept of implosion, genre space and conflict, and the comic tendencies of pivotal directors" (154).

Discussing implosion, Gehring implies that the humor in screwball comedy, by exploding inward, works "to pull things together." Screwball acts as a catalyst to unite "economically diverse classes." In poking fun at the wealthy and making them look less sophisticated than they aspire to be, screwball humbles the upper class and raises the lower class, in effect reducing the gap between the two and equalizing their positions (at least philosophically). *It Happened One Night, Vivacious Lady, The Philadelphia Story, You Can't Take It with You, The Devil and Miss Jones,* and *5th Ave Girl* are a few instances wherein humor undercuts the stuffy pretensions of the rich and blurs class boundaries.

Discussing his second key point, "genre space and conflict," Gehring iterates Schatz's theories about "Indeterminate Space." Although the setting for screwball comedies is usually the modern-day city (that is, contemporary cities at the time these films were made), the conflict between the main characters is not bound by any definite time and place, like a war film or western. Therefore, conflict between screwball characters has a nonspecific, timeless quality that can apply to people of any period and in nearly any circumstance.

To support his third point, Gehring refers to three "pivotal directors," Howard Hawks, Leo McCarey, and Blake Edwards, whose films are representative of the screwball genre. His intention is to show how films from the classical (Hawks and McCarey) and modern (Edwards) eras reflect the "conservative makeup of screwball comedy," dependent as they are on the comic theory of superiority. Hawks's *Bringing Up Baby*, *Monkey Business*, and *I Was a Male War Bride* show how the male is frequently humiliated by the female's superior role. McCarey's *The Awful Truth* and *My Favorite Wife* exemplify situations in which the man and woman take turns getting the upper hand. Edwards's *10* and *Victor/Victoria* resonate with McCarey's approach to humor, but in addition, reflect his own philosophy: "Humor is based ... on cruelty.... You have to remember that in comedy you can do *terrible* things to other people!" (159).

The element of superiority frequently occurs in noir, especially with the femme fatale assuming a position of control over the hapless male. The iconic shot in *Double Indemnity* of a naked Phyllis Dietrichson wrapped in a towel and looking down from an upper landing on a gawking Walter Neff standing at the base of her stairway represents the inequality found in these noir relationships. In other examples, Eric Stanton (Dana Andrews) willingly humiliates himself to win Stella (Linda Darnell) in *Fallen Angel*; Michael O'Hara (Orson Welles) compromises his integrity in attempting to seduce a married Elsa Bannister (Rita Hayworth) in *The Lady from Shanghai*; Al Roberts (Tom Neal) has difficulty defying the strong-willed Vera (Ann Savage) in *Detour*; and in *I Wake Up Screaming*, police inspector Ed Cornell (Laird Cregar) is so obsessed with Vicky Lynn (Carole Landis) that he forsakes his professional integrity to frame an innocent man for her murder because he blames the man for taking her from him. However, sometimes the male protagonist and his female love interest rotate in their position of superiority. Such is the case in *Out of the Past* (with Robert Mitchum and Jane Greer), *This Gun for Hire* (with Alan Ladd and Veronica Lake), and *Gilda* (with Glenn Ford and Rita Hayworth). Gehring's last point, that humor, as Blake Edwards claims, is based on cruelty, is true for screwball, while in noir, there is nothing humorous about the cruelty the man and woman inflict on each other. In *Where Danger Lives*, Margo Lannington (Faith Domergue) plays a self-consumed dominatrix. She ignores the fact that her lover Jeff Cameron (Robert Mitchum), suffers from a concussion and she manipulates him with lies and demands. And in *Nightmare Alley*, Stanton Carlisle (Tyrone Power), a phony mentalist, persuades his

Double Indemnity (1944, Paramount; Billy Wilder, director)—In noir, the eternal triangle produces tragic consequences. This particular shot conveys the relationships of the ill-fated trio: the bar imagery enclosing Mr. Dietrichson (Tom Powers, right) foreshadows the murderous trap awaiting him, as devised by the more intimate pair, his adulterous wife Phyllis (Barbara Stanwyck) and insurance salesman Walter Neff (Fred MacMurray).

wife, Molly (Coleen Gray), to help him use his sham spiritualism to deceive an old man for money, even though she pleads with him not to do it because it offends her profound religious beliefs.

Cavell's Comedy of Remarriage Applied to Screwball and Noir

In *Pursuits of Happiness: The Hollywood Comedy of Remarriage*, Stanley Cavell concentrates on seven particular films that, although usually placed under the broad heading of screwball comedies, receive his particular classification as "comedy of remarriage." This term actually encompasses many screwball comedies if we consider the number of them that frequently deal with remarriage, both as something literal—a reunion follows a divorce or separation, as in *Bedtime Story, His Girl Friday, Mr. & Mrs. Smith, The Ex-*

Mrs. Bradford, Adam's Rib, The Philadelphia Story, and *The Awful Truth*—
and also as something figurative—the two lovers are not married, but behave
as if they are, and after an extended contentious relationship, ultimately wed
(or plan to wed), as in *It Happened One Night, Bringing Up Baby, The Doctor
Takes a Wife, Bachelor Mother, If You Could Only Cook,* and *Midnight.*

Noir inverts this plot device. Whereas the relationship of the screwball
couple begins in conflict and culminates in marriage (or remarriage) as a
symbol of their hard-won bliss, the noir couple often begins the relationship
in a sexually charged union that gradually disintegrates into self-destruction
and death. *Clash by Night, No Man of Her Own, Conflict,* and *The Two Mrs.
Carrolls* start with hopeful marriages in which one partner's pent-up desires,
or secret past, or mental imbalance creates a predicament for both of them.
Gun Crazy, They Live by Night, and *Sunset Boulevard* deal with unmarried
noir couples whose alienation from mainstream society produces complications that result in tragedy. One particular example that deals with a
gamut of marital relationships is *Gilda.* The film is an extreme oddity in
this regard, containing both a common-law arrangement (Gilda and Johnny
Farrell, who had an earlier affair and, throughout the story, treat each other
with spousal contempt) and literal marriages (Gilda and Ballin Mundson,
Gilda and Johnny), not to mention the suggested homosexual relationship
between Ballin and Johnny.

In the course of the introductory remarks to his book, Cavell explains
his intention to use philosophy as the basis for his critical analysis of the seven
films under discussion. It is a valid approach that leads to some insightful
observations and conclusions about the remarriage theme that recurs so
often in screwball comedy. He also offers a broad definition of "genre":

> A narrative or dramatic genre might be thought of as a medium in the
> visual arts might be thought of, or a "form" in music.... The members of a
> genre share the inheritance of certain conditions, procedures and subjects
> and goals of composition, and that in primary art each member of such a
> genre represents a study of these conditions [28].

He touches on a number of aspects of the comedy of remarriage that relate
to screwball comedy as a whole. Originating early in the Depression years,
these films may have acted like "fairy tales" to counter the era's woes (2),
although other coincidental factors—such as "a phase in the history of the
consciousness of women" (16) and "economic issues ... [that] are invariably
tropes for spiritual issues" (5)—became an integral part of these films' thematic makeup.

According to Cavell, film noir, in contrast to offering the escapism of
a "fairy tale," imitates classical tragedy, having a cathartic effect on its audience for the problems pervading society. Issues related to the economy, sexism, and pursuit of the American Dream are examined, particularly from
cynical, pessimistic perspectives.

Thirties and Forties Films Examined by Molly Haskell

In her exquisitely crafted book *From Reverence to Rape: The Treatment of Women in the Movies,* as entertaining and informative as it is eloquently written, Molly Haskell explores the roles women played in films during the 20th century, and in the process, touches on motifs that characterize the genres of classical screwball comedy and film noir. Most of her chapters are divided by decades, and her remarks about certain films of the thirties, forties, and fifties become particularly relevant to this present study.

In discussing the thirties, Haskell frequently addresses the love-as-conflict premise, indirectly emphasizing the competitive nature of the couple as a critical staple of the genre: "The battle of the sexes is a battle of equals.... The postponements, representing the social conventions that create a distance between man and woman ... are nothing less than a metaphorical rendering of the essential ingredient of romantic love" (130). The skirmishes that delay the couple's union create a sexual tension that makes the final resolution all that more touching and satisfying.

It is crucial to screwball that this "battle" is waged between a man and woman of equal wit, will, and desire. According to Haskell, "Love is consummated in gags, [and] there is an equalization of obstacles and a matching of temperaments. A man and a woman ... rub each other with and against the grain simultaneously, and, in the friction, in the light in the other's eyes, to know themselves for the first time" (126–127). What looks like a violent collision is really a romantic *pas de deux*. In the same way that two lovers take turns assuming the dominant position during sexual foreplay, the screwball couple trades moments of one-upmanship as events move inevitably toward the desired climax. In *It Happened One Night,* for example, Peter Warne and Ellie Andrews learn something about each other and themselves as they each take turns getting the upper hand over the other during their trek northward. Walter Burns may eventually get his way in *His Girl Friday,* but Hildy Johnson parries with him verbally and intellectually, adroitly staving off several of his tactics before he succeeds. As Haskell observes, in alternating positions of control, the man and woman signify "a larger equilibrium, a world in which male authority, or sexual imperialism, is reduced or in abeyance, while the feminine spirit is either dominant or equal" (131).

Whereas the screwball couple displays matched temperaments that serve as a precondition for their eventual union in marriage, noir couples often suffer an imbalance in their dispositions and their need to dominate, a disparity that produces the ongoing tension that leads, in many cases, to their ultimate demise. *In a Lonely Place* is a good example of a relationship that is founded on mutual attraction but gradually deteriorates when doubt, mistrust, and fear creep in to erode it. Dixon Steele (Humphrey Bogart) is a volatile screenwriter suspected of killing a young hat-check girl. He and Laurel Gray (Gloria Grahame) try to support each other through the police investigation, but as their ordeal progresses and he loses more and more control of his emotions, the suspicions become overwhelming and their relationship flounders.

In his analysis of the screwball protagonist, Gehring makes the point that the character manages to find "leisure time" to court, study, and win the object of his (or her) affection. Haskell iterates this idea when she explains that game-playing for the hero and heroine "is a period of grace, of experimentation and discovery under the cover of conventions, of rules they are supposed to enact and which protect them until they are ready to act without them" (131). However effected, whether by circumstance (*The Bride Came C.O.D.*, *The Doctor Takes a Wife*) or deliberate action (*Mr. & Mrs. Smith*, *The Footloose Heiress*), this "leisure time" enables the hero and heroine to get acquainted or to rediscover each other so that their scathing scrapes can evolve into something more pleasantly romantic. In numerous screwballs involving the newspaper business, the reporter, through destiny or design, lands in a situation wherein he can give the woman his exclusive attention. This scenario begins with *It Happened One Night*, and continues with such films as *Nothing Sacred*, *Love on the Run*, *His Girl Friday*, *The Mad Miss Manton*, *Libeled Lady*, and *Design for Scandal*. Also, as noted above, noir incorporates "leisure" time, giving the noir protagonist the opportunity to explore his situation while making his way through the dark nightmare that tests his fortitude and resourcefulness.

The language specific to screwball comedies, distinctively glib and fluid, emotionally charged and boisterous, may in part have been a creative response to film's new sound technology that was introduced only a few years before. In the silent era, dialogue expressed through intertitles was deprived of inflection and tone. Talkies inspired filmmakers to take advantage of this modern technology. Crime films were enhanced when raging gunfire and screeching tires exploded from the screen and gangsters slurred slangy wisecracks at each other. Screwball comedies used language to produce a barrage of verbal gibes and vocal retorts that reflected the animosity of the combative couple while revealing their individual wit and acumen. As Haskell says, "Conversation was an index not only of intelligence, but of confidence, of self-possession" (139). Language showed the sparring power of the two lovers and symbolized the ability of the two sexes to compete equally with each other.

Stanley Cavell gives further significance to the emergence of sound:

> The year of the earliest member of our genre, 1934, is early enough for that film [*It Happened One Night*] to have had a decisive say in determining the creation of Hollywood sound film. The genre it projected, on my interpretation, can be said to require the creation of a new woman, or the

new creation of a woman, something I describe as a new creation of the human. If the genre is as definitive of sound comedy as I take it to be, and if the feature of the creation of the woman is as definitive of the genre as I take it to be, then this phase of the history of cinema is bound up with a phase in the history of the consciousness of women. You might even say that these phases of these histories are part of the creation of one another [16].

Sound film, Cavell seems to be saying, endowed women with a voice, and by their vocalizing, they defined themselves in an articulate and assertive way that made them appear more prominent, competent, and intelligent. Sound contributed to the origin of the new genre, and the genre, because of sound, contributed to society's new perception of Woman.

Haskell notes an additional consequence of the sound film in conjunction with the Production Code: while the new sound technology was responsible for giving voice to the (supposedly) new "articulate woman," the suppressive nature of the Production Code, coupled with a rash of sordid and stifling films about the Depression, prompted the emergence of the "working woman" (139). One of the benefits of woman's new prominence in society was her expanded role in the workforce. This was reflected in films in that the working woman became an integral figure in the talkies of the early thirties and the screwball comedies that emerged shortly thereafter. The working woman was the modern city woman, and she opened up a whole new area of story possibilities for filmmakers.

In the end, however, "Their mythic destiny, like that of all women, was to find love and cast off the 'veneer' of independence" (Haskell 150). In many screwball comedies in which the woman starts out in a profession that earns her status and independence, her position is viewed as "provisional," a temporary avocation that fails to contribute to "her definition as a woman" (Haskell 142). Even when she is proud of her career, she harbors a secret ambition to marry, and she eventually capitulates to tradition, as if marriage were not only her inevitable fate but her ultimate desire. Thus, Barbara Stanwyck is ready to forfeit her career as a doctor for Henry Fonda (*You Belong to Me*); Rosalind Russell is willing to sacrifice her judicial career for Robert Cummings (*Tell It to the Judge*); Ginger Rogers forsakes her nightclub act to marry James Stewart (*Vivacious Lady*); and Priscilla Lane gives away her million-dollar legacy to satisfy inflexibly chauvinistic Ronald Reagan (*Million Dollar Baby*).

Film noir began more than a decade after the sound film had become entrenched, so the impact of sound technology on the image of women seems less pertinent. However, there is no doubt that noir deals extensively with issues related to society's perception of women, whether its female characters receive treatment that is realistic or symbolic.

Haskell calls attention to a special male-female liaison that occurs with some frequency in screwball: "Frequently the father-daughter relationship ... takes precedence over the romantic interest, in a brief, platonic, mutually advantageous relationship" (143). The "father" Haskell refers to is not the female protagonist's actual father in the story, such as Walter Connolly, in *It Happened One Night* or Eugene Pallette in *My Man Godfrey*, since these fathers too often give the female a reason for rebellion. Instead, Haskell means a "father figure," an older gentleman who aligns himself with the young woman. This relationship exists between Charles Coburn and Jean Arthur in *The More the Merrier* and *The Devil and Miss Jones*, between Walter Connolly and Ginger Rogers in *5th Ave Girl*, and between John Barrymore and Claudette Colbert in *Midnight*. In these and other films, the older man acts like a fairy godfather, instrumental in helping the woman find her heart's desire—whether she is conscious of it or not—and, as Haskell says, sometimes helping himself in the bargain, as do John Barrymore and Walter Connolly, who reinvigorate connubial love in their wives. This "father-daughter" bond is one of many recurring conventions that contribute to distinguishing screwball comedy as a genre.

A Genre's Evolutionary Stages

"A film genre," notes Thomas Schatz, "is both a *static* and a *dynamic* system" (16). To belong to a specific genre, a film must retain the conventions and formulas that define its category, yet paradoxically, it is also subject to the vicissitudes of socio-political events, cultural fads, technological advances, and so on, that force it constantly to revise itself.

In respect to changing attitudes, Molly Haskell points out one particular difference between screwball's male-female relationships of the late forties and those in the thirties: "The underside—the bitterness, the sense of victimization of one partner by the other (usually husband by the wife)— begins to show through" (129–130). During the thirties, the "abuse" had a playful levity to it. In *It Happened One Night* (1934), Peter Warne tells Mr. Andrews that somebody should give Ellie a "sock" at least once a day. The comment appears to be angry sarcasm stated by a lover who thinks he has been jilted, and we accept it as a humorous gibe, not a literal intention. In *The Thin Man* (1934), Nick Charles, behind wife Nora's back, pretends he is ready to haul off and strike her, but we interpret this as the good-natured antic of a loving (and inebriated) husband. And in *Nothing Sacred*, before Wally Cook delivers a haymaker on Hazel Flagg's chin, he professes his love for her, as if this mitigates the brutality of his act. Pointing to examples of altered attitudes, Haskell recalls how Myrna Loy infantilized Cary Grant in *The Bachelor and the Bobby-Soxer* (1947), and how Ann Sheridan viewed with condescending amusement the demeaning plight of husband Cary Grant in *I Was a Male War Bride* (1949). In these and other instances, "victimization" of forties-era males differs from the treatment they received in the thirties in how it is prolonged and exaggerated while the women, for the most part, remain aloof and unsympathetic.

In discussing the evolution of male-female relationships from films of the 1930s to the 1940s, Molly Haskell touches on a key feature that applies to both screwball comedy and film noir:

> [Role reversal] was ... popular in both the thirties and forties, but in the thirties, the questioning of roles was rooted in the security of the sexual and social framework at large, in the equal importance of a "man's function" and a "woman's function" and in the emphasis on a collectivity of interests in which men and women were united, rather than divided, by their sex [132–133].

In the forties, she notes, "Women became a more serious threat to the economic hegemony of men" (133). Most films in both genres are centered on a contentious adversarial relationship between the man and the woman but with different purposes in mind. As noted above, the 1930's screwball relationship evolves from a clash in values to a harmonious settlement (or tolerable coexistence) that signifies the couple's ability to compromise, whereas the objective of the 1940's noir relationship is to expose and intensify the irresolvable animosity and strife between the sexes, producing some catastrophic outcome. Haskell notes how the intimate relationships borne out of innocent expectations and trust in the thirties evolved into alliances based on mutual suspicion, insecurity, and distrust in the forties (195–196). As examples of these later, disturbing relationships, she points to *Gaslight*, *Rebecca*, and *Suspicion*.

When Molly Haskell notes how films, from the thirties to the forties, changed in attitude, tone, and situation—that is, the way the male protagonist was treated, or the kind of relationship that men and women could expect—she is touching on a phenomenon discussed in greater analytical detail by Thomas Schatz: that genres, rather than remaining static, will, over time, progress through several stages. Looking at Henri Focillon's *The Life of Forms in Art* and his theory about the "'life span' of cultural forms," Schatz adapts that author's theories to his own on the evolution of a genre. Just as a form goes through four particular stages, a genre goes through

> an *experimental* stage, during which its conventions are isolated and established, a *classical* stage, in which the conventions reach their "equilibrium" and are mutually understood by artist and audience, an age of *refinement*, during which certain formal and stylistic details embellish the form, and finally a *baroque* (or "mannerist" or "self-reflexive") stage, when the form and its embellishments are accented to the point where they themselves become the "substance" or "content" of the work [37–38]

Schatz's analysis is evidenced in the general progress of screwball comedies, from their inception in 1934 to the close of screwball's original period, just after 1950. *It Happened One Night, Twentieth Century, The Thin*

Man, and *The Girl from Missouri* (all 1934) exemplify the informal and coincidental integration of the conventions that will become intrinsic to the genre, especially the sexual tensions in the battle of the sexes, the sexual innuendoes, and the issues related to class and wealth. The second phase, the classical stage, solidifies these conventions into a formula that delivers a more deliberate social message. *My Man Godfrey* (1936), *Theodora Goes Wild* (1936), and *Nothing Sacred* (1937) exemplify this stage by dealing purposefully with issues related to sexual propriety, social hypocrisy, and class status.

The third stage, the age of refinement, extends the classical stage by taking the genre to a more formalized level. Story construction especially, found in the likes of *The Awful Truth* (1937), *Bringing Up Baby* (1938), and

My Man Godfrey (1936, Universal; Gregory La Cava, director)—Godfrey (William Powell) is a blue-blood-turned-vagrant. After Irene Bullock (Carole Lombard) hires him as a butler, his experience in the eccentric and prodigal Bullock household pulls him out of his despair and enables him to reclaim his rightful place in society.

His Girl Friday (1940), suggests a greater entrenchment of the formula and conventions that define these films.

And finally, in the last stage of a genre, the baroque stage, the genre contains self-reflexive elements that parody and pay homage to its own origins and development. Preston Sturges's *The Palm Beach Story* (1942) and *Unfaithfully Yours* (1948) contain strictly defined structures. *The Palm Beach Story* reflects back on the screwball genre, parodying Capra's *It Happened One Night* by inverting its plotline. Gerry Jeffers (Claudette Colbert, who "happens" to be the heroine in both films) is running away from her husband, not to him, and she travels from New York to Florida, instead of the other way around. Along the way, she falls under the aegis of eccentric millionaires, the Ale and Quail Club members and John D. Hackensacker III (Rudy Vallee), rather than having to rub elbows with the common people encountered by Ellie Andrews. At the same time, there is the nod to *The Girl from Missouri* in that Gerry, like Eadie Chapman, goes to Palm Beach to snare a millionaire. *Unfaithfully Yours* is as formally prepared as the orchestral music selected by conductor Sir Alfred De Carter (Rex Harrison). Thinking he has been cuckolded, De Carter imagines how he might avenge his wounded pride. He envisions three scenarios, one involving murder, one a grand, maudlin farewell, and one a suicide, all desperate acts that push the battle of the sexes to its extreme limit. Two scenes are so grim and gruesome that the black humor balances precariously on the boundary between comedy and repulsive humor. In fact, Sturges's film may be called a noir comedy because he melds the comedy with elements from film noir, including a femme fatale, chiaroscuro lighting, and a generally dark, cynical tone.

In *People Will Talk* (1951), Cary Grant plays Dr. Noah Praetorius. He is introduced as a strange, inscrutable character who once practiced medicine in a rural town where superstitious villagers called him "The Doc" and attributed to him legendary mythic powers. His mysterious and ambiguous character is implied in a scene wherein he comforts a dying patient with the idea that death can be more pleasant than life. Noah's surname harkens back to another Doctor Pretorius (Ernest Thesiger) who, in *Bride of Frankenstein* (1935), resurrected the Frankenstein monster. In creating this connection between the two Praetoriuses, *People Will Talk* reflects back on the film medium itself while conjuring up darker implications from the horror genre. *Monkey Business* (1952) opens with director Howard Hawks, from off-screen, reprimanding Cary Grant for making his entrance too soon (and actually calling him "Cary"). The scene suggests something about the character's absentmindedness, but also inserts the self-reflexive reminder that this is a movie with real-life actors and a filmmaking crew contributing to the production.

Similarly, a generic evolution occurs in noir. During its earliest experimental stage, film noir is a conglomeration of melodrama, crime drama, and mystery. Some of the films even contain traces of screwball, such as the witty repartee, which can occur between the noir lovers and between other characters as well. In *I Wake Up Screaming* (1941), for instance, Frankie Christopher (Victor Mature) and Inspector Cornell (Laird Cregar) harass each other with the kind of sarcastic jousting found in screwball. And in *Rage in Heaven* (1941), although Phillip Monrell (Robert Montgomery) is paranoid and his comments entertain only himself, he constantly tosses mordant remarks at his wife (Ingrid Bergman) and his friend Ward Andrews (George Sanders), believing she favors Andrews to him. *The Maltese Falcon* (1941) uses cynical banter in those scenes in which Spade wisecracks with Lt. Dundy (Barton MacLane), Det. Tom Polhaus (Ward Bond), Brigid O'Shaughnessy (Mary Astor), Joel Cairo (Peter Lorre), and Kasper Gutman (Sydney Greenstreet).

Besides borrowing the idea of clever, stylized dialogue, film noir also follows screwball's lead by enlisting a coterie of eccentric characters, if not to inject humor, then at least to entertain and amuse. *A Woman's Face* (1941) contains a small band of hapless criminals who, in appearing before a magistrate to give testimony against their ringleader (Joan Crawford), are funny in spite of themselves—Herman Rundvik (Donald Meek), Bernard Dalvik (Reginald Owen), and Dalvik's wife Christina (Connie Gilchrist) comprise the bumbling gang. *Ladies in Retirement* (1941) balances between the grim and the grotesque as Ellen Creed (Ida Lupino) plots to kill her employer (Isobel Elsom) so she can remain guardian of her two mentally disturbed sisters (Elsa Lanchester, Edith Barrett) instead of sending them to a sanitarium. (The story portends certain aspects of the 1944 screwball comedy *Arsenic and Old Lace*.) Eccentric behavior provides some entertaining moments in *The Maltese Falcon*: in her row with Joel Cairo in Spade's apartment, Brigid kicks Cairo in the leg, giving the moment an air of comic farce; and in the finale, Cairo's effeminate tirade is laugh-out-loud funny. Even von Sternberg's ponderously serious *The Shanghai Gesture* (1941) contains eccentric characters who display exaggerated mannerisms to emphasize their exotic natures and bizarre habits.

In the subsequent classical stage of the mid-forties, ambiguities become more pronounced and cynicism more prevalent. Conventions develop more consistency: a flawed male protagonist often finds himself enmeshed in the machinations of an all-consuming femme fatale; guilt plagues the protagonists and affects their decisions; the labyrinth becomes a more prevalent image reflecting the protagonist's confusion and tortuous predicament; chiaroscuro techniques, such as shadows to indicate bar and web imagery, distorted silhouettes on walls, vague outlines of figures moving in and out of smoke or fog, all convey the helpless and uneasy uncertainties felt by the protagonist and transferred to the audience. Many classics of the genre appear at this time—*Double Indemnity, Laura, Mildred Pierce, Detour, Fallen Angel, Scarlet Street, Black Angel, Notorious, The Postman Always Rings Twice, The Big Sleep, Gilda, The Killers, The Dark Corner, Somewhere in the Night, Nobody Lives Forever* and *Murder, My Sweet* are among the most prominent.

The age of refinement, the period following World War II and moving into the early fifties, continued to develop and modify the motifs and themes of the previous stage in films such as *Born to Kill, The Lady from Shanghai, Gun Crazy, Sunset Boulevard, D.O.A., The Asphalt Jungle,* and *The Secret Fury.* Many noirs at this time were affected by the consequences of the war and the complications facing returning veterans who were struggling to reintegrate into society. Sometimes these issues were treated literally, sometimes figuratively. Some films noirs that touched on these matters to a small or large extent were *Crack-Up, The Chase, The Blue Dahlia, The Unfaithful, Crossfire, High Wall, The Stranger, He Walked by Night,* and *Act of Violence.*

In noir's baroque period, the early1950s to about 1960, characters take on extreme behavior, and brutality becomes more graphic. In *Kiss Me Deadly,* Christina Bailey (Cloris Leachman) is tortured to death, Carl Evello (Paul Stewart) is stabbed to death, Mike Hammer (Ralph Meeker) bangs a thug's head against a wall, Hammer crushes the coroner's (Percy Helton) hand in a drawer, Gabrielle (Gaby Rodgers) burns to death, and a final nuclear explosion suggests that humanity is without a savior to rescue it from total annihilation. *Touch of Evil* shows Police Captain Hank Quinlan (Orson Welles) carrying out a realistically grisly strangling of Uncle Joe Grandi (Akim Tamiroff); and *The Harder They Fall* and *The Sweet Smell of Success* depict despicably crooked individuals in an irredeemably corrupt world (boxing and the newspaper business). In *Cape Fear* (F. Lee Thompson, 1962), horrendous evil, personified by the ultra-sadistic Max Cady (Robert Mitchum), corrupts the upright individual, personified by Sam Bowden (Gregory Peck). The good learns that the only way it can compete with evil is to confront it with the same primitive, raw, lawless violence that it wreaks on a naïve and vulnerable society. Many of these films contain a nihilistic quality, giving the impression that the human race has degenerated to a point where it no longer qualifies for redemption.

4

Cinematic Conventions Connecting Screwball Comedy and Film Noir

Essential to distinguishing one genre from another are the conventions—particular plots, characters, themes, and iconographic elements—that come to be identified with a specific type of film, be it a western, musical, horror, science fiction, or anything else. As genres, screwball comedy and film noir reveal something more: although both are distinct genres, they correlate with each other in a number of ways. Many of the conventions that appear in screwball comedy appear in film noir, modified from the humorous treatment in the former to suit the grimmer tonal qualities in the latter. The striking relationships found in their conventions suggest a strong connection between the two genres and denote them as ironic counterparts of each other.

Male and Female Protagonists

The previous section on genre notes how Wes D. Gehring comes to terms with screwball comedy by focusing on one major component, the screwball protagonist. Gehring credits this comic antihero with five specific characteristics: leisure time to interact with the screwball female; a childlike attitude that reflects his immature and playful nature; an urban lifestyle; an apolitical viewpoint; and frustrated ambitions, especially in his relationships with women. It was also shown that these same five traits can be adapted to fit the antihero of film noir.

Besides these parallels between the male protagonists in screwball and noir, there are marked similarities in the screwball and noir females who interact with them. Females in both genres very often assume the role of what may be called a "designing woman," but while the screwball seductress, in achieving her desire (marriage), hopes also to bring happiness to the man, the femme fatale is inclined to think more about her own gain at the expense of the male. Irene Bullock (Carole Lombard in *My Man Godfrey*) and Ellen Arden (Irene Dunne in *My Favorite Wife*) know their intention to marry their men (William Powell and Cary Grant, respectively) is best for all of them. The femme fatale, meanwhile, is willing to kill the male to rid herself of him (Phyllis Dietrichson, Kathie Moffat, Helen Grayle, Norma Desmond) or let him succumb to some impending doom, as Lilith Ritter (Helen Walker) does in *Nightmare Alley*. However, some noirs counter the femme fatale with the femme blanche, the good woman whose potentially positive influence on the man sometimes succeeds, like Mary Malden (Ida Lupino) in *On Dangerous Ground* or Peg Born (Lilli Palmer) in *Body and Soul*, and sometimes fails, like Ann Miller (Virginia Huston) in *Out of the Past* or Mary Bristol (Gene Tierney) in *Night and the City*.

Screwball contains three main types of female protagonists: Aggressive Lover, Aloof Love Object, and Adversarial Partner. Each type embodies personality traits that invite conflict and contribute to the lively battle of the sexes.

The Aggressive Lover is extremely assertive and manipulative in her pursuit of the male, and she usually makes little secret of her intention. She may be paired with a male who is adamantly against any kind of relationship with her, but who, we know, must ultimately surrender to her persistence. When the Aggressive Lover instigates the relationship, she maneuvers the male toward marriage, not with malicious intent, but with the altruistic belief that, whether the man knows it or not, he will benefit from the union. Susan Vance (*Bringing Up Baby*) knows implicitly long before David Huxley that she is destined to marry him. She uses decoys and deception to keep him near her and away from his fiancée, succeeding in winning him in the end. Irene Bullock (*My Man Godfrey*) makes it very clear that she wants to marry Godfrey, and even though he hands her an unequivocal no, he finds himself before a judge in the final scene. After Edwina Corday (Claudette Colbert in *It's a Wonderful World*) decides that Guy Johnson (James Stewart) is not really a murderer, she keeps returning to help him, even though he uses all kinds of tactics to evade her. Mystery writer Paula Bradford (Jean Arthur in *The Ex-Mrs. Bradford*) moves in with her ex-husband (William Powell) to prod him to solve a murder mystery while slyly maneuvering him into remarriage.

The second type of female, the Aloof Love Object, is a beautiful woman who is admired and desired by the male, but either she is ignorant of his fascination or, if aware of it, she blatantly rebuffs him. If he actively pursues her, she does not hide her aversion to a relationship with him, much less marrying him. Her reticence may be due to awkward circumstances, her preference for personal freedom, her feeling of inferiority (or

It's a Wonderful World (1939, MGM; W. S. Van Dyke II, director)—The apple that Eve offered Adam and doomed the human race receives modified treatment when poet Edwina Corday (Claudette Colbert) shares the fruit with private detective Guy Johnson (James Stewart).

superiority) because she is below (or above) his station, her interest in another man, or her simply disliking him or not feeling attracted to him. Since we are dealing with a screwball romance, we know that this may postpone but cannot prevent the inevitable, that the two will be ideal lovers by story's end. One example is Trudy Kockenlocker (Betty Hutton in *The Miracle of Morgan's Creek*) who enjoys the company of servicemen, and has little regard for the gallant Norval Jones (Eddie Bracken) until she realizes how much he is willing to sacrifice for her. Sugarpuss O'Shea (Barbara Stanwyck in *Ball of Fire*) is a glib, fast-talking woman, who treats Professor Bertram Potts (Gary Cooper) like a foolish love-struck adolescent until his tender overtures awaken deeper feelings in her. Polly Parrish (Ginger Rogers in *Bachelor Mother*) has to decide how to handle her relationship with David Merlin (David Niven), whose father owns the department store where she works as a clerk. Connie Allenbury (Myrna Loy in *Libeled Lady*) continually rejects Bill Chandler's (William Powell) advances toward her, sure that he is trying to ingratiate himself with her for some ulterior motive—and he is, as he hopes to involve her in a scandal to stop her from suing his friend's (Spencer Tracy) newspaper. Eve Peabody (Claudette Colbert in *Midnight*) rejects cabbie Tibor Czerny (Don Ameche) to find a wealthier prospect for a husband, but Czerny is persistent and convinces her that he is a better choice than the womanizing Jacques Picot (Francis Lederer). Wilhelmina "Bill" Clark (Jean Arthur in *The Whole Town's Talking*) has no inkling that introverted "Jonesy" Jones (Edward G. Robinson) admires her from afar until he shows some spunk by kissing her and later rescuing her from his look-alike gangster, Killer Mannion (also Robinson).

The third type of female, the Adversarial Partner, is one who is bound to the man, whether by marriage or some exclusive relationship, and their association, if not marked by outright physical conflict, bristles with an ongoing exchange of sarcastic repartee. Earliest prototypes of the Adversarial Partner are resolute Ellie Andrews in *It Happened One Night* and high-strung Lily Garland in *Twentieth Century*. The most significant female protagonists in this category are those involved in divorce and remarriage: Lucy Warriner (Irene Dunne in *The Awful Truth*), Ann Krausheimer Smith (Carole Lombard in *Mr. & Mrs. Smith*), Susan Ireland (Myrna Loy in *Love Crazy*), Hildy Johnson (Rosalind Russell in *His Girl Friday*), Ellen Arden (Irene Dunne in *My Favorite Wife*), and Amanda Bonner (Katharine Hepburn in *Adam's Rib*). The Adversarial Partner fits very conveniently in the many screwball mysteries which usually involve married couples who trade quips while working toward solving a crime: Nora Charles (Myrna Loy, another female prototype, in *The Thin Man* series), Carlotta Milburn (Constance Cummings in *Remember Last Night?*), Nancy Troy (Loretta Young in *A Night to Remember*), Dixie Daisy (Barbara Stanwyck, unmarried to her foil, Biff Brannigan—played by Michael O'Shea—in *Lady of Burlesque*), and several incarnations of Garda Sloane (Florence Rice in *Fast Company*, Ann Sothern in *Fast and Furious*, and Rosalind Russell in *Fast and Loose*).

This is not to say that a female is exclusively an Aggressive Lover or Aloof Love Object or Adversarial Partner—she may be a variation of one of these types or she may exhibit traits in two or three of these categories at one time. In *Theodora Goes Wild*, for instance, Theodora Lynn (Irene Dunne) plays the Aloof Love Object for the first half of the film, rejecting the advances of Michael Grant (Melvyn Douglas) until she realizes she loves him. A minor complication in his life—he is already married—prevents him from responding to her declarations of love. But then, for the second half of the film, she becomes the Aggressive Lover trying to make him proclaim his love openly. Ellie Andrews of *It Happened One Night* shows signs of both the Aloof Love Object as well as the Adversarial Partner. And in *The Lady Eve*, Jean Harrington (Barbara Stanwyck), at different times, displays traits of each of the three types.

These three main screwball females evolve into three kinds of noir females—the Femme Fatale (or Femme Noire), the Inadvertent Femme Fatale, and the Latent Femme Fatale—who function in similar ways, but who twist their relationship with the male into something dangerous and pernicious, either because of deliberate actions done out of sinister motives, or because of unintentional behavior prompted by unusual circumstances beyond their control.

Screwball's Aggressive Lover becomes noir's trademark Femme Fatale, the manipulative Spider Woman, who fiendishly lures the male into her trap to achieve her own selfish designs, whether it be for money, for power, for revenge, or for her own unquenchable need to possess him. She is an alluring siren, fully aware of the power she wields over men. She is "bad to the bone," always dangerous, always corruptive—involvement with her generally leads to a catastrophic end for the male. Screwball's Aggressive Lover pursues the male with the intention of marrying him to their mutual advantage; noir's Femme Fatale pursues the male to exploit him for her own selfish ends without regard for his wants or needs. Some of the classic femmes fatales appear in *The Maltese Falcon* (Mary Astor as Brigid O'Shaughnessy), *Double Indemnity* (Barbara Stanwyck as Phyllis Dietrichson), *Murder, My Sweet* (Claire Trevor as Helen Grayle), *The Lady from Shanghai* (Rita Hayworth as Elsa Bannister), *Out of the Past* (Jane Greer as Kathie Moffat), *Scarlet Street* (Joan Bennett as Kitty March), *The Killers* (Ava Gardner as Kitty Collins), *Criss Cross* (Yvonne De Carlo as Anna Dundee), Annie Laurie Starr (Peggy Cummins in *Gun Crazy*), and *Angel Face* (Jean Simmons as Diane Tremayne). Less celebrated but equally treacherous and dangerously seductive are Martha Ivers (Barbara Stanwyck in *The Strange Love of Martha Ivers*), Vera (Ann Savage in *Detour*), Paula Craig (Janis Carter in *Framed*), Lilith Ritter (Helen Walker in *Nightmare Alley*), Ruth Dillon (Claire Trevor in *Street of Chance*), and Margo Lannington (Faith Domergue in *Where Danger Lives*).

Screwball's Aloof Love Object becomes, in noir, the Inadvertent Femme Fatale, both types admired and desired by a male suitor but uninterested, at least initially, in his advances. Unlike her nefarious sister, the Spider Woman, she does not vigorously pursue the male to seduce him, yet she is in some way connected to the cause of his demise (whether it be the protagonist or some other important male character). Thus she functions as a femme fatale, albeit a conditional or accidental one. Perhaps the label contains a contradiction in terms, but noir's Inadvertent Femme Fatale is, on the whole, innocent of the doom that befalls the male. Even in those situations where she is not totally guileless or innocent, she is still less sinister than the evil, aggressive, self-consumed Spider Woman. Examples include Stella (Linda Darnell in *Fallen Angel*), Nora Prentiss (Ann Sheridan in *Nora Prentiss*), Cora Smith (Lana Turner in *The Postman Always Rings Twice*), Lily Stevens (Ida Lupino in *Road House*), Peggy Dobbs (Shelley Winters in *He Ran All the Way*), Cecily Latham (Alexis Smith in *The Two Mrs. Carrolls*), Catherine "Keechie" Mobley (Cathy O'Donnell in *They Live by Night*), Lona McLane (Kim Novak in *Pushover*), Laurel Gray (Gloria Grahame in *In a Lonely Place*), Matilda Frazier (Joan Caulfield in *The Unsuspected*), and Mona Stevens (Lizabeth Scott in *Pitfall*).

Finally, screwball's Adversarial Partner becomes, in noir, a Latent Femme Fatale. She differs from the full-fledged Spider Woman in that she is neither fundamentally evil nor initially dangerous; she does not harbor some secret plan for exploiting the male, expecting to discard him once she obtains her objective. On the contrary, their relationship begins on mutually acceptable terms, but over time and because of some critical event, the relationship sours, and the woman, scorned or neglected, turns deadly as she seeks revenge by punishing the male in some way. The hostility that arises between the noir protagonist and the Latent Femme Fatale contributes to a situation very similar to that between the screwball protagonist and his

Phantom Lady (1944, Universal; Robert Siodmak, director)—Inspector Burgess (Thomas Gomez, left) tries to help sculptor Jack Marlow (Franchot Tone), who suffers from a debilitating headache, symbol of his guilt and urban angst.

Adversarial Partner, except, of course, that there is no reconciliation for the noir couple. Norma Desmond (Gloria Swanson in *Sunset Boulevard*) is a prime example; first doting on her captive lover (William Holden) and seducing him with every luxury, then killing him when he tries to leave her. Others are Lorraine Minosa (Jan Sterling in *Ace in the Hole*), who fatally stabs devious newsman Chuck Tatum (Kirk Douglas) with a nail file; Carol "Kansas" Richman (Ella Raines in *Phantom Lady*), who transforms herself into a femme fatale and causes the death of three men to save her boss (Alan Curtis) from the electric chair; and Helen Brent (Claire Trevor in *Born to Kill*), who is susceptible to the sinister urgings of her dark side, and becomes trapped in a love-hate relationship with a murderer (Lawrence Tierney).

The screwball male or screwball female, or both, in most instances, may initially resist the relationship for any number of reasons—pride, dislike, suspicion, disinterest, reluctance to get involved, even an implicit fear of what the relationship represents: adult responsibility, renouncing one's independence, lifetime commitment. In the end, the barrier is overcome and the screwball lovers surrender to their irresistible attraction for each other.

In noir, this attraction is based on a different set of principles. Molly Haskell explains how humorous hostility between the screwball lovers evolved into willful cruelty between the noir couple: "Where once sexual antagonism was a game, a pretext, a holding action until the underlying affinity could emerge, attraction is now the illusion, the decoy, the duplicitous façade" (197). Despite doubt and suspicion, the noir lovers join forces through a mutual compact—but underpinning their alliance is a selfish ulterior motive: whether driven by some base, lustful obsession or some pretentious aspiration or personal greed, each has a private agenda that requires help from the other. Phyllis Dietrichson feigns feelings of love while recruiting Walter Neff to murder her husband; later, each will betray the other. Kathie Moffat goes from Whit Sterling to Jeff Markham, then back to Sterling, and back finally to Markham because it suits her purpose each time; she eventually kills both men because they do not fit in with her scheme. "Heterosexual attraction ... still exists ... but on different terms than attractions of thirties' romances.... The difference is that the terms are no longer equal and bisexual but masculine, violent, and phallic" (Haskell 198).

For several reasons, although the screwball female protagonist prefigures the later noir Spider Woman, we would not label her a femme fatale, no matter how assertive she is. In screwball, the aggressive female mimics a femme fatale in that she leads the male down a path he may not have sought and could not have found without her insidious manipulations. "Femme fatale," literally "deadly woman," has negative connotations, which, since screwball is woven with lighter material, makes it a term more appropriate for noir. And yet, screwball's Aggressive Lover shares many of the same traits with noir's evil harpy: ambition, seductiveness, shrewdness, resourcefulness, persistence, independence, deviousness, assertiveness. The screwball temptress, however, is unlike noir's femme fatale who does not have the man's interests in mind, only her own. As often happens when one movement tries to rectify the "deficiencies" of a previous movement, noir "was a reaction against the boy-meets-girl glibness of the thirties" (Haskell 199).

Screwball's Aggressive Lover finagles the male into a marriage he opposes or fears or shirks, but it is, in the context of romantic comedy, the desirable objective, the happy ending that works best for both parties, even if the male is reluctant to admit it. This is antipodal to the objective that noir's femme fatale has in mind for herself and her male victim. Even if the Spider Woman is motivated by something she calls love, that love is perverted, diseased. What is more, the femme fatale usually intends to discard the male as soon as he no longer serves her purpose (hence the appellation Black Widow or Spider Woman). Kitty Collins in *The Killers*, Kathie Moffat in *Out of the Past*, Helen Grayle in *Murder, My Sweet*, and Elsa Bannister in *The Lady from Shanghai* may swear devotion to their male pawns, but the love they brandish is merely a lever for manipulating the man to help them achieve their private, selfish ends. On the other hand, the screwball female sees love and marriage as symbols of ultimate bliss, and even if, in her quest, she is motivated by some measure of self-interest, she is not totally oblivious to the welfare and happiness of the male who (we assume) can appreciate the advantage of surrendering to her wishes.

Plot Devices and Iconography

There is never a question that in screwball comedy the central conflict revolves around the screwball couple. Noir, however, varies the import it gives to the conflict between its male and female protagonists: sometimes they are at the heart of the conflict (Johnny and Gilda in *Gilda*; Annie Laurie Starr and Bart Tare in *Gun Crazy*; Johnnie Aysgarth and Lina MacLaidlaw Aysgarth in *Suspicion*) and sometimes more emphasis is placed on one character than the other (Sam Spade with Brigid O'Shaughnessy in *The Maltese Falcon*; Jeff Markham with Kathie Moffat in *Out of the Past*; Stan Carlisle with Lilith Ritter in *Nightmare Alley*). However, even when this latter situation occurs, the dynamics in the relationship of the noir couple still carry significance for the story. Whatever the focus of the conflict, it is enhanced by a number of plot devices that recur frequently, both in screwball comedy and film noir.

The **labyrinth** is both a visual and conceptual device in screwball and noir. Physically, the city, the primary setting of both genres, acts like a labyrinth, an arena of endlessly merging streets, tall obstructions, and constricted byways, where characters become entangled in their predicament and each other (screwball's *The Impatient Years* and noir's *Night and the City*). In addition to the city, specific settings may function like a labyrinth—an apartment (screwball's *The More the Merrier* and *Adam's Rib*; noir's *The Blue Gardenia*) or mansion (the Bullock mansion in screwball's *My Man Godfrey* and various abodes in noir's *Rebecca, Suspicion, Notorious,* and *Murder, My Sweet*); a ship (screwball's *The Lady Eve* and noir's *Journey into Fear*); a hotel (screwball's *Easy Living* and noir's *Kiss Me Deadly*) or funhouse (noir's *The Lady from Shanghai*). In the winding maze, characters cannot see everything that lies ahead nor can they be prepared for it. They are forced to make quick decisions when, after taking some unexpected turn, they confront sudden dangers and abrupt surprises. The labyrinth stands for unpredictability that contributes to mystery, suspense, and angst. At the same time, whether in noir or screwball, it acts as a metaphor for the protagonist's confused state of mind and reinforces the complexity of the storyline that, rather than progress in a linear way, constantly assaults us with convoluted twists and tortuous angles.

Amnesia is a device that surfaces in a few screwball comedies, but more frequently in film noir. In the comedy *I Love You Again*, William Powell plays George Carey, a dashing con artist who realizes, after getting conked on the head, that for the past several years he has been living his life as prim and proper model citizen Larry Wilson. Carey discovers that "Wilson" owns some sizable bank accounts and he plans to make a full withdrawal. However, he meets "Wilson's" wife, Kay (Myrna Loy), who is in the process of divorcing him because of his stiff and stingy life style. He is instantly attracted to her and so he changes his plans. In his amnesiac state, Carey had abandoned his criminal ways and was able to make money legally. Now, however, with his memory restored and his interest in Kay aroused, especially as he is about to lose her, he reforms on his own—he discovers that Kay finds his true self more appealing than the conservative "Wilson" and that he can prosper well enough in a new legitimate business.

In the quasi-fantasy *Remember?*, Jeff Holland (Robert Taylor) marries Linda Bronson (Greer Garson). His job in an advertising firm interferes continuously with their attempts to go on a honeymoon, and after an exceptionally heated argument, they decide to get a divorce. The divorce will not be finalized for three months, and before that time is up, their friend Skye Ames (Lew Ayres), who has access to a new drug that erases memory, slips the powder into their drinks. They forget they know each other and that they are waiting for their divorce to be finalized. When they meet accidentally, they fall in love during what they think is their first encounter. This time, though, Jeff refuses to let his job take precedence over his honeymoon plans and it appears as if their future together looks secure—especially since Linda announces that she is pregnant.

Both screwball films use amnesia to suggest that life can be a do-over, that people can reform and that the mistakes committed the first time around can be pushed aside and replaced with more acceptable habits and behaviors. However, whereas *I Love You Again* presents amnesia as the less attractive existence and reality as the more desirable one, *Remember?* treats amnesia in an opposite manner, making reality the less appealing state, and the new life, with true reality forgotten, the more advantageous condition.

Noir uses amnesia in a similar way but with more philosophical ramifications. Amnesia can create a dual identity for a character, producing a kind of Jekyll-and-Hyde syndrome and suggesting that good and evil can exist within one person (something implied in *I Love You Again*). In films such as *Street of Chance, Spellbound, Somewhere in the Night, Nightmare, Fear in the Night, Fall Guy,* and *Crossroads,* characters are caught between their conscious intention to do the right thing and their fear that they harbor a secret subconscious desire to ignore their scruples and succumb to evil, usually by committing murder.

Street of Chance (1942, Paramount; Jack Hively, director)—Frank Thompson (Burgess Meredith) may blame his troubles on his amnesia, when, in fact, his dilemma stems from the femme fatale, Ruth Dillon (Claire Trevor).

Characters' **motives** are essential to the theme of any story, and several key ones recur in both noir and screwball. In noir, characters are driven by one or more of four incentives: money, lust, power, and revenge. These motives are transparent in most noirs—money and lust in *Double Indemnity*; money, lust, and revenge in *The Killers*; revenge in *Act of Violence*; money and power in *The Unsuspected*, *Night and the City*, and *Ace in the Hole*; lust, power, and revenge in *Out of the Past*, *Born to Kill*, *Phantom Lady*, and *Fallen Angel*; money (and to some degree, lust and power) in *The Asphalt Jungle*. It is as if all the evils that could corrupt humanity were represented by these four prevailing motives.

Ironically, these same four motives can be applied to screwball characters, with the difference that lust is replaced by its more venerable counterpart—love—and power is replaced by its complementary ambition—status. Love is, of course, the ultimate quest of the romantic couple; and it receives different treatment in different situations. The suitor must persist against a stubborn love object until the love object realizes that the two of them are meant for each other: Irene Bullock fawning over her reclaimed butler in *My Man Godfrey*; Susan Vance seducing dull-witted David Huxley in *Bringing Up Baby*; and Jonesy Jones admiring winsome Wilhelmina Clark from afar in *The Whole Town's Talking*. Or both parties may begin as strangers who develop an adversarial relationship, until repeated collisions force them to take a second look at each other and admit their love: Peter Warne and Ellie Andrews in *It Happened One Night*, Polly Parrish and David Merlin in *Bachelor Mother*, Guy Johnson and Edwina Corday in *It's a Wonderful World*, and Tony Anthony and Nancy Fleming in *Next Time I Marry*. In still other plots, the couple may at first be in love (and even married), but something fractures the relationship, and they must work contentiously toward reconciliation: David and Ann Smith in *Mrs. & Mrs. Smith*, Tom and Gerry Jeffers in *The Palm Beach Story*, Lucy and Jerry Warriner in *The Awful Truth*, and Theodora Lynn and Michael Grant in *Theodora Goes Wild*.

While love is always the primary motive for the screwball couple, it often appears in the company of at least one of the other three motives. Revenge, for instance, enhances the conflict in those comedies of remarriage where some crisis has caused a schism and turned the two lovers into combatants. In the course of their battles, the male and female protagonists take turns at one-upmanship, first one, then the other getting the better of the partner. *The Awful Truth*, *Mr. & Mrs. Smith*, *My Favorite Wife*, and *His Girl Friday* exemplify this kind of give-and-take abuse. In *Unfaithfully Yours*, wherein the conflict exists solely in the mind of the jealous husband, the imagined battle of the sexes leads to the ultimate revenge: murder.

Money, as previously noted, is an issue in screwball comedy that signifies the economic gap between upper and lower classes. As a motive, money may fuel the conflict in two contradictory ways: first, a gold digger or gigolo, on a quest for a prosperous mate, comes to realize that love is more precious than wealth and he or she forsakes the rich life for the more romantic option; or second, a character who makes a principle of poverty may righteously fault another character for having excessive riches; however, the righteous character manages in the long run to compromise that idealistic code and marry the wealthy nemesis.

As an example of the first case, *Hands Across the Table* presents two protagonists who nurture the same private ambition, to marry money that will guarantee them a life of comfort and ease. Manicurist Regi Allen (Carole Lombard) tells Theodore "Ted" Drew III (Fred MacMurray) of her dream to marry a millionaire, and he tells her that he has fallen from the ranks of the rich, but expects to recover his losses because he is engaged to a wealthy young lady. In the midst of the Great Depression (1935), their ambitions seem a very practical quest. However, after they become more acquainted with each other, they gradually renounce their original intentions—Ted breaks his engagement, and Regi, who is being courted by kindhearted millionaire Allen Macklyn (Ralph Bellamy), ignores his advances. Instead, the two would-be mercenaries opt for each other, choosing love over money. There is a long list of films in which characters are motivated by wealth, until they decide that love, for all its impractical unpredictability, is really more valuable than material riches: *The Palm Beach Story*, *The Girl from Missouri*, *The Bride Walks Out*, and *Midnight* are among the many examples.

Notwithstanding its practical benefits, wealth can become a liability when one of the lovers takes an idealistic stand against it. *It Happened One Night*, *Smartest Girl in Town*, *Double Wedding*, and *Take a Letter, Darling* are examples of films in which one person's money becomes an impediment to the screwball relationship. In *Holiday*, for instance, Johnny Case (Cary Grant) falls in love with beautiful Julia Seton (Doris Nolan), and only after their whirlwind courtship does he discover that she is the daughter of a wealthy businessman. He has been nursing the romantic whim to travel aimlessly for a year or so to experience the world and learn more about himself. When he realizes that his fiancée and her father are trying to control him with the lure of a prominent business position and future wealth, he abandons his betrothed and winds up with the less materialistic Linda Seton (Katharine Hepburn).

There is a small category of films that treat the wealth motive in a special way. These films follow the pattern established by *My Man Godfrey*, wherein one member of the screwball couple, unbeknown to the other, comes from the rich upper class. Like Godfrey, Butch Baeder (Craig Reynolds) in *The Footloose Heiress* portrays a tramp who actually comes from a proper line of blue-bloods, but for personal reasons, has rebelled

Holiday (1938, Columbia; George Cukor, director)—Johnny Case (Cary Grant) is forced to decide between two women, Julia Seton (Doris Nolan, left), whom he thinks he loves, and Julia's sister Linda (Katharine Hepburn), whom he is fated to love.

against them. Thus, money is not his objective. In trying to tame shrewish Kay Allyn (Ann Sheridan), his motive is more the enjoyment that comes from his position of power, dominating her and getting her to respond to his directives. Two more examples, *If You Could Only Cook* and *The Devil and Miss Jones*, build their plots around this same situation in which the wealthy male delays revealing his true status. On the other hand, while the screwball male may keep his wealth a secret from the female, the screwball female cannot hide her wealth from the male. In films such as *It Happened One Night, Love on the Run, Next Time I Marry*, and *Take a Letter, Darling*, the screwball male is armed with a foreknowledge of the woman's affluence. The logic behind this is that the male, to create audience empathy, must show industry, ambition, and strength independent of the money the woman might bring to their relationship. Thus, even if he does not show outright repugnance for the woman's wealth (as in *It Happened One Night*), he must at least show casual indifference to it (*The Bride Came C.O.D.*).

Without a show of disdain for his sweetheart's money, the male risks becoming dubbed a Cinderella Man, as happens to reporter Stew Smith (Robert Williams) when he marries heiress Anne Schuyler (Jean Harlow) in Frank Capra's pre-screwball comedy *Platinum Blonde*. (Capra uses the epithet again in *Mr. Deeds Goes to Town* with the disparaging connotation that the man has fallen into his fortune without working to earn it.)

The last motive, status (associated with power and wealth but also distinct from them), can be critical in noir when it lures a character into a situation that proves lethal. For instance, Joe Morse (John Garfield) in *Force of Evil*, and Vicky Lynn (Carole Landis) in *I Wake Up Screaming*, are characters who, unsatisfied with their current success, try to reach beyond it, and in the process, create havoc for themselves and those around them. In screwball, however, a craving for status generally receives indirect emphasis, perhaps because it carries negative connotations that could undercut the audience's empathy with the screwball couple. If status should be an issue in screwball, it is usually relegated to the peripheral characters to indicate their selfishness, self-importance, or pretentiousness. In those comedies involving a romantic triangle, the character who eventually gets ousted is the one overly concerned with social status. John Sloan (Reginald Gardiner) in *Christmas in Connecticut*, Camille Lansing (Marcia Ralston) in *Ever Since Eve*, and Mr. Hooper (Edmund Gwenn) in *The Devil and Miss Jones* display a pompous preoccupation with status, making them unworthy of their love objects.

George Kittredge (John Howard) in *The Philadelphia Story* may be an industrious self-made man, but his obsession with the new social ranking he expects to gain from marrying Tracy Lord (Katharine Hepburn) exposes him as a conceited, news-hungry snob. In *Vivacious Lady*, Peter Morgan, Sr. (Charles Coburn), president of Old Sharon College, appears anxious about the fragility of reputation, unlike his son, Peter, Jr. (James Stewart), who is proud of his new bride, Francey (Ginger Rogers), a nightclub entertainer. In *Bachelor Mother*, when Freddie Miller (Frank Albertson) loses his status as floorwalker in Merlin's Department Store, he blames Polly Parrish (Ginger Rogers). He tries to create trouble for her and David Merlin (David Niven) by sending a letter to David's father, J. B. Merlin (Charles Coburn), suggesting that David is the father of Polly's illegitimate child. But J. B.'s pride in having a grandson overrides any threat of scandal and social embarrassment.

Mirrors, a convention in many films, are used to indicate duplicity, duality, or an alter ego, and they carry similar meanings in screwball and noir. In *It Happened One Night*, for instance, when Andrews' detectives arrive at the auto camp and Peter and Ellie act like a bickering couple, she sits in front of a mirror while she pretends to be someone she is not. Later, at home, while preparing to marry King Westley, she is reflected in a mirror in her bedroom, dressed in her bridal gown, while her father says, "Ellie, you've changed." She has matured from a "spoiled brat" who acts rashly against parental rules to a young woman who makes decisions sensibly and deliberately.

Mirrors are even more prominent in film noir. In many films, the femme fatale shows her reflection in a mirror to imply her duplicity, her sensual beauty a veneer that hides her black and self-centered soul. In *Double Indemnity*, Walter and Phyllis are reflected in a mirror when they first meet, suggesting the complicity in their treachery. In *Psycho*, Marion Crane (Janet Leigh) appears in several mirrors to imply that even a fundamentally good and innocent person can have a dormant wicked side with the potential to commit unlawful acts.

Shadows perform a similar iconographic function as mirrors, doubling the character but usually implying a hidden sinister side, not merely a dual nature. Shadows serve a more significant function in noir than in screwball—which is expected since noir melds its dark style with its cynical themes. In particular, those films directed and photographed by the many European émigrés, so deeply influenced by German Expressionism, depended on chiaroscuro—deliberate combinations of light and shadow—to evoke emotional tonalities and convey characters' psychological states. Screwball mysteries, such as *The Thin Man* series, the *Fast Company* series, *The Lady of Burlesque*, *The Mad Miss Manton*, and so on, make broad use of shadow to enhance their mysterious, suspenseful atmosphere, whereas mainstream screwball comedies keep this visual effect to a minimum, if they use it at all.

Thematic Motifs

Fate is an active agent throughout film noir. Its ambiguous presence raises the age-old, unresolved debate about whether our actions are subject to predestination—a force that predetermines our destiny even while we hold the illusion that we are making our own decisions—or are governed by self-determination—our free will to control our methods and options for achieving our ends—or are simply struggles in a series of random accidents. In some films, characters acknowledge fate's influence, such as in *Detour* when Al Roberts (Tom Neal) comments on the futility of our making choices in this world: "That's life. Whichever way you turn, Fate sticks out a foot to trip you.... Yes. Fate, or some mysterious force, can put the finger on you or me for no good reason at all." Roberts' words describe the very force at work in *Sunset Boulevard*. Down on his luck, Joe Gillis is driving along when, by chance, he sees the two men who want to repossess his car. He speeds away, only to have his car blow a tire. He pulls into the first available driveway that leads to the decrepit mansion of Norma Desmond—

and his fate is instantly sealed. In *The Dark Corner*, detective Brad Galt (Mark Stevens), frustrated when his investigation reaches a dead end, laments to his secretary (Lucille Ball), "I feel all dead inside. I'm backed up in a dark corner, and I don't know who's hitting me." That unnamed, invisible assailant is fate, beating and buffeting him about.

Many noirs imply the intervention of fate without naming it explicitly. In *The Big Heat*, Detective Sergeant David Bannion (Glenn Ford) escapes death when his wife dies in a car bomb explosion meant for him. Her death turns him into a ruthless avenging angel bent on capturing his wife's killers. *Kiss Me Deadly* begins with Christina Bailey (Cloris Leachman) planting herself in the middle of a country highway and forcing Mike Hammer (Ralph Meeker) to swerve his car off the road. The intersection of their two lives forces Hammer into an intrigue that kills one of his closest friends and nearly kills him and his girlfriend Velda (Maxine Cooper), events that happened because he had met Christina.

Fate also plays a role in screwball comedies, especially when we consider that it is related to coincidence, chance, and accident. In *Twentieth*

Sunset Boulevard (1950, Paramount; Billy Wilder, director)—Norma Desmond (Gloria Swanson) throws a private New Year's Eve party for herself and her script consultant Joe Gillis (William Holden). Situated between the photographs of his pathetic employer, Gillis is slow to realize just how entangled he is in her snare.

Century, the coincidence of Lily Garland taking the same train as Oscar
Jaffe gives him the opportunity to devise ways of tricking her into signing
a contract for his next Broadway play. In some films, first meetings can
present an ironically fateful aspect. In *It Happened One Night*, not only do
Peter Warne and Ellie Andrews take the same bus, but they are also forced
by chance to share the same seat; and unusual circumstances compel them
to stay together throughout the story. In *The Doctor Takes a Wife*, feminist
writer June Cameron (Loretta Young) "happens" to meet medical professor
Dr. Tim Sterling (Ray Milland) while they are on vacation at the same
resort. Coincidentally, their individual circumstances lead them to make a
mutually beneficial pact to pretend they are married, a situation that contributes to the complications that follow. In *Next Time I Marry*, Nancy
Crocker Fleming (Lucille Ball) literally points the finger of fate at WPA
road laborer Tony Anthony (James Ellison) when, out of several choices,
she selects him as a candidate for her temporary marriage to a "plain American" which, according to her father's will, is a prerequisite for her to receive
her inheritance. Even physical obstructions cannot thwart destiny. The
Walls of Jericho—Warne's flimsy blanket in *It Happened One Night* transformed into literal walls in *The More the Merrier* and *Come Live with Me*—
must eventually topple, enabling the separated lovers to unite. The moral:
People destined to love each other will manage to consummate their relationship no matter what obstacles are put in their way.

Guilt is a critical motif in film noir. The existential dilemmas facing
the characters depend on their awareness of right and wrong and their anx-
iety and regret in making the wrong choices. Walter Neff in *Double Indemnity* shows signs of guilt by narrating his story into a Dictaphone, treating
his friend Barton Keyes (Edward G. Robinson) as his confessor while he
unburdens his sins to him. Dixon Steele (Humphrey Bogart) of *In a Lonely
Place* is a man haunted by demons. He knows he has a violent temper,
regrets its flare-ups, but cannot control it nor openly apologize for it. It is
his raging outbursts that make him a prime suspect in a murder case, and
it is what destroys the one chance he has for happiness with a devoted
woman (Gloria Grahame). In *The Lady from Shanghai*, Michael O'Hara
(Orson Welles) narrates the story in flashback. At the beginning, he claims
to adhere to certain ethics, especially not wanting to flirt with a married
woman. But he quickly abandons his principles, becoming romantically
involved with Elsa Bannister (Rita Hayworth), wife of famed attorney
Arthur Bannister (Everett Sloane), and accepting five thousand dollars to
help George Grisby (Glenn Anders) fake his death so he can bilk money
out of his insurance company. O'Hara escapes with his life and says he
intends to recover his lost values. (Unfortunately in noir, crime leaves an
indelible mark on the soul and a person seldom gets the chance to restore
his or her life to what it was before the fall. In O'Hara's case, he is wounded

The Lady from Shanghai (1947, Columbia; Orson Welles, director)—In the famous Crazy House sequence, Michael O'Hara (Welles) confronts Elsa Bannister (Rita Hayworth) in the Hall of Mirrors, where he finally comes to recognize her as the duplicitous femme fatale.

on the hand, the wound—symbolic of Christ's stigmata—leaving a scar that will always remind him of his moral lapse.)

Guilt is an apparent motif in screwball comedies as well. The two combatants savagely rake each other over hot coals before being soothed and saved by a declaration of love. But with reconciliation must come repentance and forgiveness, on both sides, before the lovers can proceed to marriage (or remarriage). And perhaps that is what makes the happy ending so satisfying, not only the marriage or the prospect of marriage, but the genuine remorse and exoneration that the marriage represents. In *My Favorite Wife*, Nick Arden's (Cary Grant) biggest crime is indecision, and this leads to uncomfortable situations for everyone. Not until he and legitimate wife Ellen (Irene Dunne) are trapped in a compromising circumstance and he dons the Santa suit and makes her laugh does the barrier collapse— all is forgiven and reunion is possible. In *The Awful Truth*, the same two actors face a similar quandary and resolve it in a nearly identical manner.

In *Mr. & Mrs. Smith*, David (Robert Montgomery) learns that, because of some legal discrepancy, he and Ann (Carole Lombard) are not legally married. Suddenly, he thinks of her as his mistress and he entertains the idea of having illicit sex with her. Ann, ignorant of his carnal fantasies, expects him to correct the marital confusion, and when he doesn't, she punishes him for his depravity by throwing him out of their apartment. For the rest of the story, he repents for his indiscretion and seeks her forgiveness. Meanwhile, she provokes David's jealousy by dating his law partner (Gene Raymond, a leading man in a number of early screwballs). The film ends with some ambiguities about the relationship, but it is obvious that they have forgiven each other and intend to reconcile and remarry.

The guilt in screwball comedies does not appear as damaging as in noir because the contented couple in the end gives the impression that happiness and order have been attained or restored. Still, guilt motivates the characters to repent for their vindictive or devious or selfish behavior, and their repentance along with the other characters' forgiveness enables us to accept them as redeemable human beings. Nearly all screwball comedies use this motif. A prominent example is *The Philadelphia Story*, in which Tracy Lord (Katharine Hepburn) has to learn humility, meekness, and tolerance for others' shortcomings. As a study, she is no less deserving of character analysis than her more serious noir counterparts, the title characters in *Mildred Pierce*, *Nora Prentiss*, *Gilda*, and *Laura*, all of whom are burdened with doubts about their behavior.

Possessiveness is another motif that, depending how it is used, has the potential for comic or tragic consequences. It leads to humorous situations in *Twentieth Century* when Oscar Jaffe assumes the role of a Svengali (the ironic allusion points to the title character Barrymore played in 1931) who tries to wield excessive control over actress Mildred Plotka, immediately exercising his dominance by changing her name to Lily Garland. In *My Man Godfrey*, Irene Bullock exaggerates her overwrought condition in an effort to divert Godfrey's attention from her beautiful sister (Gail Patrick) to herself. And in *Affectionately Yours*, philanderer Rickey Mayberry (Dennis Morgan) becomes suddenly obsessed with keeping his wife (Merle Oberon) after he learns that she intends to divorce him.

Film noir, on the other hand, emphasizes the catastrophic costs of unbridled possessiveness. Pathetic Louise Howell Graham (Joan Crawford) in *Possessed* is headed for an emotional collapse because of her unhealthy infatuation with David Sutton (Van Heflin). The classic *Sunset Boulevard* accentuates Norma Desmond's (Gloria Swanson) gnarled, grasping hands as symbols of the fatal clutch of the femme fatale; she promises to satisfy a man's (William Holden) concupiscence but at the expense of his freedom and his identity. In *Laura*, the alluring title character (Gene Tierney) stands between two possessive men. Waldo Lydecker (Clifton Webb) would rather kill her than let her denigrate herself by associating with lesser men than he. Detective Mark McPherson (Dana Andrews) falls in love with her portrait and, after he meets the real-life facsimile, becomes her obsessive protector.

Pride, a positive trait when linked to dignity, self-respect, or a sense of accomplishment, manifests itself in screwball and noir as uncompromis-

Laura (1944, 20th Century–Fox; Otto Preminger, director)—Laura Hunt (Gene Tierney) goes from victim to suspect when undaunted detective Mark McPherson (Dana Andrews) takes her to headquarters for a third degree. The policeman is unidentified in this publicity still.

ing hubris, appearing in the likes of narcissism, vanity, conceit, and aloofness. In screwball, it is a human foible that can be conquered or circumvented, whereas in noir, it is a tragic flaw that portends disaster for certain characters. Sometimes characters' feelings of superiority can be blamed on the possession of an inordinate amount of money, power, or status, but sometimes the pretentiousness comes from the nature of the characters themselves, particularly if they adhere to some immutable self-prescribed code.

Whether one of the screwball protagonists is guilty of pride or whether the couple encounters it inside or outside their relationship, it is a trait that complicates the conflict already going on between them. In *The Bride Walks Out*, pride operates within the relationship to create problems for the screwball couple. The husband (Gene Raymond) is a struggling civil engineer who is adamant against letting his wife (Barbara Stanwyck) take a job outside the home. His inflexible attitude, coupled with their financial bind, puts a strain on their marriage. *Vivacious Lady* offers an example of pride impacting the screwball couple from outside their relationship. College president Peter Morgan, Sr. (Charles Coburn), prizes his lofty social standing and lets his ultra-conservative attitude govern the way he treats his son's new bride, a nightclub singer who does not measure up to his values. A film wherein destructive pride works from both inside and outside the relationship is *Holiday*. Liberal-minded Johnny Case must decide whether to uphold the lofty ambitions that his lover, Julia Seton, and her father, Mr. Edward Seton (Henry Kolker), attempt to impose on him. He rebels and Julia's more understanding sister Linda (Katharine Hepburn) captures him on the rebound.

In the most extreme cases, hubris tends to erode the humanity of some characters; they become embalmed in their own self-importance, dead in their ability to show consideration for others. They are used to having their own way and assume that everyone should fall in line with their way of thinking. They are stiff, stodgy, sanctimonious characters who cling to hackneyed standards that interfere with the union of the romantic couple. Mr. Edward Seton and Peter Morgan, Sr., fit in with this crowd, along with Mr. and Mrs. Anthony Kirby (Edward Arnold and Mary Forbes in *You Can't Take It with You*), Hopsie Pike (Henry Fonda in *The Lady Eve*), and Professor Rodney Elwell (Hume Cronyn in *People Will Talk*). Screwball comedy, however, borrows from Shakespeare's romantic comedy in that most of the time it finds a way to reform these stubborn, pretentious characters and, unless they are beyond redemption (like Prof. Elwell), to welcome them into the marriage circle at the end. Mr. Anthony Kirby joins Mr. Vanderhof in a harmonica duet, signifying that his spirit has been reclaimed. Hopsie Pike relaxes his staunch moral code and earns the right to reunite with his lost love. And in *Topper*, the title character suffers from

The Philadelphia Story (1940, MGM; George Cukor, director)—In the finale, Macaulay Connor (James Stewart, right) is willing to marry Tracy Lord (Katharine Hepburn, left) to spare her the embarrassment of lacking a groom for her wedding. However, C. K. Dexter Haven (Cary Grant, looking on) will intervene to set things right since he is better suited to marry Tracy, while Connor will find a better prospect in Liz Imbrie (Ruth Hussey).

his wife's obsessive concern with propriety. It takes his misadventures to jar her out of her narrow-mindedness, enabling her to appreciate the more enjoyable aspects of mischievous nonconformist behavior.

Film noir treats hubris as a more deadly character flaw. Vain characters are set up as objects of foolishness, as in screwball, but without the humorous implications. The self-important person who thinks himself above the common masses must eventually collapse under the weight of his own top-heavy arrogance. The final shot of Billy Wilder's *Ace in the Hole* (a.k.a. *The Big Carnival*, 1951) signifies this terrible fall from the glorious heights of egocentricity to the ground level of common reality. Sleazy, ambitious newspaperman Chuck Tatum (Kirk Douglas) is responsible for the death of a man trapped in a cave-in because he tried to prolong the man's predicament for the sake of his story. After the man's wife stabs him with a nail file, Tatum returns to the newsroom where, framed in an extreme low-angle shot, he topples forward, hitting the floor, his face suddenly in an extreme close-up to the camera, his eyes staring vacantly.

We find that film noir contains a host of arrogant characters who bring destruction to themselves and to many around them, whether innocent or not. Victor Grandison (Claude Rains) in *The Unsuspected* displays a hubris that validates his superiority and drives him to murder several naïve people in his family. The nihilistic *Sweet Smell of Success* has ambitious hustler Sidney Falco (Tony Curtis) ingratiating himself with ruthlessly powerful gossip columnist J. J. Hunsecker (Burt Lancaster). Together they plan to ruin the reputation of Hunsecker's sister's fiancé (Martin Milner), but pay the price with their own downfalls. *All the King's Men* shows idealist Willie Stark (Broderick Crawford) rising to political prominence, but with the acquisition of political power, he becomes as corrupt as the politicians he earlier condemned. And *Sunset Boulevard* presents Norma Desmond as a forgotten silent-screen star still nurturing an undying vanity that deludes her into believing she can cheat time, physically and professionally, and prevents her from confronting reality.

Obsession and **alienation**, according to Silver and Ward in their encyclopedia on film noir, are the two key elements defining the noir protagonist. Taking desire to its unholy extreme, obsession perverts what would otherwise have been a natural, wholesome quest—love becomes lust, need becomes possessiveness, ambition becomes avarice—and a character's aspirations become a warped vision of the American Dream. Going after a twisted, tainted version of the ideal dream can only bring devastation to the seeker. Thus, Walter Neff and Phyllis Dietrichson (*Double Indemnity*), Bart Tare and Annie Laurie Starr (*Gun Crazy*), Jefty Robbins (*Road House*), Louise Howell (*Possessed*), Stanton Carlisle (*Nightmare Alley*), and Geoffrey Carroll (*The Two Mrs. Carrolls*) pursue what they believe will fulfill their happiness, but their priorities are distorted and their quest brings calamity to them and to innocent people around them.

Alienation is either something the protagonist seeks willingly or something that is thrust upon him or her because of uncontrollable circumstances. Most detectives operate as loners by choice. Spade, Marlowe, Hammer, Jeff Markham, and Jim Wilson (*On Dangerous Ground*) may have a helpmate or two, but generally they walk the mean streets alone, confront the evil unknown on their own terms, and take their lickings stoically. Alienation comes with the job; it is a condition the hardboiled detective accepts because he knows he doesn't quite belong in elite social circles—Bogart's Marlowe is uncomfortable sitting in General Sternwood's hothouse (*The Big Sleep*); Dick Powell's Marlowe gets lost in Grayle's mansion and needs the butler to show him the exit (*Murder, My Sweet*); Jeff Bailey, gas station owner, dons his trench coat to become Jeff Markham, private detective, aware that ordinary society will never accept him even if he married Ann Miller (*Out of the Past*). If he does not make any exceptionally big blunders, the detective knows that, although he must sustain a few scars, he can survive on his own in the concrete jungle.

Alienation in domestic noirs, on the other hand, is an unhealthy condition that can be fatal for the characters. One or both of the noir lovers become separated from society by design or circumstance, usually because they are plotting some crime or rebelling against the social order. Once Walter Neff and Phyllis Dietrichson make their murder pact (*Double Indemnity*), they alienate themselves from everyone else and become an isolated society of two. In *They Live by Night*, Bowie, on the run from the law, takes the innocent Keechie with him. At different moments in the film, he contradicts his impression of "normal" people, one time sounding as if he and Keechie are above them, and at another wishing he and she could be like them. Unable to reconcile any kind of existence in the "normal" world, they are singled out for a tragic conclusion.

In screwball comedy, the battle of the sexes is very much dependent on these same elements of obsession and alienation. Obsessions can take a variety of forms, and when characters get caught up in extreme behavior, they create the farcical madcap situations that pervade the genre. Love, the desire to possess the other, and revenge, the desire to punish the other, are the two most obvious obsessions. In *Mr. & Mrs. Smith*, David Smith's inexorable campaign to reclaim his wife is counterpoised by Ann Smith's deep desire to avenge herself on him, most pointedly by securing David's law partner as her divorce attorney and dating him to arouse David's jealousy. Jean Harrington starts out in *The Lady Eve* as a con artist who expects to swindle money out of Hopsie Pike. Instead, he quickly becomes enamored with her and she with him and their worlds revolve solely around each other. When Hopsie learns that Jean is a member of a gambling ring, he deserts her without hearing her explanation. Love turns to hate and Jean transforms herself into the Lady Eve Sidwich who becomes fixated on avenging the wrong he did to her.

Obsessions can also take the form of idiosyncratic behavior, such as that of David and Susan in *Bringing Up Baby*: Susan is obsessed with convincing David that he loves her; David is obsessed with finding his missing dinosaur bone. In *Twentieth Century*, the two lovers combat each other with explosive displays of exaggerated emotions and excessive rants. In *Footsteps in the Dark*, rich Francis Monroe Warren II (Errol Flynn) has a secret fetish, to follow the police on their calls so he can get first-hand information for the crime novels he secretly writes.

Alienation is inherent in the relationship of the screwball couple. While the two lovers concentrate primarily on each other's whereabouts and comings-and-goings, they distance themselves from everything else—job, friends, activities. In *My Favorite Wife*, Nick Arden had by chance met

Bianca Bates aboard ship while searching for his first wife, Ellen, who had disappeared in a shipwreck. On the same day that Nick has Ellen declared legally dead (after being missing for seven years), he marries Bianca. Miraculously (and fatefully), Ellen appears just in time to disrupt the newlyweds' honeymoon. From then on, the lives of the two estranged spouses become enmeshed in a series of personal predicaments to the exclusion of everything else. In *Tell It to the Judge*, Marsha Meredith (Rosalind Russell) has divorced Pete Webb (Robert Cummings), thinking he cheated on her, and Webb cannot help pursuing her to explain the mistake and get her to remarry him. After fleeing a police raid on a gambling house, they take a rowboat out to a lighthouse island where, in isolation (except for lighthouse keeper, Alonzo K. Roogle, played by Clem Bevans), they have time to focus on each other and rekindle their relationship. They remarry, and the same series of events that broke up their first marriage begin coincidentally to repeat themselves as Pete gets waylaid and Marsha thinks he ran away with another woman. In all of these films, it is about the relationship. The two lovers keep each other at the center of their attention no matter what extraneous events they have to deal with in the meantime. They create a private world unto themselves while they clash and claw their way toward reconciliation.

Setting

Both screwball and noir take place in a modern-day urban setting. That is, their stories occur in the cities of the 1930s, '40s, and '50s, when the films were produced. Noir offers some exceptions with period costume dramas that are infused with noir stylistics (*Gaslight*, *Experiment Perilous*, *The Woman in White*) and transgeneric noirs (noirs that overlap other genres), such as westerns (*The Ox-Bow Incident*, *The Gunfighter*), science fiction (*Minority Report*), and war films (*The Steel Helmet*), but these are few, and for the most part, classical noir is a product of then-current times.

Screwball comedies, on the other hand, are exclusively contemporary in their setting. There is something about the nature of the battle of the sexes that demands that the films reflect the attitudes of the current society. These are not character studies—the films do not explore the universality of human nature; rather they focus on the dynamic of love as it fits into the context of modern life. These films are concerned with the influence of urban environment on current life styles and the vicissitudes occurring in romantic relationships tested by unconventional conditions.

A number of screwball comedies may shift the action between the city and the country (or a small town), usually to imply some fundamental contrast between the two venues. One contrast has to do with the popular, widely accepted myth that the country nurtures human kindness and considerateness that the city tends to crush with steel-toed boots. The country becomes a kind of Forest of Arden, where lovers are free to express themselves in a way they could not while under the constraints of the city. There are many examples where a brief or extended hiatus in a rural or small-town setting contributes to the union of the disputing lovers: *It Happened One Night, It's a Wonderful World, Come Live with Me, Design for Scandal, Adam's Rib, Tell It to the Judge, Christmas in Connecticut, Mr. Blandings Builds His Dream House, My Favorite Wife, The Awful Truth*.

Several screwball comedies approach the city-country myth ironically. One of the first to satirize the myth and show that rural America is not the bastion of innocence it is purported to be is *Nothing Sacred*. Wally Cook (Fredric March), reporter for the *New York Star*, travels to Warsaw, Vermont, to write a story on a young woman (Carole Lombard) dying of radium poisoning. He encounters several townsfolk who are money-grubbing, inhospitable, and rude, and when later he learns that Hazel Flagg has lied to him about her dying just so she could get a trip to New York, he realizes that country folk are not only as devious and materialistic as city slickers but have an even more gifted talent for it.

Theodora Goes Wild presents a number of comparisons between rural and urban settings. Theodora Lynn (Irene Dunne) is a product of Lynnville and a descendent of its founders. She appears to conform to the provincial attitude of the small town, but, in fact, she secretly writes scandalous novels, protecting her reputation under the pseudonym of Caroline Adams. Michael Grant (Melvyn Douglas) is an artist who lives in New York, and when he meets Theodora on one of her visits to her publisher, she charms him and he follows her back to Lynnville. Michael convinces her to break away from the repressive constraints of Lynnville's priggish and narrow-minded women. However, when Theodora tells Michael she loves him, he suddenly realizes he did not mean for this to happen. He deserts her and returns to the city. Heeding Michael's encouragement, Theodora sheds the insular thinking of Lynnville, follows Michael to New York, and audaciously announces to the newspapers that she is the provocative writer Caroline Adams. Michael explains that he is married and intends to get a divorce, but he has to wait until after the upcoming election because his father is a political candidate and the scandal could ruin him. Scandal, it seems, knows no boundaries, running rampant in both country and city; gossipmongers paradoxically disapprove of it and welcome it as grist for their rumor mills. Although the city is filled with more energy and chaos than the country, the belief that the country is populated by gentlefolk living a quiet, simple, honest life is satirized by the bigoted town characters who exhibit biased thinking and sanctimonious scruples, and in editor Jed Waterbury (Thomas Mitchell), whose Lynnville newspaper thrives on sensationalism just as much as big city publications.

Night and the City (1950, 20th Century–Fox; Jules Dassin, director)—Harry Fabian (Richard Widmark, right) displays his skills as a con artist by duping unsuspecting tourists (Eddy Reed, left, and MacDonald Parke) to visit his employer's club.

In film noir, movies like *Deadline at Dawn, Night and the City,* and *D. O. A.* reinforce the idea that big cities are dangerous, deadly places, and that small towns and country residences are healthier, more nurturing environments. *The Asphalt Jungle* suggests this idea at the end, when Dix (Sterling Hayden), dying from a gunshot wound, tries to return to the happier place of his youth, a horse ranch in the country. He reaches his childhood home in time to die in the pasture, the horses sniffing him out of idle curiosity, suggesting that youth and innocence, once lost or forfeited, cannot be reclaimed.

Many noirs also employ a new message, that rural villages and small towns are not immune to the crime and wickedness already corrupting the big cities. Hitchcock's early noir, *Shadow of a Doubt,* makes this clear when Uncle Charlie, the Merry Widow Murderer, leaves the city to visit relatives in small town Santa Rosa. Arriving at the station, the train that carries him spews clouds of black smoke into the air, polluting the clean country sky and signifying the malevolence its dissolute passenger brings with him from the city. Similar suggestions occur in other noirs, among them *Gun Crazy, Ace in the Hole, Fallen Angel, The Hitch-Hiker, Road House*, and *On Dangerous Ground*.

Tonal Quality

Have an audience glimpse but a few films from the noir genre and one of the first things they notice is the patent cynicism that runs systemically through their visual and thematic elements. The sensation most viewers experience is probably similar to that felt by André Bazin and his disciples when they first reveled in the postwar trove of American films that defined a dark side of human nature heretofore unprecedented in filmmaking. These films belonged unmistakably to the crime genre, but were distinct in their crude, crooked, and caustic themes, so much so that Nino Frank dubbed them "films noirs," making them close kin of the notorious French Series noires. The label was appropriate, delineating a genre separate from mainstream crime films.

Ironically, screwball comedy flirts with a similar pessimism, but clothes it in comic sarcasm so the cynical tone may not appear as obvious or as profound. The similar pranks and devious ploys that lead to tragedy for the noir protagonist and femme fatale produce humorous consequences for the screwball male and female. Walter Burns (*His Girl Friday*) is as sinister as any noir antagonist in his attempt to manipulate events so that Hildy Johnson will forego her wedding and remain with the newspaper. Similar underhanded and deceptive tactics are practiced by Bill Chandler (William Powell) in *Libeled Lady*, Jeff Sherman (Walter Pidgeon) in *Design for Scandal*, Jennifer (Veronica Lake) in *I Married a Witch*, Hazel Flagg (Carole Lombard) in *Nothing Sacred*, Mac MacGregor (Rosalind Russell) in *Take a Letter, Darling*, and many other screwball characters who they try to maneuver their romantic counterpart into doing what they want—which, in most cases, is to get married.

Many minor characters also step forward to voice a cynical contempt for whatever they observe; their critical comments contribute to that undercurrent of pessimism flowing just below the surface of the comedy. Alexander Bullock (Eugene Pallette) in *My Man Godfrey* views his family as a liability, which he makes clear in his sarcastic remarks about them. Muggsy Murgatroyd (William Demarest) in *The Lady Eve* is the epitome of cynicism; he has no faith in humanity and is skeptical of everyone. No one surpasses Franklin Pangborn as the effete, effeminate snob who thinks his station, no matter what it is, places him above everyone else. In nearly every role he plays, he openly expresses his distaste for the common and the vulgar. Some of his more prominent roles: Mr. Douglas in *Design for Living;* Guthrie (coordinator of the scavenger hunt) in *My Man Godfrey;*

Van Buren (clothing store salesman) in *Easy Living*; apartment manager in *Vivacious Lady*; and Higgins in *5th Avenue Girl*.

In some screwballs that involve the romantic triangle, there is the woman who starts off engaged to the screwball protagonist, but then has to compete with a new woman who enters his life. This fiancée, destined to lose in the contest for the man, usually exhibits a haughty, contemptuous air, automatically making her unlikable and proving she is not meant for him. She has a hard, cynical, materialistic outlook on the world, a contrast to the more romantically inclined female protagonist who ends up in the arms of the male lover. The various actresses who play this thankless role are always beautiful, suggesting that outward beauty is not enough to make her a prize worth having: Doris Nolan (*Holiday*), Marcia Ralston (*Ever Since Eve*), and Rita Johnson (*The Major and the Minor*), to name a few. One standout actress who became strongly equated with this condescending image is the stunningly gorgeous Gail Patrick, a reliable performer who always brought class and sophistication to the part even while she delivered her lines with venomous sarcasm. She adopts this same character in several screwball comedies: Cornelia Bullock in *My Man Godfrey*, Marilyn Thomas in *The Doctor Takes a Wife*, Bianca Bates in *My Favorite Wife*, and Isobel Kimble Grayson in *Love Crazy*.

The dynamics operating in the eternal triangle in film noir is the antithesis of what it is in screwball comedy. If the noir protagonist is initially in a relationship with a woman, she is generally the "right" woman. But he cannot appreciate what he has and he makes the mistake of straying outside that respectable circle to pursue the "wrong" woman. To satisfy an insatiable, idealistic desire, he wanders out of a peaceful Eden and into a perilous jungle. The world that was originally in balance for the protagonist goes suddenly awry. Unlike in screwball where the female protagonist acts like "the other woman" to save the male protagonist from a grim fate, in noir "the other woman" represents disaster: whether a Spider Woman, Inadvertent Femme Fatale, or Latent Femme Fatale, she lures the male into the dark quagmire from which he cannot escape. Nora Prentiss (*Nora Prentiss*), Mona Stevens (*Pitfall*), Diane Tremayne (*Angel Face*), and Margo Lannington (*Where Danger Lives*) are a few of the noir women who mislead the noir man from his former sedate but secure existence.

Whereas noir wears its cynicism on its sleeve, screwball tucks it just under the cuff. Screwball comedy masks its cynicism with a veneer of humor: comical circumstances disguise dismal and dour motifs, and resolutions in marriage create the impression of a happy ending. Yet there is always a subtle, nagging ambivalence: the momentary joy of marriage or reunification of the lovers diverts attention from the prospects of a life of feuding, albeit a "good-natured" ongoing battle between the romantic pair. After witnessing a 90-minute battle of the sexes on the screen, can we expect the future to be much different for Ellie Andrews and Peter Warne (*It Happened One Night*) or David Huxley and Susan Vance (*Bringing Up Baby*) or Hildy Johnson and Walter Burns (*His Girl Friday*)? A central irony in *It Happened One Night* is that the image of combative spouses, not the blissful picture of "two people in love," is considered the accepted standard. Peter and Ellie's phony row to fool the detectives is perceived as normal behavior; Danker (Alan Hale) interprets Peter and Ellie's squabbling as an ordinary spat between newlyweds; and the cranky wife and her milquetoast husband who own the auto camp represent the fated relationship expected of most marriages. Even in the final scene taking place at a third auto camp where the elderly owners appear friendly and pleasant, the wife stands taller than her husband, dominant to him, and she doubts whether Peter and Ellie are married, since "they don't behave like married folk"—in other words, their show of kind and considerate affection for one another is abnormal married behavior. Perhaps Ellie and Peter (and most screwball couples in the final frame) represent the hope that marriage does not have to decline typically and inevitably into a state of acrimony, hostility, and intolerance where one partner tries to gain dominance over the other.

Screwball films do not always end with marriage. Even when they tend to imply that an exchange of vows is imminent, they may hint at the close that the couple has the opportunity to engage in a pre-marital liaison. This is not cynicism per se, but by giving the audience a conspiratorial wink, these films flout the Production Code while entertaining the lewd and vulgar instincts of the crowd. Thus, at the end of *Mr. and Mrs. Smith*, David Smith (Robert Montgomery) finagles his estranged wife Ann Krausheimer (Carole Lombard) into an uncompromising position. Her crisscrossed skis suggest the X-rated physical union they are apt to under-take that night before they have a chance to legitimize their marriage in the morning. And at the end of *Twentieth Century*, Lily Garland (Carole Lombard, again) and Oscar Jaffe (John Barrymore) have reconciled their dispute and reestablished their romantic union, a relationship that was never sanctioned by holy—or secularly legal—wedlock.

One of the most morally ambiguous endings occurs in Preston Sturges's *The Lady Eve*. Charles "Hopsie" Pike (Henry Fonda) enters the cabin of his former love Eugenia "Jean" Harrington (Barbara Stanwyck) under the impression that he is married to someone else and that he is com-mitting adultery, although the audience (and Jean) is fully aware that she had married Hopsie after assuming the false identity of Lady Eve Sidwich. How are we to interpret this? If a person thinks he sins, doesn't he commit a sin even when his actions are not intrinsically sinful?

Back and forth, the same situations that produce laughs for screwball comedy convey a sense of doom and despair in film noir. The laughs in screwball, however, are ambiguous: the humor is the result of outrageously absurd situations, yet further examination shows that accompanying the comedy is the underlying implication of something more serious. In his perpetual drunken state, Nick Charles (*The Thin Man*) acts like a buffoon who shows bartenders how to concoct drinks to music or feigns throwing a vicious punch at his unsuspecting wife. In the world of screwball, his drunkenness codes him as a playful eccentric. The main irony is that he still functions like a charming and competent individual, accomplishing his deeds with aplomb, bravado, and skill. Yet we have to ask why he is drunk: the stress of his new responsibilities from overseeing his wife's inherited businesses?; the monotony of a new lifestyle that transitioned from an active life as a detective to an empty life as figurehead of several companies?; the freedom of the wealthy leisure class with the money and opportunity to imbibe at will? Drunkenness, in itself, is a despicable, wretched condition—Nick Charles, Doc Enoch Downer (*Nothing Sacred*), and George and Marion Kerby (*Topper*) may stumble about in a drunken haze that makes them appear like comical and entertaining figures in screwball comedy, but noir characters set themselves up for misfortune. Consider Jeff Hartnett (Van Heflin) as a pathetic poet in *Johnny Eager*; Marty Blair (Dan Duryea) as a broken-down songwriter in *Black Angel*; Charlie Waterman (Robert Warwick) as a has-been actor in *In a Lonely Place*; and Stanton Carlisle (Tyrone Power) as an exposed con artist in *Nightmare Alley*. Screwball films use drunkenness to color their characters with eccentricity; noir films use drugs and booze to create characters who are pathetic, vulnerable, endangered, or lost.

On the whole, screwball comedy disguises its cynicism with a humor derived from eccentric characters, complicated plotlines, sarcastic dialogue, and bizarre ironies; film noir filters similar components through a darker lens and stains them with a gray tinge that more cruelly and adamantly reflects the cynical, hostile nature of the world.

5

Comparative Analyses of Films from the Two Genres

One approach to this study could have been to compare the screwball comedies and noirs made by individual directors. However, a survey of the two genres discloses that, other than Billy Wilder, few directors made significant forays into both areas. Howard Hawks, for instance, is a mainstay in screwball comedy, directing one of the first (*Twentieth Century*), several important ones throughout the era (*Bringing Up Baby, His Girl Friday, Ball of Fire,* and *I Was a Male War Bride*), and one of the last (*Monkey Business*), yet he directs only one important noir, *The Big Sleep.* The same is true of Mitchell Leisen, who made several distinguished screwball comedies, including *Easy Living* and *Midnight,* but turned out only one noir, *No Man of Her Own* (1950). On the opposite extreme is Alfred Hitchcock, whose suspense films often bleed into noir—*Shadow of a Doubt, Spellbound, Notorious, The Paradine Case, Rope, Strangers on a Train, Rear Window, The Wrong Man,* and *Vertigo*—yet he made only one screwball comedy, *Mr. & Mrs. Smith.* Such is the case with other outstanding directors of the era—Michael Curtiz, Jack Conway, Lloyd Bacon, Richard Thorpe, Curtis Bernhardt, William Keighley, Preston Sturges, George Cukor, and Fritz Lang—who, prolific as they were, did not work enough films in both genres to merit a practical comparison. Had he not succumbed to an untimely death, W. S. "Woody" Van Dyke II might have served as the ideal model for this study. He directed one true noir, *Rage in Heaven,* and a number of important screwball comedies, including four screwball mysteries in *The Thin Man* series which foreshadow some of the noir stylistics to come and provide evidence that he would have handled film noir quite adeptly.

Rather than analyzing the films of one director, we will still examine some specific noir and screwball films that share remarkably comparable qualities. The previous chapter discussed the general conventions that are common to screwball comedy and film noir. This present chapter offers a comparative analysis of films that use related conventions in their different generic contexts.

The Lady Eve (Preston Sturges, 1941) and *Out of the Past* (Jacques Tourneur, 1947)

> *You see, Hopsie, you don't know very much about girls. The best ones aren't as good as you think they are and the bad ones aren't as bad. Not nearly as bad.*
>
> —Jean Harrington in *The Lady Eve*

> ANN MILLER (referring to femme fatale Kathie Moffat): *She can't be all bad. No one is.*
> JEFF MARKHAM: *Well, she comes the closest.*
>
> —From *Out of the Past*

The most apparent point of comparison between *The Lady Eve* and *Out of the Past* lies in their plots which are divided into two distinct sections defined by the leading female character who assumes a dual role. In both cases, an alluring seductress in the first half of the story plays a sincere romantic love interest for the male, but in the second half of the story, she becomes a vengeful and vicious femme fatale bent on the male's vilification and destruction.

In *The Lady Eve*, Eugenia "Jean" Harrington (Barbara Stanwyck) drops an apple like a bombshell right onto the head of Charles "Hopsie" Pike (Henry Fonda) as he prepares to board her cruise ship from his tender. Hopsie is the son of Horace Pike (Eugene Pallette) and heir to the Pike's Pale Ale fortune. He has been studying snakes in a remote jungle and now returns to civilization. Jean is, in effect, marking him as her personal target in the gambling scheme she and her cardsharp father, Colonel Harrington (Charles Coburn), will employ to bilk him out of a considerable sum of money. However, a turning point occurs when Hopsie invites Jean into his stateroom to show her his snake Emma. Jean thinks he is using an imaginative variation on a man's standard ruse to get a girl into his room, but when she sees the creature slithering out of the sleeve of his robe lying on the bed, she panics and runs away, dashing through the ship's winding corridors, all the way to her own room. Superficially, her reaction shows a typical aversion to snakes; yet if the snake is considered a phallic symbol, her fear of it might suggest her fear of sex and of losing her virginity. Her sense of self-confidence and control are shaken by this unexpected situation. Although Hopsie told her truthfully what she would find in his room, her previous experiences conditioned her to interpret his comment differently. Instead, here is a man who tells the unembellished truth. Her initial plan to fleece him down to his expensive flannels falls apart for her.

Hopsie follows Jean back to her stateroom, symbolically making his way through the labyrinth to the lair of the seductive "monster." With Jean stretched out on a divan and Hopsie sitting on the floor beside her with his head cradled in her arms, the camera lingers on this two-shot for three minutes and 15 seconds, during which time the bonds of a trusting and meaningful relationship are formed. (Her perfume makes him "cockeyed," one of many code words of these comedies, like "screwball," "nuts," "crazy," "mad," "cuckoo," and "screwy," to remind us of the mental state of the protagonist-lovers.)

Unexpectedly for her, Jean falls in love with Hopsie and forsakes her plans to con him, even trying to protect him from her father. In one of those fateful coincidences on which complex screwball (and noir) plots depend, two things occur. Jean would have told Hopsie of her shady past, but she promises her father not to, so that he and his accomplice Gerald (Melville Cooper) can still cheat other unsuspecting passengers on the ship. At the same time, Hopsie's friend and bodyguard Ambrose "Muggsy" Murgatroyd (William Demarest) learns the true profession of the three gamblers and prompts the steward to inform Hopsie who the Harringtons really are.

When Jean meets the enlightened Hopsie at the bar, she doesn't yet know he knows, and she utters one of the key themes of the film related to his limited, unrealistic perception of women: "You see, Hopsie. The best ones aren't as good as you think they are and the bad ones aren't as bad." Her maxim derives from the wisdom of observation and experience. She may be exonerating herself, but only because she loves Hopsie and knows she is right for him. It is his lack of experience, his cloistered life dedicated to herpetology, that prevents him from sharing Jean's insight and compels him to cling so tenaciously and inflexibly to his expectations of the ideal woman. Like Tracy Lord (Katharine Hepburn) in *The Philadelphia Story*, no personal flaw can he brook, no imperfection can he tolerate. At first glance, Hopsie seems like an affable buffoon who deserves to be laughed at—he is the brunt of slips and spills, including the first time he meets Jean, who purposely sticks out her foot to trip him, and he docilely complies with her instructions thereafter—but he possesses a righteous arrogance, a trait that reveals his priggishness and diminishes his humanity. This is his tragic flaw; and Jean exploits it to exact her revenge.

To avenge her injury, the jilted woman plans to attack Hopsie in a way that will inflict the greatest pain: by undermining his lofty, impractical notion of what his ideal mate should be. And so, in the second half of the film, Jean drapes herself in a new identity, the Lady Eve Sidwich. She uses but a thinly veiled guise—no wig or heavy makeup, only a fake English accent. Although Muggsy is not fooled, the superficial ruse deceives Hopsie who argues with him, using the strange ironic logic that she looks too much like Jean to be "the same dame." Hopsie becomes enthralled with her, and

Eve seduces him in his home, gets him to propose to her, and marries him. On the train taking them to their honeymoon destination, Eve unloads her phony romantic history, an inventory of male suitors whom she had known; she recalls with relish the enjoyable times she had with them. This arouses Hopsie's righteousness and he walks out on her, or rather slides out, for when he scrambles off the train, he slips in the mud.

Remorseful in victory, Jean/Eve has a change of heart. She wants to talk with her husband, but he refuses, thinking her a tarnished woman. Hopsie returns to the cruise ship for another tour (perhaps hoping he might run into Jean). As she did the first time she got his attention, Jean sticks out her foot as he passes her table and trips him up. He immediately admits his mistake in losing her. They retire to her cabin. As the door closes on their romantic reunion, Hopsie tries to be honest with her, confessing, "I'm married." Jean replies, "So am I, darling"—as if their common marital status is supposed to justify their "adultery." In one of the most bizarre endings for a screwball comedy, the door opens and Muggsy furtively exits, as if he

The Lady Eve (1941, Paramount; Preston Sturges, director)—As part of her plan to avenge herself on ex-lover Charles "Hopsie" Pike, Eugenia "Jean" Harrington (Barbara Stanwyck) poses as Lady Eve Sidwich and ingratiates herself with Hopsie's father (Eugene Pallette).

had been secretly investigating her by searching her room. His last line, "Positively the same dame," suggests that he has not found conclusive evidence and has only his intuition upon which to rely. It also suggests that no matter how different one woman may seem from another, she is always "the same dame."

Like Jean/Eve, Kathie Moffat (Jane Greer) lurks at the center of *Out of the Past,* and the divided structure reflects her two personalities. The story begins in a pleasant small town named Bridgeport, where Jeff Bailey (Robert Mitchum) owns a gas station and courts local nice-girl Ann Miller (Virginia Huston). Like Hopsie, who boards the cruise ship after leaving the jungle primeval, Bailey is an outsider, a mystery to everyone, as Ann says when they are at the lakeside fishing and enjoying each other's company. Bailey's assistant, a deaf mute known only as The Kid (Dickie Moore), calls him back to the shop to talk with some stranger who knows him. Joe Stephanos (Paul Valentine), an acquaintance from "out of the past," reminds Bailey that he has some unfinished business with a former employer. Bailey is reluctant to go, but resigns himself to it. He leaves that night for Tahoe and brings Ann along for the ride. This becomes an excuse for the lengthy flashback that allows Bailey to tell her his problem and confess his sordid role in an unpleasant history.

Bailey is really private eye Jeff Markham, who worked with partner Jack Fisher (Steve Brodie). Markham was hired by Whit Sterling (Kirk Douglas) to retrieve runaway girlfriend Kathie Moffat, who shot him and stole $40,000 of his money. To intimate the power he wields and his potential to exercise forgiveness or cruelty, Sterling compares his girlfriend to a horse he bought after it lost a race that cost him a heavy wager. Markham assumes that Sterling bought the horse to shoot it, but Sterling rebuffs this assumption, saying he put the horse out to pasture where it is living a comfortable, contented life.

In this exchange, Jeff plays something of the knight-errant watching out for the damsel in distress. Although their banter is light and playful, Markham and Sterling are jousting with each other. Markham suspects a vicious streak in his client and wants no part of subjecting a woman to it, even if she did wrong to shoot him and steal his money. This speaks of Markham's ethical standards.

In their relationship with women, both Jeff Markham and Charles Hopsie Pike exhibit a sense of values that reflect their personal and professional code. Markham assumes the role of a savior protecting Kathie from Sterling's wrath, while Hopsie plays Prince Charming in the "Cinderella scene" where he fits the "slipper" on Jean's foot. The two relationships are consummated in similarly symbolic ways: figurative erotic imagery circumvents the Production Code to suggest a sexual interlude between the male and female. In *The Lady Eve,* Hopsie and Jean stand at the rail near the bow of the ship, trading terms of endearment and finally kissing. The

Out of the Past (1947, RKO; Jacques Tourneur, director)—In the second phase of his relationship with the femme fatale, Jeff Markham (Robert Mitchum), alias Jeff Bailey, ponders his mistake with Kathie Moffat (Jane Greer) who, appropriately, wears a black outfit as a symbol of her treacherous nature.

music swells and the camera-eye shifts to a shot of the ship's prow plowing through the water and creating a frothy wake. In *Out of the Past,* Markham and Kathie escape a tropical shower by running to her cabana where they towel off each other's head. They kiss on the couch. Markham tosses away the towel, a breeze blows open the door (the sexual invitation), and the camera cuts to an objective shot outside the cabana, tracking away from the open door to the surrounding gardens. The implied consummations confirm the lovers' commitment to their relationships.

At climactic moments, both men learn something of their lovers' feet of clay. Markham is in the throes of a fistfight with Fisher when Kathie shoots and kills the partner, then runs away. Markham finds her bankbook and discovers the entry for $40,000, proving that she lied and had really stolen Sterling's money. In a similarly abrupt way, Hopsie learns the truth about Jean from documented evidence, a photo and a written notation that discloses her secret about her and her father being gamblers. Hopsie hurts himself by adhering so adamantly to his code, showing a lack of flexibility in rejecting the woman who fails to meet his ideal. Ironically, this is the inverse of how Markham seals his fate by forsaking his professional code and succumbing to the tantalizing wiles of the femme fatale. Both behaviors are extreme and undermine the men's self-respectability. Before Markham first makes love to Kathie on the beach, she warns him about getting involved with her. He plunges ahead anyway, saying, "Baby, I don't care." While he means that he believes she is worth whatever Sterling might do to him, his decision also implies that for her, he is willing to forsake his professional integrity by betraying a client. Eventually, though, both Markham and Hopsie reject the loves of their life for a similar reason: they cannot commit to a woman who turns out to be different from their original impression and from their imagined and unrealistic idealization.

The second half of *Out of the Past* begins when Ann deposits Markham at the wrought-iron gate outside Sterling's Tahoe mansion and drives away. Inside, Sterling reintroduces Markham to Kathie at breakfast. Markham now knows what she is, and so their relationship cannot return to what it was. She swears that her love for him is unchanged, which we later learn is a lie because she works with Sterling to frame Markham for the murder of accountant Leonard Eels (Ken Niles).

Like Kathie Moffat, Jean Harrington as Lady Eve Sidwich has plans for getting even with her traitorous lover. Shifting their roles from lover to Nemesis, Kathie and Eve define the essence of the classic femme fatale: they seduce and devastate the male purely for their own selfish ends.

At the conclusion, although Markham agrees to run away with Kathie, we see what she does not: while she goes to pack their bags, he walks to the phone, lifts the receiver, and dials some unidentified party. Minutes later, we realize he must have contacted the police, who have set up a road-block in response to his call. Kathie shoots Markham and the police shoot Kathie. All through the film, Markham has exuded the air of a defeated man resigned to his fate, even though he appears to fight against the inevitable, going through the motions of one trying to rig the outcome the way one rigs a horse race. He wants to make a deal with Eels, but Eels is killed by Stephanos; he steals the affidavit that accuses him of killing Fisher and burying his body in the woods, but Sterling's men get it back; he returns to Tahoe to negotiate a truce with Sterling, but after Kathie kills Sterling, Markham loses his leverage and Kathie claims complete control over him. He capitulates and then makes that phone call, as if to indicate that he has finally given up all hope of ever erasing his past and is willing to seal a suicide pact just to be done with life.

Just as Markham returned to Kathie, Hopsie in *The Lady Eve* returns to Jean, the woman he knew and loved in the first half of the film. There is a surrender and a commitment that he could not make in the first half. Hopsie has learned to overcome his petty righteousness; Markham has reclaimed his former sense of right. Both men succumb to their fate, in a way paying the price (marriage, death) for the way they misused their code.

The Palm Beach Story (Preston Sturges, 1942) and Gilda (Charles Vidor, 1946)

Sex has everything to do with it.
—Gerry Jeffers in *The Palm Beach Story*

Put the blame on Mame, boys.
—Gilda in *Gilda*

In *Hollywood Genres*, Thomas Schatz notes four stages in the evolution of a genre: experimental, classic, modified, and baroque/self-reflexive (See Chapter 2). *The Palm Beach Story*, appearing about midway through the classical screwball cycle, contains modified characteristics that anticipate the more bizarre and outrageous elements of the form in its later stage. In fact, it not only parodies the earlier models; it is a near inversion of one of the first screwballs, Capra's *It Happened One Night*. Consider: Ellie wants to go from Florida (Miami) to New York (Long Island) to reunite with her alienated husband; Gerry wants to flee from New York City to Florida (Palm Beach) to get a divorce from her husband. Ellie rides on a bus, accompanied by unemployed drifters and the struggling working class; Gerry rides a train, escorted by an assortment of eccentric millionaires. Ellie begins her trip to New York by diving off her father's yacht; Gerry ends her trip to Palm Beach by riding in luxury on John D. Hackensacker's yacht. Ellie gets an annulment from her husband and marries the reporter; Gerry abandons her designs to marry a millionaire and returns to her husband. Writer-director Preston Sturges seems to deliberately invert the original Capra-Riskin formula as a comment on the genre.

Gilda comes close to the middle of the noir cycle and shares points of comparison with Sturges's film. For one, they both emphasize a fundamental idea common to screwball and noir: that the female has physical seductive powers which she uses to manipulate males to do her bidding. Whereas men had seized control of politics, industry, and business, women decided to seize control of men.

Preston Sturges trumps male chauvinism by endowing his female characters with this power and having them flaunt it openly. In 1948's *Unfaithfully Yours*, Sir Alfred De Carter (Rex Harrison) becomes manically obsessed with the idea that his wife (Linda Darnell) has used her charms to seduce his handsome male secretary, Tony Windborn (Kurt Kreuger). In his 1941 *The Lady Eve*, Sturges exaggerates the female's consciousness of her sexual powers when, in the dining room scene after Hopsie first comes aboard the cruise ship, every available woman—young and old, attractive or not—flirts with the heir to the Pike fortune, batting her eyelashes or dropping her handkerchief to make his acquaintance. Later, Jean, as Eve Sidwich, uses her feminine wiles to charm Hopsie's father and then seduce Hopsie for a second time.

In *The Palm Beach Story*, Tom (Joel McCrea) and Gerry Jeffers

The Palm Beach Story (1942, Paramount; Preston Sturges, director)—The triple wedding in the finale is reminiscent of Shakespeare's *A Midsummer Night's Dream*, where dues ex machina brings all the lovers together for a mass marriage, and love is based simply on visual, physical attraction rather than some deep meta-physical rationale. Tom (Joel McCrea) and Gerry (Claudette Colbert) acquaint their twins with John D. Hackensacker (Rudy Vallee) and Princess Centimillia (Mary Astor), while Toto (Sig Arno, far right), abused and snubbed, appears indignant.

(Claudette Colbert) have an argument about an odd, elderly man who came to their apartment, took a liking to Gerry, and gave her enough money to pay all their bills. Tom cannot fathom any man giving her money for no reason:

> TOM: I mean, sex didn't even enter into it.
> GERRY: Oh, but of course it did, darling. I don't think he'd have given it to me if I had hair like excelsior and little short legs like an alligator. Sex always has something to do with it, dear.

The question she answers for her husband is not only why this one man she met—the Wienie King (Robert Dudley)—was so willing to help her but also why most men she meets take time to give her assistance. Is it that she has encountered a cadre of kind, considerate males eager to come to the aid of any damsel in distress? No, it is because she is a *beautiful* damsel in distress. After the Wienie King, there is the cab driver who drives her to Penn Station without charge. (Frank Faylen plays the cabbie, a stereo-typical role for him. If he had actually collected fares in all the movies in which he played a hack, he could have retired a wealthy man.) At the gate of the departing train, members of the Ale and Quail Club, millionaires all, pass her and glance at her with knowing, flirtatious smiles. She answers their inquiries about her dilemma, and when they realize she needs help, they purchase a train ticket for her and adopt her as their mascot. Finally, there is John D. Hackensacker (Rudy Vallee), who is sincere in his overtures to Gerry, but they are overtures inspired by Gerry's beauty, which is *the* essential ingredient in prompting men to respond to her needs.

This same motif runs throughout *Gilda*. Whatever her motive, because her husband Ballin (George Macready) is not satisfying her emotional or sexual needs, or because she wants to make Johnny (Glenn Ford) jealous, Gilda (Rita Hayworth) constantly flirts with men willing to abet her in her extramarital romps. She is completely aware that her beauty gives her a power over men, that she can get them to respond to her wishes—everyone, that is, except Johnny, who keeps fighting bitterly with her for being what she is (or so he thinks she is) and playing the temptress the way she does.

Gilda's and Gerry's awareness of the seductive power of their beauty is reminiscent of a scene in *Murder, My Sweet* (1944) wherein Spider Woman Helen Grayle (played by classic femme fatale Claire Trevor) trades quips with Philip Marlowe (Dick Powell) who tries to neutralize her allure by acting nonchalant:

> HELEN: I like men, all kinds of men. I find men attractive.
> MARLOWE: I imagine they meet you halfway.

Helen expects men to succumb to her charm, and she cleverly maneuvers them to do what she wants. Marlowe senses her attractive power and resists it, but his self-confidence unwisely leads him to give her a little too much leeway and he pays a price. (He thinks he is in control of the situation, but his plans go amok when a gun is fired close to his eyes and the powder burns temporarily blind him. Blindness signifies the flaw plaguing many an overconfident detective: their failure to see the complete truth behind the pretense.)

One of the most revealing demonstrations of the woman's power over men is Gilda's striptease. In a striptease, the woman places herself on center stage and makes herself the sole focus for the male's intense, undiluted gaze. She is momentarily a seductive exhibitionist who has utter control over the mind and desire of the male voyeur. Gilda whets the base appetite of the crowd, flaunting her sexiest movements while singing "Put the Blame on Mame." She takes off her gloves and necklace, throws them to some approving gentlemen, then invites someone to help her with her zipper. Two men from the audience eagerly oblige, but Johnny's bodyguard (Joe

Sawyer) intervenes. It appears that, if not for the interruption, Gilda would have carried the striptease to its anticipated consummation. However, later, when we learn of Gilda's true personality, that she never actually committed adultery while married to Ballin and that her outlandish sexual behavior was all a pretense to get back at Johnny (for some slight that is never explained), we understand that she is not the oversexed seductress she seemed to portray.

Ironically, Rita Hayworth will take part in a similar but inverted scene ten years later in *Pal Joey*, in which she plays Vera Simpson, an entrepreneur backing Joey Evans (Frank Sinatra) who wants to open a nightclub. Trying to thwart Joey's romantic aspirations for singer Linda English (Kim Novak), Vera orders Joey to fire her, unless he is willing to let Linda do the striptease segment. Linda fools both of them by agreeing to do it, but just as she is about to take off her last layer of garments, Joey stops the performance. Vera later tells Linda that Joey's stopping her from undressing at rehearsal was one of the great love scenes. In a similar way, Johnny's disapproval of Gilda's striptease verifies his romantic claims on her. Argumentatively, he may be keeping her from looking foolish or protecting her for his boss Ballin—but more likely he is protecting her for himself, displaying love's vanity and possessiveness in the guise of bitter resentment and self-righteousness.

Tom Jeffers exposes similar feelings of jealous resentment when his wife tells him that the Wienie King, without any conditions, offered her a wad of money. When he questions her with the sarcastic remark, "I mean, sex didn't even enter into it," he puts into words the very thought in Johnny's mind as he observes Gilda dating a string of extramarital suitors.

Both Gerry Jeffers and Gilda break up with their man and then use their sex for different reasons. When Gerry flees her husband, she makes it sound like a practical sacrifice: she believes that, if he were on his own, he could live more comfortably and perhaps make a success of himself; and she gives herself the opportunity to make "connections" while she is still young. Gerry is confident in how to use her sex and anticipates what men will do to please her. There is no animosity in the separation: Tom wants her back because he loves her and he pursues her with that intent; Gerry runs out with ambivalent feelings, believing it is necessary for their future success and happiness but still feeling deeply for Tom and showing a reluctance to leave.

There is an unexplained backstory concerning Gilda and Johnny. They have had a relationship and separated at some earlier date before the film begins. Although the time of their breakup and the reason for it is not revealed, he holds an intense grudge against her, as if she had committed some extremely heinous wrong, real or imagined, that caused him to sever their relationship. In the present, they express mutual dislike, even hatred, for one another. Johnny's feelings are explicit and clear; Gilda's are guised in sarcasm and feigned ignorance. Gilda's reason for using her sexual allure differs from that of Gerry: she taunts Johnny for the purpose of reaping some kind of personal vengeance.

After their respective breakups, the two women get caught between two men, the one they tried to desert who is an outcast of sorts (Tom, a failure as an architect, and Johnny, a lone, displaced gambler), the other one wealthy and secure (Hackensacker and Ballin). Eventually, the woman "remarries" the failure/outcast, suggesting that money is not the most important objective, nor the thing to ensure the greatest happiness.

Both *The Palm Beach Story* and *Gilda* have ironic endings. Screwball comedies, in general, use marriage in the finale to signify the happiness achievable in the male-female relationship. Noir, in an ironic way, makes a similar assertion by inverting the outcome: failure and tragedy prove that the characters have chosen the wrong way to go after the American Dream; the couple might have been happy enough if they had been satisfied with what they had. Although *Gilda* inserts a familiar "happy ending" (oddly abrupt and not totally satisfying), the conclusion, in a way, suggests the conventional noir lesson: the lovers redeem each other by rekindling their love and returning to America to reclaim their dream, but they have put each other through a world of misery before realizing the worth of what they once had.

In his approach to comedy, Sturges is very much aware of the ambivalence in the cliché happy ending. To suggest this fact, he *begins* the film with the happy ending to some previous, unexplained story that shows two people (Tom and Gerry) getting married. The ending of this introductory scene is enclosed in two captioned frames, the first reading "...and they lived happily ever after..." followed by the question "...or did they?" The madcap events that precede the opening wedding show what the screwball characters went through to reach that point. The rest of the film, then, reveals the aftermath of that wedding and how reality alters fairy tale expectations. But when the story proper also ends in a double marriage, a bride and groom arriving like *dei ex machina* to marry the rich John Hackensacker and his sister Princess Centimillia (Mary Astor), the scene reprises the beginning with its two captioned frames and suggests that happy endings are an illusion—married couples, rich or not, have no immunity against life's travails that will assault them after their glorious but brief honeymoon. The audience laughs, but the implication is hardly less cynical than the tragic consequences found in noir.

Besides its parallels with *The Palm Beach Story, Gilda* also bears some marked similarities to Ernst Lubitsch's pre–Code, pre-screwball comedy *Design for Living* (1933). First of all, the main female protagonists in both films coincidentally have the unusual name of Gilda, although the Hayworth character pronounces it with a "hard" G and Hopkins calls herself

Gilda (1946, Columbia; Charles Vidor, director)—Gilda Mundson (Rita Hayworth in one of her iconic poses) performs a strip tease, using the sensual power of her body to taunt and defy her estranged lover, Johnny Farrell (Glenn Ford, not shown).

"Jilda." The differences in the pronunciation suggest basic differences in the characters. Hayworth's character is "gilded" in the sense that she is an exquisitely fashioned golden idol, yet her gorgeous exterior is merely a thin veneer for a vulnerable, thinking, feeling woman who is trying to disguise her damaged emotions. The name of the Hopkins's character may be related to the word "gill" (pronounced "jil"), which means girlfriend. At the same time the name resonates with the word "jilt," a woman who cruelly discards a man. Hopkins' Gilda in *Design for Living* is a girlfriend to two men, but she also jilts both of them in a double betrayal.

A significant comparison concerns the situation in which the two women find themselves: each stands as the desirable object in a tug of war between two men who are extremely close friends. Hopkins's Gilda meets the two friends at the same time: George Curtis (Gary Cooper) and Tom Chambers (Fredric March). She is drawn to them both, but in the heat of passion, she disappoints Tom by marrying George, only later to have an extramarital fling with Tom. Hayworth's Gilda marries Ballin after she already had a volatile relationship with Johnny, and Ballin suspects that the hate between her and Johnny is an even more intense emotion than love. Shortly after Ballin is presumed dead, Johnny marries Gilda, pretending to love her but really intending to use the marriage as a way to control her.

The comedy ends with the suggestion that the three friends will continue their ménage à trois, unlike the film noir, which eliminates Ballin as a competitor and enables Johnny and Gilda to pair off with hope for a romantically fulfilling future. The dynamics among the three people are at the center of both films, particularly the confused desires, the revolving jealousies, and the intriguingly convoluted circumstances. Lubitsch handles his material with scandalous levity; Vidor takes the same material and treats it as a study in sexual obsession and frustrated passion.

The Whole Town's Talking (John Ford, 1935) and *I Wake Up Screaming* (H. Bruce Humberstone, 1941)

MISS CLARK: *I've always wanted to go abroad.*
ARTHUR FERGUSON JONES: *Yes, so have I.... Shanghai, for instance. I've always wanted to go to Shanghai. Say, I've got a stamp from Shanghai.*

—From *The Whole Town's Talking*

JILL LYNN: *What's the good of living without hope?*
LT. ED CORNELL: *It can be done.*

—From *I Wake Up Screaming*

Stifled romantic dreams haunt a particular character in both Ford's screwball comedy and Humberstone's film noir. The key difference is that in Ford's film, the protagonist appears content with his unfulfilled expectations; in Humberstone's film, the antagonist is a bitter man whose lone-liness and despair arouse our pity. Both men burn with an obsessive love for a woman, but they have difficulty declaring their love. Their obsession is so strong that they keep a picture of their beloved on the wall of their apartment where they can secretly pay homage to her. In the meantime, the two men suffer some form of alienation because of their personality and demeanor, one being extremely shy, the other physically repulsive. This combination of obsessive love and alienation contributes to the events that disrupt their previously tolerable life style.

Ford's film is debatable as a screwball entry—the serious dramatic aspects dominate the humorous elements, but the incongruous personalities of introverted Arthur Ferguson "Jonesy" Jones (Edward G. Robinson) and extroverted Miss Wilhelmina Clark (Jean Arthur) are similar to those found in such screwball comedies as *Ball of Fire* and *The Miracle of Morgan's Creek*. At the same time, the story contains many satirical barbs ridiculing social hypocrisy, which links it to other screwball comedies of the era, such as *Nothing Sacred* and *Theodora Goes Wild*. The emphasis on drama is probably due to the film's being adapted by screenwriters Robert Riskin and Jo Swer-ling from a story by W. R. Burnett (also an accomplished screenwriter), all of whom had reputations for writing outstanding dramas—including some films noirs—rather than laugh-out-loud comedies. (Riskin becomes most famous for his work with Frank Capra, contributing to some of the director's classic films, *It Happened One Night, Mr. Deeds Goes to Town*, and *You Can't Take It with You.*)

Jones has stolen a photo of Miss Clark from the office and hung it in his apartment where he gazes on it to inspire the poetry he writes anony-mously to her. In his poetry he christens her with the romantic name of Cymbaline. (The name may allude to some historic or literary figure, although it is not clear to what or whom. Spelled differently is Cymbeline, the King of Britain in the Shakespeare play of that title, but any connection is vague.) Jones has been a loyal employee of the J. G. Carpenter Company for eight years, predictable in his punctuality and dependable in his work ethic. The office manager Mr. Seaver (Etienne Girardot, whose diminutive stature makes him a physical foil in many screwball comedies) brags of Jones's sterling record to Mr. Carpenter (Paul Harvey), who tells him to give Jones a raise and to fire the next person who walks in late in order to set an example for the other employees. As coincidence would have it, Jones had just bought a new alarm clock and it fails to wake him in time for work. When he arrives late, Seaver faces a dilemma: whether to reward Jones with a raise or punish him with dismissal. He doesn't know what to do with "the both of you," so he delays a decision.

This idea of two Joneses, a good and a bad, foreshadows the fact that Jones greatly resembles a notorious criminal, Killer Mannion (also Robinson). As Jones's double, Mannion represents the dark, lawless side of the meek, subservient accounting clerk. Mistaken for the ruthless killer, Jones is arrested and subjected to a cruel and unjust police grilling. When the police finally learn of their mistake, it is Jones who apologizes to them instead of the other way around. (The scene is an example of the tail wagging the dog, satirizing the haughty, impersonal attitude of public agencies toward the people they are supposed to serve.) To avoid confusion in the future, District Attorney Spencer (Arthur Byron) issues Jones an official letter validating his true identity.

Mr. Carpenter, who could not recognize Jones by sight and failed to vouch for him during his ordeal with the police, suddenly becomes friendly with his employee when he realizes how much free publicity his firm can gain from Jones's instant fame. Reporter Healy (Wallace Ford) suggests to Carpenter that his newspaper could run a series of articles on Jones's per-

The Whole Town's Talking (1935, Columbia; John Ford, director)—Wilhelmina "Bill" Clark (Jean Arthur) points out the uncanny likeness between meek Arthur Ferguson "Jonesy" Jones (Edward G. Robinson) and his double, the outlaw Killer Mannion (also Robinson), whose picture appears in the newspaper.

sonal opinion of Killer Mannion, and Carpenter summons Jones to his office to persuade him to comply. (Like the previous altercation between Jones and the police, the Healy-Carpenter conspiracy satirizes how the media and people in power exploit a situation for their own advantage and profit.) Drinking and smoking with the two men, Jones submits to their plan. He gets drunk, then returns to the office where he uncharacteristically grabs Miss Clark, kisses her passionately on the lips, and calls her Cymbaline. Miss Clark tells a colleague that she always knew Jones had gumption in him and needed only a push to bring it out. Jones's brazen behavior foreshadows his later inadvertent heroics in rescuing Miss Clark from Mannion's mob.

When Jones returns to his apartment that afternoon, his look alike killer is waiting for him. (The split-screen effect with Jones in the same shots as Mannion is executed with convincing technical precision, and Robinson shows uncanny genius in portraying the extremes of malice and subservience in his two characters.) Mannion learned from the newspapers about the letter and he plans to use it at night to fool the police and return it to Jones to use during the day. He stays in Jones's apartment to keep an eye on him.

Miss Clark negotiates with Healy to get money for Jones's articles. She visits Jones's apartment to give him his first paycheck and runs into Killer Mannion. She thinks he is Jones until she notices his gun hanging from a chair. She leaves to phone the police, but while she is in the phone booth, one of Mannion's thugs abducts her. Mannion also kidnaps Mr. Seaver and Jones's Aunt Agatha (Effie Ellsler) who has come for a visit. Mannion devises a scheme to have Jones gunned down by the police so they will think they killed Mannion and stop looking for him. However, when Jones returns to the gang's hideout before Mannion, the gang thinks that he, Jones, is their boss. Jones gives the order to shoot "Jones" as he walks through the door. They do so. The real Jones grabs a machine gun and forces the gang into a back room. He frees the captives just as the police arrive. He is declared a hero and earns the $25,000 reward. In the final scene, Jones has married Miss Clark and they are setting off for their honeymoon on the *U. S. S. Shanghai* to the exotic land he always dreamt of seeing.

Although publicity agent Frankie Christopher (Victor Mature) is the protagonist of *I Wake Up Screaming,* it is the antagonist, Police Lt. Ed Cornell (Laird Cregar), who is the more interesting character and begs closer scrutiny after the murder of Vickie Lynn (Carole Landis), Christopher's latest protégé. Cornell is a steadfast member of the police department. He is respected for his diligence and his arrest record, although his methods have provoked some criticism. His extreme attention to the murder case of Vickie Lynn demonstrates the mark of a devoted cop who is tenacious in seeking justice, until we learn from Vickie's sister Jill (Betty Grable) that Cornell had been behaving like a Peeping Tom, leering at Vickie through the window of the restaurant where she worked as a waitress. His suspicious behavior makes him a leading murder suspect even though he insists that Frankie Christopher is the murderer.

Christopher is a sports promoter. When beautiful Vickie Lynn waits on his table, he quickly recognizes her potential as a celebrity. He persuades her to let him act as her agent and she becomes an instant success. An offer to act in a movie comes from Hollywood and she decides she has become important enough to leave Frankie and set out on her own. The day before she is to leave, she is murdered. Cornell claims that Christopher killed her because he felt she betrayed him.

This whole time, a third suspect is at large, Harry Williams (ubiquitous noir character actor Elisha Cook, Jr.), the desk clerk at the apartment house where the Lynn sisters had lived. Christopher enlists the police to help him trick Williams into confessing the crime. Williams confesses and also admits that Cornell knew he was guilty, but told him to keep quiet. Obviously, Cornell had a personal dislike for Christopher and wanted to frame him for the murder.

Christopher sneaks into Cornell's apartment where he discovers various pictures of Vickie Lynn hanging on the walls and a small altar set up in honor of the dead woman. Cornell enters without seeing Christopher. He walks to the altar and replaces the old flowers with fresh ones. Christopher steps forward and asks why Cornell tried to frame him when all the time he knew that Williams was guilty. Without a fight, Cornell admits that he worshipped Vickie and hates Christopher for taking her away from him by filling her head with dreams of fame and fortune. Cornell slumps in a chair and Christopher realizes that the detective has taken a dose of poison. The final shot shows Frankie Christopher riding off in his car with Jill Lynn.

The noir *I Wake Up Screaming* shares a number of common points with the screwball *The Whole Town's Talking*. First of all, Cornell, like Jones, harbors a secret love for a woman, but his loathsome looks, like Jones's introverted personality, prevent him from expressing his feelings openly. Both men lament their inhibitions, but manage to live comfortably with them as long as they can dream fancifully about their beloved. Cornell and Jones substitute the real woman with her photograph that feeds their fantasies.

The two films incorporate a doubled character, Jones with Mannion and Cornell with Christopher. In *The Whole Town's Talking*, Miss Clark appears to like Jones, and she suspects he hides a more forceful nature beneath his shy demeanor. Her presumption proves correct after he gets drunk in Carpenter's office and kisses her in front of everyone. Later, in

I Wake Up Screaming (1941, 20th Century–Fox; H. Bruce Humberstone, director)—Frankie Christopher (Victor Mature) works as a promoter for Vicky Lynn (Carole Landis, center), but when she is murdered and he becomes a prime suspect, he relies on her sister Jill (Betty Grable) for help.

Jones's apartment, she mistakes Mannion for Jones, and when he kisses her—until she realizes who he actually is—she welcomes what she believes is the virile side of the milquetoast. In the end, Jones's heroics, despite a second fainting spell, convince her that he possesses the assertive trait she wants to see in a man and so she marries him. The irony of the Mannion character is that his evilness is bound up with his confidence, suggesting that positive attributes, such as leadership, decisiveness, and assertiveness, may depend for their existence on negative traits, such as selfishness, brusqueness, and even brutality.

Just as Jones and Mannion are doubles, so are Cornell and Christopher, and in a similarly contrary way. Cornell nurtures a secret love for Vickie, but he knows that he lacks the charm and the looks to win her. Christopher, on the other hand, has the prepossessing manly flair to attract women, yet his relationship with Vickie is strictly business. Cornell, like Jones, plays the hero for Vickie, once rescuing her from a masher. She shows she is grateful, although they never share more than conversation over coffee. Cornell's revenge on Christopher is based as much on his envy of Christopher's charisma and manly appeal as it is on his grief over losing Vickie.

While Jones and Mannion represent the good and evil that can reside within a single individual (the Jekyll-and-Hyde correlation), Christopher and Cornell stand for opposing concepts that are contending with each other, charisma and confidence rivaling alienation and despair. At the same time, Cornell is himself both the good cop and bad cop. He has done his job faithfully and efficiently for many years, but now, a situation has warped whatever sense of ethics he may have possessed: he willfully tries to frame an innocent man to appease his jealousy over a woman who rejected him. Interestingly, in this very early film noir, Lt. Cornell, in using his power to manipulate justice, anticipates Capt. Hank Quinlan (Orson Welles in *Touch of Evil*), the corrupt cop in one of the last noirs of the classical period.

Other conventions are also evident. The city as labyrinth appears in both films. *I Wake Up Screaming* opens with an establishing shot of New York City. Later, when Frankie Christopher tries to avoid being picked up by the police, he shows Jill how to use the city as a giant playground or funhouse with limitless nooks and crannies for hiding. In *The Whole Town's Talking*, Jones must make his way from Mannion's hideout to the bank and back again. Location shots show him lost in the waves of people walking on the sidewalks; and danger is ever-present: he barely escapes being struck by cars when he weaves through traffic to cross the street.

Fate is critical in both noir and screwball, and these two films give it prominence in the many coincidences that occur. Vickie and newspaper columnist Larry Evans (Allyn Joslyn) enter her apartment when Harry Williams is there. Williams hides in the closet until Evans leaves, and then kills Vickie. When Jill comes home soon after, she finds Christopher hovering over Vickie's body just after she was killed, so it appears that he could have killed her. In *The Whole Town's Talking*, fate manifests itself in the doubling of Jones and Mannion and in their coincidental appearances where one is mistaken for the other. Fate also plays a key role in the string of connected coincidences that occur at the end. Mr. Hoyt (Donald Meek) had earlier seen Jones in a restaurant, thought he was Mannion, and called in the police to arrest him. Contributing to the climactic finale, Hoyt again spots Jones on the street and follows him from the bank to the Mannion hideout, and again informs the police where to find him. By chance, Jones happens to get back to the hideout just ahead of Mannion and the gang mistakes him for their boss, so that Jones is able to have them shoot the wrong man. The police arrive, shortly after they are summoned by Mr. Hoyt, and round up Mannion's gang. Jones, beneficiary of these fortunate coincidences, is declared a hero.

The Doctor Takes a Wife (Alexander Hall, 1940) and *Sunset Boulevard* (Billy Wilder, 1950)

> *The modern woman can match the modern man fiber for fiber and still have a rib left over.*
> —June Cameron in *The Doctor Takes a Wife*

> JOE GILLIS: *You're Norma Desmond. You used to be in silent pictures. You used to be big.*
> NORMA DESMOND: *I am big. It's the pictures that got small.*
> —From *Sunset Boulevard*

Central to the plot of screwball's *The Doctor Takes a Wife* and noir's *Sunset Boulevard* is the live-in arrangement established between the man and woman for mutually advantageous purposes. Both relationships are immersed in irony. For one, the women have achieved greater celebrity and financial security than their male companions who are struggling to gain a foothold in their professional careers. At the same time, the male protagonists falsely assume that they are dictating the terms of their liaisons. It takes a sequence of unexpected events for them to realize just how indebted they are to the women.

True to the usual complexity of a screwball comedy story line, *The Doctor Takes a Wife* develops this relationship around a series of intricate complications. The hero and heroine first meet in typical screwball fashion—an antagonistic altercation presages their battle of the sexes. June Cameron (Loretta Young) is a feminist author who defends the dignity and courage of the single, independent female. She is vacationing in a resort hotel in upstate New York when she receives word from her publisher that she has to return immediately to the city. While she argues in the lobby with the hotel clerk about securing a ride, Dr. Timothy Sterling (Ray Milland) asks her to lower her voice because he is making a long-distance phone call. Instead, she ignores his request, planting the seeds for their ongoing rivalry. Ironically, Tim has a car and is preparing to return to New York. Without preamble, June throws her bags into his convertible and makes herself his unwanted passenger. A college teacher, Sterling is doing a study of migraine headaches and so has with him a model of a head in a carrying case. June discovers the head and dubs it "Chester," much to Tim's annoyance.

Along the way, June wants to stop to send a telegram. While she is in the telegraph office, Tim observes a wedding taking place. He doesn't notice that a boy sent to attach the "Just Married" sign to the married couple's car has accidentally attached it to his. The telegraph operator, a spinster who admires June's championing single women, spots the sign and thinks June has betrayed her cause. She quickly broadcasts the news that June has secretly married.

In New York City, the porter takes June's bags out of the car and inadvertently grabs Chester's case. When Tim realizes the error, he follows June up to her room and demands the case back. June claims it is hers, and when she tries to wrestle it from him, the case accidentally opens, the head falls out, and the nose breaks off. Tim demands payment for the damage, but June refuses. Tim holds up his thumbs and declares that their shortness signifies his inexorable stubbornness. Like the "severed" head and the broken nose, the short thumbs have phallic significance, suggesting, if not complete impotence, then diminished sexual power. Sexual prowess is replaced with overt physical and verbal aggression.

Tim refuses to leave, and instead, roams around the room, placing varied artifacts in his pockets and tallying their worth. He discovers the liquor cabinet and downs several glassfuls as compensation—getting extremely drunk in the process. He falls asleep in June's bed and cannot be wakened, even after June's publisher-fiancé Johnny Pierce (Reginald Gardiner, the perennial bridesmaid in these relationships) arrives and tries to help her.

The Doctor Takes a Wife (1940, Columbia; Alexander Hall, director)—June Cameron (Loretta Young) points an accusing finger at Dr. Timothy Sterling (Ray Milland) sleeping contentedly in her bed while her book agent and fiancé, John Pierce (Reginald Gardiner), considers the circumstances.

The next morning, newsmen arrive to get the scoop on the marriage, see Tim in his undershorts, and assume that the rumor is accurate. Pierce is more mercenary than romantic. He convinces June to substantiate the rumor in order to write a book on marriage. He tells her that, after the book is published and bought up by her adoring public, she can go to Reno for a divorce.

June agrees to the ruse, but Tim does not. He leaves to resume his post as college instructor, but learns from his father, Dr. Lionel Sterling (Edmund Gwenn), that Dean Lawton (Paul McAllister) has promoted him to full professor on the basis of his recent marriage. Tim realizes that the new position means more money, which will enable him to marry his fiancée, Marilyn Thomas (Gail Patrick, playing the ever elegant but shallow other woman). He returns to June's apartment where he consents to the charade, failing to reveal the real reason for changing his mind, and instead giving the impression that he is only doing it as a favor to her. In this way, he can exploit her guilt, usurping her bed (while she sleeps on the couch) and demanding more space for his clothes in the closet and bureau (while removing hers).

Tim's having the upper hand does not last long. His colleagues on the faculty visit his apartment to celebrate his marriage. The senior Dr. Sterling tells June how fortuitous his son's marriage is because it earned him the promotion. June now realizes what prompted Tim's compliance with the fake marriage and she reclaims her bed and bureau drawers.

June and Tim are constantly at odds with each other until an unexpected event occurs. On their way to the country to visit a colleague of Tim's, they are stopped by a police officer who had noticed the MD license plate and says that a neighboring woman ready to give birth is in need of a doctor. Tim dutifully makes the house call, but the birth is complicated and they have to stay all night. June willingly helps out the family, cooking for them and preparing hot water when Tim asks for it. This is a turning point in their relationship. Afterwards, both show mutual respect and appreciation for each other. When they return to the apartment, June constantly attends to Tim, making up his bed and heating up his milk before bedtime.

Just when they seem on the verge of an armistice, there is a sudden complication. Tim guiltily relents to go through with his marriage to Marilyn. He accompanies Marilyn to a party to announce their engagement. However, June shows up, and without saying a word, begins to knit baby clothes in front of everyone. The people draw their own conclusions, just as they did when they assumed Tim and June had married. By this time, Tim and June are oblivious to scandal and are happy for the excuse to marry.

In *Sunset Boulevard*, the fateful meeting of Joe Gillis (William Holden) and Norma Desmond (Gloria Swanson) depends, as it did for Tim Sterling and June Cameron, on an automobile. In fact, the initial conflict in *Sunset Boulevard* centers on an automobile: Gillis has failed to meet his payments and the finance company threatens to repossess his vehicle. For him, the automobile is a symbol of independence and self-determination. As long as he can evade his creditors, he remains free and in control of his life, if only just barely. When the repo men, driving along Sunset Boulevard, spot Gillis driving his car, they give chase. At high speed, Gillis's car suffers a blowout. He is forced to turn off the road and into a random driveway, which turns out to be the home of former silent film star Norma Desmond.

Just as June and Sterling's relationship was initiated by a misunderstanding, the relationship between Norma and Gillis begins when she mistakes him for an undertaker. As a symbol of the baroque and the bizarre to which her life has devolved, her pet monkey has died and she is planning an oddly dignified and decorous burial. In one respect, Gillis's coincidental arrival at the moment of the monkey's funeral suggests that he is about to replace the monkey as Norma's exotic pet. In another respect, the monkey represents the grotesque child she could have birthed had an offspring resulted from her perverted relationship with her ex-husband Max von Mayerling (Erich von Stroheim), a once-great film director who has been reduced to serving as her butler and personal factotum.

Norma as the classic Femme Fatale and June as screwball's complementary Adversarial Partner play parallel roles. Both women convince the man to live in their home, and the man, devious in his own way and believing he stands to benefit more from this arrangement, complies. An interesting similarity in the two films is that both male protagonists reject the initial arrangement and walk out on the female, but then have a change of heart and return, deciding that living with the woman serves a better purpose at the moment.

Like Tim Sterling, Joe Gillis wheedles his way into the woman's home by giving the impression that he is doing her a favor: he offers to edit Norma's screenplay, which he knows is a flop, but pretends is salvageable, giving her false compliments while planning to pocket her money. Both men operate from hubris, underestimating the female and thinking they can capitalize on an opportunity to profit (visions of status and money) from their association with her. Abruptly, they realize their mistake. Guilt affects their capitulation to the female's whims—Sterling loses his leverage in dictating the routine in June's apartment; Gillis plays the gigolo and becomes Norma's kept lover. Before he yields, however, Gillis actually makes a valiant attempt to sever the relationship. He abandons Norma on New Year's Eve. While walking out the door, he accidentally snags his watch chain on the handle, a clear implication that, once invited into Norma's lair, he is chained to her permanently. He goes to a party at the home of his friend Artie Green (Jack Webb) who tells him he can move in and stay there as long as he wants. But when Gillis phones Norma to have his clothes sent to him, Max the butler tells him that Norma tried to commit suicide. Gillis rushes back to the house and finds a weepy Norma in bed. He moves toward her, and her long spindly fingers, like the talons of some predatory bird, grasp him and pull him down. Guilt has brought him back to her, but the nature of that guilt is difficult to define. The guilt may originate in some pity he feels for her pathetic condition, or it may be that, after his original attempt to deceive her, he feels a need to atone for his petty crime. In any case, Gillis represents the quintessential Wilder protagonist, the male who "prostitutes" himself, forfeits his ideals for the material gain that is suddenly offered him. (Compare other Wilder characters, C.C. Baxter in *The Apartment* [1960], and Harry Hinkle in *The Fortune Cookie* [1966].)

Romantic triangles that occur in the two films end predictably for

Sunset Boulevard (1950, Paramount; Billy Wilder, director)—Her breakdown complete after shooting Joe Gillis, Norma Desmond (Gloria Swanson) prepares for her close-up for an imaginary Mr. Cecil B. De Mille.

their respective genres, happily in the screwball comedy, tragically in the film noir. In *The Doctor Takes a Wife,* perhaps the romantic triangle is more of a "square" in that June is involved with John Pierce while Sterling is affianced to Marilyn Thomas. Marilyn appears flighty and frivolous and Pierce places mercenary goals above romantic ones. Thus, June and Sterling, despite their contentious beginning and the controversies in their makeshift relationship, are destined to forsake their original partners for the more suitable relationship with each other.

Sunset Boulevard, like *The Doctor Takes a Wife,* expands the romantic triangle to a four-cornered intrigue. Gillis sneaks out of Norma's clutches at night, trying to rejuvenate his foundering career as a writer by co-writing a script with studio reader Betty Schaefer (Nancy Olson). Betty, meanwhile, is in a serious relationship with Gillis's good friend, Artie Green. The writing collaboration starts innocently enough, but suddenly both realize that they mean more to each other than simply co-writers. Gillis, however, makes the supreme sacrifice: he gives Betty a tour of Norma's mausoleum, knowing he cannot have her after he shows her the life he has been living; then after Betty leaves, he ends his affair with Norma. Unfortunately for him, Norma is not so easily snubbed: "No one ever leaves a star. That's what makes one a star." Rather than allow him to desert her, she shoots him. It's difficult to say who is the parasite and who the host, since in this deranged symbiotic relationship each member preys on the other while serving as the other's sustenance. In the ironic pitilessness of film noir, *Sunset* teases its protagonist with the faint hope of finding love and redemption, and then takes it away.

Ball of Fire (Howard Hawks, 1941) and *Scarlet Street* (Fritz Lang, 1945)

> PROFESSOR BERTRAM POTTS (to Sugarpuss O'Shea): *Make no mistake, I shall regret the absence of your keen mind; unfortunately, it is inseparable from an extremely disturbing body.*
> —From *Ball of Fire*

> KITTY MARCH (to Johnny Prince about Chris Cross): *If he were mean or vicious or if he'd bawl me out or something, I'd like him better.*
> —From *Scarlet Street*

Central to the stories of *Ball of Fire* and *Scarlet Street* is the formation of an ironic liaison between a naïve, idealistic gentleman and a profligate, worldly woman. Around this situation, both films fashion their plots which contain many parallels: the gentleman's infatuation with the lady is sudden, profound, and innocent; the woman, meanwhile, already in an illicit relationship with a man, has no intention of forming an intimate association with this newcomer; her secret lover, however, convinces her to pretend she loves the gentleman in order to wrangle some benefit out of him (money, evading the police); the gentleman eventually learns the truth and gets revenge on the male lover (and in the case of *Scarlet Street,* on the woman as well).

Hawks's film obviously parodies *Snow White and the Seven Dwarfs,* as indicated by several allusions to that fairy tale, but for its thematic issues, *Ball of Fire* relates more meaningfully to Shakespeare's *Love's Labors Lost.* In the Bard's play, four men take an oath to isolate themselves from the world for three years, devoting themselves to study and shunning the company of women. However, their noble pursuits are soon upset when four ladies arrive at the castle for a visit and capture the attention of each of the four men. This same premise—the noble and idealistic pursuit of knowledge diverted by romantic love—exists in Hawks's film, wherein eight men (seven bachelors and one widower) have cloistered themselves under the aegis of the Totten Foundation for the sole purpose of dedicating their lives to completing an encyclopedia. After nine years of diligent, uninterrupted concentration on their goal, Bertram Potts (Gary Cooper) unwittingly invites Sugarpuss O'Shea (Barbara Stanwyck) into their midst. Although the focus is on the relationship between Sugarpuss and Pottsie, her presence disrupts everyone's work. The men all take a liking to her—like the dwarfs with Snow White—and they fawn over her and allow themselves the luxury of being distracted from their task. She recognizes their naiveté about the world and finds them amusing, but she never belittles them or treats them condescendingly. When they are having trouble with certain dance steps, she obliges them by teaching them the Conga, the current dance craze. This is a paradox in men who are so advanced intellectually but so backward in the ways of the world. And therein lies one of the main themes.

One day, a garbage man (Allen Jenkins) strolls inside, thinking the foundation is some kind of school and looking for answers to a quiz contest he wants to enter. When he addresses the eight men with his street slang, they cannot understand him, and Potts, the grammarian who handles all things linguistic, realizes that he cannot complete his section on slang until he goes out into the streets to hear how people really talk. His rare excursion leads him to a nightclub, where he meets singer Sugarpuss O'Shea. He is enthralled with her extensive array of slang. He tries to recruit her as a consultant for his research, but she refuses. He gives her his card as he leaves.

Sugarpuss is the girlfriend of mobster Joe Lilac (Dana Andrews). Two of Lilac's henchmen (Dan Duryea and Ralph Peters) tell Sugarpuss that she has to hide from the police who want to ask her about Joe's whereabouts the night before. Her testimony could implicate Lilac in a murder, but she thinks that Joe is innocent. The henchmen take her in a cab, intending to drive her to Lilac's warehouse, but she is afraid of the rats. She finds Potts's card in her scarf and goes there instead.

Ball of Fire (1941, RKO; Howard Hawks, director)—Sugarpuss O'Shea (Barbara Stanwyck) adopts a sultry pose in a sequined outfit like the one she wears when she first dazzles Pottsie (Gary Cooper, not shown) and his fellow researchers.

Sugarpuss finagles her way into the Totten Foundation and immediately wins the sympathy of Potts's fellow researchers. She gives Bertram the nickname Pottsie and likens the seven elderly men to the seven dwarfs and herself to Snow White. Pottsie is moved by Sugarpuss's presence, but he resists her charm because she endangers the completion of their encyclopedia. When the housekeeper Miss Bragg (Kathleen Howard) delivers an ultimatum, "Either she goes or I go," Sugarpuss shows Pottsie the yum-yum kiss by placing several books on the floor so her face can reach his, and planting several kisses on his lips. Pottsie is convinced. He tells Miss Bragg goodbye. Miss Bragg, however, stays in spite of this. In the meantime, Lilac decides that the best way to prevent Sugarpuss from testifying against him is to marry her. He has his henchmen deliver an engagement ring with a stone the size of a baseball.

Pottsie also decides to propose to Sugarpuss. He hides his ring under a breakfast server, a much smaller stone than Lilac's. Lilac chooses this moment to phone Sugarpuss, calling himself her "Daddy." Pottsie asks the "father" for Sugarpuss's hand in marriage. Lilac encourages Pottsie's misunderstanding because it suits his plans. Although Sugarpuss is against it, Lilac tells her to have the eight men accompany her to New Jersey. With them, she has a better chance of getting past the police roadblocks to reach Lilac.

Of the seven professors, Professor Gurkakoff (Oscar Homolka) is the only one with a driver's license, expired though it is. He has an auto accident and they have to stay at a motel for the night, delaying their trip. Sugarpuss starts to have doubts about Lilac. Lilac and his gang show up to get her, revealing the truth of their relationship. Lilac punches his rival in the stomach and Pottsie, broken-hearted, believes that Sugarpuss only used him and his friends for her own selfish designs. The professors return to the Totten Foundation to resume their work on the encyclopedia. Suddenly, Lilac's two henchmen enter the Foundation and place the men at gunpoint. It turns out that Sugarpuss has refused to marry Lilac and he has sent his men to hold the professors hostage until she agrees to go through with the wedding.

While she and Lilac are exchanging vows, the professors use their wits to outsmart the mobsters. They subdue them and then get into the garbage man's truck and race to the scene of Sugarpuss's marriage, arriving in time to halt the ceremony. On the way there, Potts reads about the art of boxing. He challenges Lilac to a fistfight, but Lilac quickly knocks him down. Pottsie picks up the book from the ground and tosses it away. With renewed determination he charges Lilac, knocks him down, and throttles him handily. Lilac and his men are all thrown into the garbage truck and hauled away.

Back at the Totten Foundation, all of the professors surround Sugarpuss. She advises Pottsie not to marry her, but the professors argue why they should marry and offer reasons validated by their areas of expertise: mathematics, history, geography, literature, physiology, and law. Pottsie intervenes after grabbing several books and telling his colleagues, "As a grammarian, I know when words cease to be of use. There remains one argument." He places the books on the floor, makes Sugarpuss stand on them so she can reach up to him, and seals their relationship with a lengthy kiss.

The central conflict in *Scarlet Street* depends on a premise very similar to that of *Ball of Fire*. A mild-mannered, self-effacing bank clerk, Chris Cross (Edward G. Robinson, emulating his earlier role as introverted Jonesy in *The Whole Town's Talking*), becomes enamored with a conniving street-wise femme fatale Kitty March (Joan Bennett), who lures him into a romantic intrigue. The smitten bank clerk quickly and easily succumbs to her pretentious charms, and she takes advantage of him, working with her lover Johnny Prince (Dan Duryea) to siphon money out of him. When Cross discovers her betrayal and her loathing repugnance for him, he kills her. Prince is accused of the murder and Cross's testimony confirms his guilt. Cross's conscience, however, haunts him, endlessly replaying in his head the tender words of love he overheard between Kitty and Johnny. He wanders the streets alone, totally alienated in his obliviousness of people around him, accompanied only by the disembodied voices of the two dead lovers.

The story begins in the small banquet hall of a Greenwich Village restaurant where Chris Cross receives a gold watch for his 25 years of faithful service. He has earned the respect of his co-workers and he basks in the praise of his boss, J. J. Hogarth (Russell Hicks). Foreshadowing Cross's pathetic affair with Kitty March is the illicit relationship Hogarth enjoys with his mistress, who waits for him in a car outside the restaurant. Hogarth exits with a flourish and his employees clamber to the window, ogling the mistress and envying their boss's good fortune. Hogarth's affair seems to predispose Cross to the idea that, given the opportunity, he would welcome a similar liaison of his own.

Cross and his friend Charlie (Samuel S. Hinds) sneak out of the party. It is raining, and Cross delays his return home so that he can share his umbrella with Charlie who wants to catch a bus. After missing one bus, they stand on the curb under the umbrella and Cross remarks, "I wonder what it's like ... to be loved by a young girl like that.... Nobody ever looked at me like that, not even when I was young." Cross's generous gesture toward his friend has taken him into unfamiliar streets where he gets "turned around." From a distance, he spies a man assaulting a woman— this is Johnny Prince, manhandling Kitty March—and, in a rare act of rash bravado, the bank clerk rushes the man, strikes him with his umbrella, and knocks him unconscious. While Cross runs to get a policeman, Prince revives, and it is obvious that Kitty is sympathetic toward him, for she points the policeman in the wrong direction.

Fate is evidently at work here—the rain prompts the good-natured Cross to share his umbrella with his friend, and his kindness is an ironic tragic flaw responsible for detouring him toward his dreadful destiny: rather than following a direct route home, he is led to an altercation with Prince and an intrigue with Kitty. The wet, winding city streets represent the noir labyrinth, and Kitty lurks like a hungry Minotaur in its passages. Cross invites her into a bar for a cup of coffee, and playing in the background is the song "Come to Me, My Melancholy Baby," which becomes the Siren's mellifluous song, luring the unwary traveler onto the dangerous rocks. *Ball of Fire* shows fate insinuating itself in a similarly innocuous way with the timely entrance of the garbage man. His free and easy use of slang inspires Pottsie to take his research into the streets (again, the labyrinth) instead of relying on the limited information he gets from reading books. After a lengthy montage sequence, depicting his venture through the maze of New York avenues, garnering lists of slang words and phrases from the city's various denizens, Pottsie ends up in the nightclub inhabited by Sugarpuss O'Shea, the Aloof Love Object playing the alluring Siren—although one far less deadly than noir's femme fatale. She sings "Drum Boogie" with the Gene Krupa Orchestra, tantalizing Pottsie by her use of slang and her dazzling sequined outfit.

In both *Scarlet Street* and *Ball of Fire*, the romantic triangle materializes because the desirable woman is already involved with a shady character before the naïve idealist arrives. Prompted by selfish motives, both male villains actually encourage their women to fuel the fantasy of the love-struck innocent. Even though Kitty has the initial impression that Cross is a rich artist, she has no intention of leading him on. It is Prince, rather, who forces her to use her feminine wiles to ensnare Cross, hoping to finagle money out of him. Joe Lilac exploits the innocent male lover for a less venal motive. Pretending he is Sugarpuss's father living in New Jersey, he tells her to let Pottsie think he can marry her there. This way, Pottsie and his colleagues can escort her over the George Washington Bridge, unwittingly dodging the police so that Lilac can marry her and keep her from testifying against him.

Scarlet Street contains a double romantic triangle. Besides the Cross-Kitty-Prince entanglement, there is the Cross-Adele-Higgins triangle. Cross's wife, Adele, is supposedly a widow, her detective husband having drowned while trying to save a woman. However, Detective Higgins (Charles Kemper) suddenly reappears and tries to extort money from Cross, threatening to make himself known to Adele if Cross does not pay him. Ironically, his threat feeds into Cross's plans, for Cross is looking for some excuse to leave Adele so he can marry Kitty. Cross becomes the author of two diabolical plots. First, he arranges for Higgins to sneak into his bedroom to get his money while, unknown to Higgins, Adele is asleep. Higgins's entrance wakes Adele and, as they get reacquainted, Cross sneaks out of the apartment permanently to ask Kitty to marry him. Much to his astonishment, he finds her with Prince. He confronts her, only to become the brunt of her mockery and revulsion. The revelation is too much to bear. He grabs an ice pick used previously by Prince and he stabs Kitty in bed, a symbolic consummation of their perverted relationship. Prince is arrested for the murder, and at the trial, Cross carries out his second deception, distorting the facts by feigning ignorance and letting his rival be sentenced to death in the electric chair.

The male protagonists in *Ball of Fire* and *Scarlet Street* share many qualities. For one, they are associated with the arts, signifying their sensitive, creative side: Bertram Potts is a grammarian, linguist, and writer; Cross enjoys painting, although what once was his foremost ambition has been reduced to a hobby indulged on Sunday afternoons. Both men are likable and friendly, and they lead quiet, unassuming lives somewhat removed from the frenetic hubbub of life. Yet each is responsible for shaking himself out of his usual routine when he deviates from his customary habits and goes on an adventure in which he meets a beautiful and exciting woman. This woman will change his life. She is unscrupulous, recognizes his gullibility, and uses him for her own advantage. His susceptibility can be blamed in part on his adherence to archaic romantic ideals that are not acknowledged or respected in the modern world, to his lack of experience with women, and to his celibacy or implied impotence.

Pottsie is celibate but not impotent. His inexperience with women and his concept of an idealistic romantic love give him shy, childlike qualities in his interaction with Sugarpuss. His confused reaction when she first enters his house wearing only her sequined outfit, and his need to apply a cold compress to the back of his neck after she delivers the yum-yum kiss, are moments that reflect his immaturity in love. However, when he needs to assert himself, such as disagreeing with Professor Oddly (Richard Haydn) on how to handle his new bride and then assuming a dominant role over her at the end, he shows that his manliness is merely latent. Cross is different. The film provides more situations to suggest that he is impotent. As a henpecked husband, he submits sheepishly to his shrewish wife, afraid even to assert himself when she threatens to throw out the one thing most important to him, his paintings. In one scene he argues with Adele while brandishing a large carving knife, threatening, it seems, to reclaim his lost masculinity. But when he steps into the doorway and drops the knife, it sticks in the floor and he appears trapped between two worlds—between Adele and Kitty—suspended between them, paralyzed and emasculated.

Scarlet Street (1945, Universal; Fritz Lang, director)—Femme fatale Kitty Marsh (Joan Bennett) assumes a lofty position above the fawning Chris Cross (Edward G. Robinson) and looks down on him with contempt. The scene evokes some parallels with *The Lady Eve* in the scene in which Hopsie, helping Eve don her shoes, bows before the superior female.

With Adele, he wears his apron while cleaning up the Sunday dishes. With Kitty, he willingly complies with her deceit in putting her name on his paintings. (She tearfully confesses she did it to make money without asking him for it.) He says, "Why, it's just like we were married—only I take your name." In effect, he takes on the traditional role of the woman, the dutiful helpmate behind the "successful" artist. Art critic David Janeway (Jess Barker) had assumed it was a man who did the paintings, but when he discovers that the artist is Kitty, he alters his interpretation to the idea that she is a woman with the strength of a man. Obviously, Cross was able to express his masculinity through his painting, his forsaken career, but not through his existence as the meager bank clerk he has chosen to become.

Guilt is a critical element in both screwball and noir, but the guilt associated with screwball characters receives far different treatment from that attributed to characters embroiled in a noir relationship. In screwball, the guilty party always earns forgiveness and redemption (e.g., David Smith in *Mr. & Mrs. Smith* and Trudy Kockenlocker in *The Miracle of Morgan's Creek*). In *Ball of Fire*, Sugarpuss and Joe Lilac are the guilty parties. First, Sugarpuss, in search of a hideout, takes advantage of Pottsie and the professors by preying on their gullibility and hospitality, thus disrupting their productive routine. Later, anxious to reunite with Lilac, she agrees to use Pottsie and the professors to achieve that end. However, she has a conscience. She knows she is using them unfairly. During the motel scene wherein Pottsie enters Sugarpuss's room by mistake and refutes Professor Oddly's admonition to be particularly gentle with the new bride, he asserts his intention to love her with an ardent, aggressive, physical passion, and she realizes he genuinely loves her. She immediately forfeits her allegiance to Lilac.

Joe Lilac is a villain without any redeeming qualities. When he meets the professors for the first time at the New Jersey motel, he punches the defenseless Potts in the stomach out of pure meanness. Then, when Sugarpuss refuses to marry him, he sends his henchmen to threaten and hold the professors at gunpoint in their home until she consents. Using science and their wits, the professors overpower the two gunmen. They recruit the garbage man to drive them in his truck to New Jersey to rescue Sugarpuss. On the way, Potts reads about the art of pugilism, but these are formal and archaic techniques once practiced by the likes of John L. Sullivan. When he confronts Lilac, Potts still gets knocked off his feet. Only after he throws the book away does he attack Lilac with wild abandon, his arms flailing, and this time he wins. Lilac and his gang are thrown into the garbage truck to be hauled to the police station. Lilac receives his punishment, a beating from Potts and the expectation of a criminal sentence. Potts, meanwhile, has learned that books may offer a cornucopia of theoretical knowledge, but there is something to be said for knowledge gained through practical experience.

In noir, guilty parties must be punished, even if their crime is committed in ignorance or if it bears the taint of some minor indiscretion. Al Roberts (Tom Neal) in *Detour* and Frank Bigelow (Edmond O'Brien) in *D.O.A.* are examples of noir protagonists who stumble innocently into situations that lead to their undoing. All of the main characters in *Scarlet Street* are guilty of some transgression that deserves retribution. Cross's shrewish wife, Adele, keeps an oversized portrait of her "dead" husband, Higgins, in their living room, hovering over their heads like a reproving reminder that she idolizes him to the belittlement of her current husband. Higgins, meanwhile, is guilty of absconding with money from the drowning victim he tried to save, deserting his wife, and pretending he was dead. They both get their comeuppance when Higgins returns and he and Adele rediscover each other.

Kitty and Prince pay the ultimate penalty, death, not only for their scheme to take money from Cross, but for other offenses as well. Kitty may not have wanted to cheat the meek bank clerk at first, but she goes along with all of Prince's plans. Prince tries to sell Cross's paintings and pass Kitty off as the original artist. He is guilty of other crimes, too, such as his mistreatment of Kitty and his avarice when he callously pawns her jewelry after he finds her dead. Their punishment is severe. Cross stabs her with an ice pick, then contributes false testimony at Prince's trial to frame him for the murder he did not commit.

The most ironic—and the most devastating—of the punishments falls on Chris Cross—devastating because he lives with a guilt that has demoralized him, crushed him, and turned him into an emotionless zombie, a walking dead man, without any sense of self or connection to life. On the eve of Prince's execution, Cross rides a train on which he meets and talks with reporters who have been following the Prince trial. Tom Crocker (Syd Saylor) expounds on his theory of crime and punishment: "Nobody gets away with murder.... No one escapes punishment. I figure we have a little courtroom right in here [he points to his chest], judge, jury, and executioner.... The problem just moves in here where it can never get out, right here in solitary.... So you go right on punishing yourself. You can't get away with it. Never." Whether it is Crocker's speculation that inspires Cross to internalize his guilt is not certain, but up to now Cross appears smugly indignant about his actions, comfortably righteous in his revenge. After Crocker's speech, Cross begins his mental breakdown. He hears the disembodied voices of his victims, Kitty and Prince, uttering terms of endearment that Cross overheard in the apartment: Kitty saying, "I love you, Johnny" and Prince calling her "Crazy Legs." The whispered sentiments become unbearable and he tries to commit suicide, but neighbors in the flophouse where he lives rescue him. After that, he wanders aimlessly about the city streets, friendless, isolated, dazed. The final shot of him walking along the sidewalk amid a crowd of pedestrians who dissolve into nothingness is as despairing and nihilistic a statement as Macbeth's words about life being "a tale / Told by an idiot, full of sound and fury, / Signifying nothing."

Thematically, *Ball of Fire* and *Scarlet Street* focus on the development of the male protagonist from a retiring milquetoast to a determined man who assumes more control of his circumstances. Pottsie demonstrates this when he takes charge in the final scene of *Ball of Fire*. He overrules the romantic metaphors of his fellow professors by grabbing several large volumes from the table, stacking them on the floor, and pulling Sugarpuss onto them so she can reach up to him with a lingering kiss. In the same way that he learned the limitations of his self-help book on boxing when he fought with Lilac, he has discovered that books are inadequate in imparting all knowledge, and that some kinds of knowledge—especially practical knowledge—is better attained through personal experience. Chris Cross also takes charge of his situation, but with different results. At the beginning of the film, Cross and his friend Charlie are standing under his umbrella waiting for a bus when Cross expresses his desire to have a young girl look at him as one looked at his boss, J.J. Hogarth. Charlie says, "When we're young we have dreams that never pan out, but we go on dreaming." Cross responds: "When I was young ... I dreamt I was going to be a great painter some day." Instead, he has bartered his dream for financial security as a bank cashier. He has betrayed his dream. He appears to be quietly resigned to his fate, but his jealousy toward Prince gradually festers until Kitty's admission of her love for Prince and repugnance for Cross pushes Cross over the line of temperance. In killing Kitty, he vents all the frustration he has been storing up for years—never having a young girl look at him lovingly, forfeiting his dream to be an artist, submitting humbly to the demands of his scolding wife, and seeing despicable men like Prince get a woman he does not deserve. He thinks he is justified in murdering an unfaithful woman and perjuring himself to get the court to convict a deserving criminal. But guilt becomes a persistently oppressive force on his conscience. He chose the wrong way to exercise his power, and he did it for perverted reasons. He cannot hope to revel in the joy of his success. Fate will not let him.

Midnight (Mitchell Leisen, 1939) and *The Secret Fury* (Mel Ferrer, 1950)

> EVE PEABODY: *I landed a lord—almost.*
> TIBOR CZERNY: *Almost?*
> EVE: *The family came between us. His mother came to my hotel and offered me a bribe.*
> TIBOR: *You threw her out, I hope.*
> EVE: *How could I, with my hands full of money?*
>
> —From *Midnight*

> GREGORY KENT: *I wish your father were alive to see you today [Ellen's wedding day].*
> ELLEN EWING: *He'd like your taking his place.*
> GREGORY KENT: *I've always tried to do that, Ellen. And anything I can do for you is only a small measure of repayment for the many things your father did for me*
>
> —From *The Secret Fury*

Both *Midnight* and *The Secret Fury* share a similar central conflict: a woman is caught between a love interest and a phony husband, and the clash between reality and fantasy creates a confusing and complex situation that affects everyone associated with the female protagonist. In the screwball comedy *Midnight,* the woman (Claudette Colbert) is caught in an outrageous romantic triangle wherein the phony husband truly loves her and pretends he is married to her to keep her from marrying the wrong man. In the film noir *The Secret Fury,* the woman (Colbert, again) is the victim of a hoax in which a phony husband is fabricated by a vengeful antagonist as part of a conspiracy to drive her insane.

Like *Ball of Fire,* Leisen's *Midnight,* produced two years earlier, is written by the screenwriting team of Billy Wilder and Charles Brackett and borrows its central premise from a fairy tale. Whereas the later film parodies *Snow White and the Seven Dwarfs, Midnight* turns to *Cinderella* for some of its basic motifs. Eve Peabody (Colbert) appears to have been dropped from the sky. She arrives in Paris by train, an American who, in Monte Carlo, had pawned her suitcase with everything she owned after she gambled and lost. She has only the evening gown in which she is dressed. Immediately, she runs into Tibor Czerny (Don Ameche), a taxicab driver. She wants him to drive her around Paris while she auditions at the local nightclubs—she is a blues singer—and if she gets a job, she promises to pay him double. He snubs her at first, but it is raining, and when he sees her spend her last coin on a newspaper to serve as an umbrella, pity moves him and he reluctantly accepts her offer. Unable to find work, she lets him treat her to dinner. Their table-talk reveals their divergent attitudes toward money: she, intent on marrying a symbol of permanent financial security, and he, content with having just enough to live a comfortable lifestyle. Czerny, despite a cantankerous demeanor, has taken a liking to her and invites her to his apartment as a place to sleep for the night. She says no— and although she suspects him of having an ulterior motive, she will later admit that she really trusted him, but feared falling in love with someone who could not guarantee her wealth and a well-stocked wardrobe. So for now, she bolts out of his cab and evades his pursuit.

Coincidentally, she mingles with a crowd of people preparing to enter some social gathering. She sneaks into the affair under false pretenses, passing off her pawn ticket as her invitation. Inside, the concert proves boring, and a stranger, Marcel Renaud (Rex O'Malley), invites her to make up a foursome for bridge. She meets Marcel's sister Helene Flammarion (Mary Astor) and rich, debonair Jacques Picot (Francis Lederer). Helene's husband Georges (John Barrymore) enters shortly thereafter and the conversation makes it clear that Helene and Jacques are having an affair, but Helene is growing jealous as Jacques appears to be taking a sudden interest in Eve.

Up to now, fate has been a factor in guiding Eve from Czerny to the social event, to the bridge game, and to Jacques. However, Georges intervenes in the role of a fairy godfather when he slips money into Eve's purse so she can pay her bridge losses. Then, when Jacques offers to take her home to the Ritz, where she claims to live, Flammarion overhears and calls ahead to get her a room. She is shocked when she finds the room magically waiting for her, but she accepts her good fortune, including the clothes that arrive the next day, along with a private chauffeur. Flammarion appears and explains his if she will entice Jacques away from his wife so he can get Helene back. Jacques is rich, and Eve finds the venture agreeable. She accepts his invitation to the Flammarion mansion where they are planning a ball on the weekend.

Czerny, meanwhile, plays the handsome prince searching for the beautiful Cinderella who momentarily entered his life and then ran away. From another cabbie he learns of her whereabouts and he plots to reclaim her.

At the ball, Eve is succeeding in winning Jacques's favor, but she warns Flammarion that "every Cinderella has her midnight." Helene had got hold of Eve's pawn ticket and sent to Monte Carlo for the pawned suitcase. Inside the case, she discovers a photo of several chorines, one of whom looks strikingly like Eve. She is about to make a public exposé of Eve's subterfuge when fate intervenes again: Tibor Czerny enters the ball under the pretense that he is Eve's husband and that they are royalty from Budapest. Helene retracts her threat.

Midnight (1939, Paramount; Mitchell Leisen, director)—Tibor Czerny (Don Ameche, center) presents his "wife" the Baroness, actually the American Eve Peabody (Claudette Colbert), with a phony telegram, saying that their "daughter" Francie is ill. He uses it as a ruse to fool Georges Flammarion (John Barrymore) so that he and Eve can make their escape.

Czerny tries to convince Eve that they are meant for each other, but she does not like the prospect of a future without a reliable bankroll, and she rejects his offer. At breakfast, Czerny says he learned that their daughter "Francie" is sick, and they need to return home. Eve places a phony phone call to see if "Francie" is all right, but shortly afterwards, the butler announces that the phone has been out of order all morning. Eve is forced to admit that she faked the phone call, that they have no daughter. She then embellishes her story with the notion that Czerny is mad. Czerny reenters the scene, driving his cab and wearing his work clothes. Everyone assumes that this is one of his imagined roles. Jacques becomes indignant that Czerny should try to take Eve away. They struggle and Czerny is knocked out. When he recovers he insists on a divorce.

At their divorce proceedings, Czerny feigns madness and the judge (Monty Woolley) rules that Eve cannot divorce her husband because he is insane. All the parties leave satisfied, Flammarion arm-in-arm with Helene and Jacques by himself, smiling broadly as he chalks off his loss to experience. Czerny ambushes Eve as she leaves the courtroom and whisks her off to be married.

The Secret Fury may not be one of the better-known noirs, but it is deftly constructed and well-acted, an intriguing mystery with many of noir's technical and stylistic requirements. Like her character in *Midnight,* Claudette Colbert is at the center of the story, playing female protagonist Ellen Ewing. However, unlike her screwball counterpart who co-authored the intrigue in which she found herself, Ellen is the victim of a sinister plot woven by someone else.

The film begins with Ellen preparing for her wedding. When she finally stands at the altar, ready to exchange marriage vows with David McLean (Robert Ryan), a strange man brusquely interrupts the service to claim that Ellen is already married to a Mr. Lucian Randall (Dave Barbour). This untimely revelation shocks everyone, especially Ellen, who knows she has never been married before. As in *Midnight* the announcement that a fictitious husband exists creates an awkward, disruptive moment for the heroine whose life has been moving smoothly toward a commonplace objective. Eve Peabody, because she only pretended to be married to Tibor Czerny, never foresaw the untimely appearance of her "husband" at the Flammarion ball. Neither, for that matter, could Ellen have predicted that anyone would interrupt her marriage, protesting that she already has a husband. Both situations suggest the impact of the extraordinary on the ordinary and the past on the present.

The Secret Fury borrows a few pages from author Cornell Woolrich's (a.k.a. William Irish) *Phantom Lady,* in which a man, accused of killing his wife, maintains he was not home at the time, having gone to a musical revue with some woman he met in a bar. The nameless woman cannot be found (hence the title), and several witnesses contradict his story, corroborating each other's observation that, although they did, in fact, see him, he was quite alone. The testimonies turn out to be an elaborate conspiracy which is uncovered by the convicted man's secretary. *The Secret Fury* deals with the same subterfuge. That Ellen was married to Lucian Randall is verified by an array of witnesses—the man who interrupts the marriage; a justice of the peace (Percy Helton), who claims he performed the marriage; the jp's wife and their housekeeper, who claim they witnessed the marriage; and a maid (Vivian Vance) at the hotel where Ellen and Randall supposedly went on their honeymoon. The eyewitnesses are plentiful and positive, sounding most convincing, but just as in Woolrich's story, they are complicit in a conspiracy devised by a warped mastermind bent on revenge against the unsuspecting protagonist. When Randall is shot and killed, Ellen becomes the prime suspect.

In most noirs, the male is the victim of the seductive and corrupting femme fatale. *The Secret Fury,* however, reverses these conventional roles with Ellen playing the victim caught between her fiancé, David McLean, who remains loyal and steadfast, and her sham husband, Lucian Randall, acting as the agent for the family's duplicitous solicitor, Gregory Kent (Philip Ober). Ellen is an accomplished concert pianist, who, we learn, had collapsed under the strain of her last concert tour. That she has forgotten her marriage to Randall receives credence because of this previous mental breakdown, an incident that helps Kent's scheme. Again, the past exerts its influence on the present.

Gregory Kent, the vengeful mastermind of the plot to drive Ellen insane, is the family solicitor. No reason to suspect him is ever given until the end, when he divulges his motive to Eve. The story he tells is that Ellen's father had him committed because he thought him mad. However, after several years in a sanitarium, he was released when Ewing realized his mistake. Unfortunately, those years in the sanitarium had the effect of actually inducing insanity. Ewing had died, so Kent is content to wreak his vengeance on the daughter of his nemesis. Hence, Kent's words in the above epigraph, spoken to Ellen on her wedding day, take on an ironically menacing meaning. The question that arises is whether we are to believe Kent, that he was normal before his incarceration and that his confinement in the sanitarium is what caused his mental imbalance and obsessive vindictiveness. Or should we view Kent's bitter machinations as proof that Ellen's father was justified in having him committed, that he was always mad and was released not because Ewing had made a mistake, but because Ewing thought he was cured? It is an ambiguous issue that cannot be resolved from the story. By extension, the implications are that Kent represents ourselves, certain that we are sane and willing to blame anyone else for our foibles and idiosyncrasies.

The confusion between reality and fantasy is too much for Ellen (as, in a way, it is for Kent), both for her questionable marriage to Randall and her alleged murder, and so she suffers a mental breakdown and has to be institutionalized. David, however, does not lose faith in her. She had told him she was at her beach house on the day the witnesses say she supposedly married Randall. David visits the beach house and discovers the conch shell she said she found that day. He explores the beach and also discovers the boat she had seen a fisherman painting. The boat was upside-down, and the name appeared to her as "NOOSNOW." (She pronounces it "noose now," but it is possible to see it as "new snow.") When David sits on the sand to rest, he notices a boat moored nearby named "MONSOON." Reflected in the water, however, the word upside-down is the name Ellen had seen, and he realizes that she must be telling the truth. (Although this is not a true blooper because it was done as a deliberate process shot, the reflected name that David sees in the water is "NOOSNOW" when what he should have seen was "WONSOON" with the "S" and "N's" inverted. Instead of having David come upon the upside-down boat, the filmmakers may have tried to create some suspense by delaying his discovery of Ellen's evidence; at the same time, the natural reflection of "WONSOON" may not have appeared obvious enough as a clue.)

In the sanitarium, doctors plan to monitor Ellen's brainwaves. We learn the source of the film's title when Dr. Twining (Elisabeth Risdon) explains to a fellow physician how the resulting graph of the patient's brainwaves should contain sharp peaks which she calls "mountains of secret fury," suppressed irrational acts of aggression. However, when Ellen takes the test, Dr. Twining is surprised to see that Ellen manifests no signs of hidden aggression. The "secret fury" lies beneath the sophisticated and kindly exterior of the family solicitor, Gregory Kent, who has patiently and ingeniously plotted revenge against his former employer by punishing his daughter.

David visits the sanitarium with Kent. Ellen receives his hopeful news with little effect. Later, however, she escapes and confronts Kent, who is living in her home. He had a habit of breaking matchsticks into small zigzag shapes. She noticed these broken matchsticks in the office at the sanitarium, connected them with the broken matchsticks she had seen at Randall's apartment before he was killed, and concluded that Gregory Kent is the murderer who framed her for Randall's death. She has a gun that she took from her aunt's drawer, but unexpectedly, Kent appears unafraid. In fact, after he explains why he plotted against her, he is eager to sacrifice his life, wanting Ellen to kill him so she will go to prison for murder. She runs away and tries to hide in the attic. Kent follows her there. David arrives in time to fight briefly with Kent. A large mirror in a heavy, baroque frame stands upright, supported by a timber. (In a bit of foreshadowing, Ellen had visited the attic on her wedding day and almost knocked the

The Secret Fury (1950, RKO; Mel Ferrer, director)—Before the marriage ceremony is thwarted, Ellen Ewing (Claudette Colbert, second from right) enjoys a brief moment of bliss with her fiancé David McLean (Robert Ryan, center). Her aunt Clara (Jane Cowl) and former boyfriend, District Attorney Eric Lowell (Paul Kelly, second from left) stand beside them as the bishop (Clifford Brooke) looks on.

mirror down on herself. Bad luck should have been thwarted, but Ellen suffered an ordeal anyway.) Kent knocks against the support and—in one of the most bizarre deaths in any film—he is crushed to death by the weight of the monstrous antique. He screams as his own image squashes him, signifying a suicide, the man killing himself. The implication is that his hatred—his secret fury—corrupted him psychologically and spiritually, and was responsible for his death.

In respect to characterization, the exchange noted in the above epigraph between the screwball couple reveals the crux of their personalities and the reason for their battle of the sexes:

EVE: I landed a lord—almost.... His mother came to my hotel and offered me a bribe.
CZERNY: You threw her out, I hope.
EVE: How could I with my hands full of money?

Czerny is a principled idealist, but obstinate and righteous. Eve is a would-be gold digger, determined to find a rich husband but, as we learn, too sentimental to believe that money is all that matters. Czerny makes an overture that could initiate their relationship, but Eve runs away, afraid of succumbing to the charms of a mere taxi driver. When she meets the wealthy Jacques, she alternately teases and flirts with him, appearing coy but intending ultimately to get him to propose marriage. She is playing the Aloof Love Object, caught between the shunned Tibor Czerny, her destined lover, and Jacques Picot, her tenacious suitor. She might have gone through with her mercenary motives, but Tibor's timely arrival sways her from making this mistake. Ironically, Jacques is as much an obstacle between Eve and Tibor as Tibor is between Jacques and Eve. As an actress, Colbert had faced this same situation before, in Preston Sturges's *The Palm Beach Story*, wherein she runs away from her husband, only to have him pursue and finally reclaim her. This same theme of a character's internal conflict between heart and head appears in *Hands Across the Table*, in which both screwball lovers admit to forsaking love in favor of the more practical plan to marry someone who can offer financial security. Coincidentally, their venal designs dissolve when love emerges between them.

Fate is extremely active throughout both films. In *Midnight*, Eve arrives in Paris when it is raining. The rain is the reason Czerny takes pity on her and drives her around for several hours looking for a job, during which time he falls in love with her. When she runs away from him, she (by chance) encounters a crowd of socialites making their way into a concert and so she blends in with them. Inside, she prepares to sit in one chair, but a patron's dog is already there and barks at her, and so she moves next to Georges Flammarion, who will assume the role of her fairy godfather and help her finagle a relationship with Jacques Picot. Later, at the Flammarion home, Helene Flammarion suspects that Eve is not who she says she is, and just when she thinks she has the evidence to expose her, Tibor Czerny coincidentally makes his entrance to reinforce her façade as his wife.

The Secret Fury plays with a system of coincidences contrived by Gregory Kent to enmesh Ellen in a psychological trap. Yet fate works in her favor, too, when David finds the conch shell and the *Monsoon* by accident. Ellen happens to see the broken matchsticks in two different places, enabling her to make the reasonable connection that uncovers Kent's plot. And, of course, there is the ending in which the hero arrives at the last moment to rescue the heroine from the clutches of the clever villain.

Guilt is apparent in both films as well. Each member of the screwball couple has a reason to feel guilty, Eve more than Tibor. Tibor rudely shuns Eve when she asks for his help, but when he sees her struggling in the rain with a newspaper for an umbrella, he guiltily changes his mind and accepts her terms of driving her around to get a job. His invitation for her to sleep in his apartment sounds suspicious, but we eventually learn he was sincere, especially since Eve later admits that she trusted him, but didn't trust herself not to fall in love with him before she met someone with money. For a time, at the Flammarions, he goes along with the ruse that he is her husband, but he is too admirably honest and he tries to expose their pretense by telling the Flammarions who he and Eve really are.

Eve's guilt is more profound, particularly because she forsakes true love for gold digging. She is also guilty of a litany of lies: she uses a pawn ticket to fake her way into the social event (to get out of the rain and escape Tibor); she lies to the Flammarions and Jacques; she teases Jacques and leads him on with the intention to marry him; she pretends that Tibor is her real husband and that they have a daughter, Francie; she concocts the story about Tibor's insanity; and she lies in the courtroom about being married to Tibor and wanting a divorce. In comedy, however, we perceive these subterfuges less as guilty behavior than as plot machinations that contribute to the humorous ironies.

In *The Secret Fury,* Ellen is completely innocent of any wrongdoing, which makes her ordeal an example of the noir principle that virtue cannot guarantee immunity from ill, that fate allots adversity randomly and without reason. In the noir world, the punishment does not have to fit the crime—all humans are susceptible to misfortune befalling them—as exemplified by the trials heaped on the (basically) innocent protagonists in *Detour, D.O.A,* and *Strangers on a Train.* Ellen's guilt is inherited, the sins of the father falling on the child—but her father's guilt is ambiguous since we have only Kent's account to confirm this. If Kent were truly insane when Mr. Ewing had him committed, his testimony is the biased misperception of a madman. The guilt resides with Kent—and the fantastic image that shows him being crushed by his own reflection in the ornate mirror suggests that he had nurtured a hatred until it festered in him like a cancer and consumed and destroyed him. This is the price he pays.

Both films impose an abnormal mental state on one of the characters as a plot device. In *Midnight,* Eve Peabody wants Jacques and her other friends to believe that Czerny is delusional and capable of violence, and so she fabricates a story about his unstable mental condition. Czerny insists that he is sane at this time, but later in the courtroom scene, he uses his supposed madness to prevent Eve from "divorcing" him. Her scheme may have backfired on her, but in the end, they both get what they really want, each other. In *The Secret Fury,* Ellen's breakdown is induced through a kind of relentless brainwashing by her nefarious antagonist. Gregory Kent creates a fictional past, which witnesses confirm and Ellen denies, implying that she suffers from amnesia, a recurring noir device that allows for the exploration of a character's identity and existential qualities.

Finally, there is the issue of obsession. Several characters in *Midnight* exhibit this trait to different degrees. Georges Flammarion is set on getting his wife back. Helene Flammarion is intent on keeping Jacques for herself. Jacques is suddenly enamored with the newcomer who enters their social circle. And Czerny is obsessed with finding the woman he knew only for one night and then, like Cinderella, disappeared out of his life. Eve makes a deliberate decision to forsake a true romantic relationship for one that promises a more luxurious life style. Hers may be an obsession, a self-deluding belief that money makes a better choice than true love, but in the end she abandons that self-defining principle easily enough to make the more emotional—ironically, the more rational—choice. All the other characters, too, seem to overcome their obsessions—Jacques for Eve, Helene for Jacques—to find contentment in the new order of things.

In *The Secret Fury*, the obsession lies with the antagonist instead of with the protagonist as it often does in noir, where it serves as a kind of tragic flaw in the main character. Kent's obsession, his warped motive, is not revealed until the end, when he is desperate to have Ellen shoot him so she can be convicted for murder. A similar example of this strange kind of paranoid obsession occurs in an earlier film, *Rage in Heaven*, in which the insanely insecure Philip Monrell (Robert Montgomery) kills himself to frame his charismatic friend Wade Andrews (George Sanders) for murder, so that he might be executed, thus depriving his wife, Stella Monrell (Ingrid Bergman), of the man whom he jealously believes she loves more than him.

His Girl Friday (Howard Hawks, 1941) and *Road House* (Jean Negulesco, 1948)

> BRUCE BALDWIN (Hildy's fiancé): *You know, Hildy, [Walter Burns isn't] such a bad fellow.*
> HILDY JOHNSON: *No, he should make some girl real happy.... (Under her breath) Slap-happy!*
> BRUCE: *He's not the man for you. I can see that. But I sort of like him. He's got a lot of charm.*
> HILDY: *Well, he comes by it naturally—his grandfather was a snake.*
> —From *His Girl Friday*

> LILLY STEVENS: *Are you gonna let [Jefty] run your life always?*
> PETE: *Oh, you don't understand. Jefty needs to have somebody around. He—he needs a friend. Nobody's all good. Nobody's all bad.*
> —From *Road House*

Screwball comedies often complicate their basic plots with the eternal triangle, positioning either a woman between two men or a man between two women. *It Happened One Night*, *Mr. & Mrs. Smith*, *Ball of Fire*, and *Too Many Husbands* are examples of the former; *My Favorite Wife*, *Vivacious*

Lady, The Major and the Minor, Ever Since Eve, and *Bringing Up Baby* are examples of the latter. Destiny requires that the intended true lovers eventually unite; the third party is exiled into oblivion unless lucky enough to pair with another mate.

Film noir frequently exploits these triangular dilemmas. In the more pessimistic noirs—such as *Rage in Heaven, Out of the Past, Black Angel, Criss Cross, The Killers, Double Indemnity, Where Danger Lives,* and *The Chase*— this is a forbidden obsessive love that must end in tragedy for one or more of the participants. (*The Chase* is an anomaly in that it offers two endings, one supposedly a dream and the other a reality—ambiguity leaves it to the viewer to decide which is which.)

The screwball comedy *His Girl Friday* and the film noir *Road House* place a woman between two men, creating a competitive situation that becomes the central conflict in their stories.

His Girl Friday evolved from two previous incarnations, initially as a play entitled *The Front Page,* written by the acerbically witty team of Ben Hecht and Charles MacArthur, and then as a 1931 film adapted from their play. These first two versions place two newspapermen at odds with each other. In the early film, Pat O'Brien plays crack reporter Hildy Johnson who is planning to quit his job to get married. Editor Walter Burns (Adolphe Menjou) is a conniving, self-serving tyrant who feels that Hildy is too valuable to lose, so he plots to prevent the marriage. Burns convinces Hildy to write one last story. The assignment delays the wedding, but once completed, Burns with feigned exuberance sends Hildy off to get married. However, he trumps his well-wishes with another frame-up to postpone the marriage and keep Hildy working for the paper.

His Girl Friday follows a similar trajectory with the significant difference that ace reporter Hildy Johnson undergoes a sexual mutation, transforming the original Burns-Johnson feud into a seminal example of screwball's battle of the sexes. This modification from a conflict between two males to a conflict between a male and female is attributed to director Howard Hawks, who claims to have seen what was essentially a love story in the 1931 film.

Reporter Hildy Johnson (Rosalind Russell) visits the newsroom one last time (or so she thinks) to tell boss Walter Burns (Cary Grant), who is incidentally her ex-husband, that she is leaving for good by marrying insurance salesman Bruce Baldwin (Ralph Bellamy) and moving to Albany to live with him and his mother. Burns feigns a gracious acquiescence to her intentions, while all the time plotting to sabotage her plans and keep her wedded to his paper. She is too valuable to him, for one thing, and for another, he knows that newspaper ink runs through her veins and that deserting her news desk for a sedate life as a housewife would be disastrous for her. So Burns does everything he can to implicate Baldwin in shady criminal acts, planting counterfeit money on him and framing him for "mashing." Hildy, however, is wise to Burns's tricks and, at almost every turn, manages to foil his little diversions. At the same time, she has agreed to cover a "final" story for Burns, a murder case in which Earl Williams (John Qualen) sits on death row because of a miscarriage of justice. Hildy learns that he is merely a scapegoat for the political anglings of the sheriff (Gene Lockhart) and the mayor (Clarence Kolb). Hildy's findings, coupled with ironic circumstances, enable Burns to gain the upper hand on the political bosses. In the meantime, Baldwin's mother (Alma Kruger) has arrived, only to be subjected to Burns's nasty manipulations. Baldwin comes to realize that Hildy loves the paper more than she does him. He and his mother depart indignantly, and Hildy and Burns, acknowledging the unbreakable bond between them, make plans to remarry. But nothing has changed. Burns, evidently not a sentimental man, exits the press room, leaving Hildy to carry her own suitcases down to the car.

The parallels between *His Girl Friday* and *Road House* are not obvious at first because they occur as a number of variations. *Road House,* for instance, like *His Girl Friday,* wastes no time in presenting the intricate romantic triangle at the beginning, but whereas the central female, Hildy, introduces Bruce to Walter and sets in motion their three-way entanglement, it is the male, Jefty Robbins (Richard Widmark), owner of the road house, who invites female entertainer Lily Stevens (Ida Lupino) into the mix, disrupting his relationship with Pete Morgan (Cornel Wilde), his friend and manager of the club. Significantly, the traits embodied by Walter and Bruce are divided into different proportions between Jefty and Pete, the latter two men at times resembling one or the other of Hildy's male rivals.

Road House begins with Lily and Pete facing off in an abrupt, antagonistic meeting. He walks into his office to find a strange woman sitting in his chair, her stockinged feet carelessly resting on his desk while she plays solitaire. She projects an uninhibited, self-confident, and world-weary demeanor as if she controls the space she inhabits and couldn't care less what he or anyone else thinks. She explains that Jefty has hired her to sing in the lounge. Pete is familiar with his friend's habit of going on a jaunt and returning with new female entertainment for the road house, only to give Pete the job later of getting rid of her. Although Jefty claims that this girl is different, Pete tries to point her out of town, but she slaps his face and announces her intention to stay.

In respect to their opening moments, *Road House* and *His Girl Friday* not only introduce the three members of the triangle, but also contain similarities in scene and character. Hildy bounds into Walter's office to trade caustic but cordial witticisms in a comparable way that Lily trespasses on Pete's privacy, rouses his ire, and exchanges sarcastic barbs with him. Hildy

Road House (1948, 20th Century–Fox; Jean Negulesco, director)—When Jefty Robbins (Richard Widmark, center) angrily commands Pete Morgan (Cornel Wilde) to give Lily Stevens (Ida Lupino) a bowling lesson, he fails to realize that the bowling alley serves as a symbol of sexual arousal and entanglement.

presents Walter to Bruce, who, as the antithesis of the conniving editor, proves to be reserved, responsible, phlegmatic, and dull. When Jefty arrives to interrupt the tense meeting of Pete and Lily, he possesses something of Walter's personality, being rash, unpredictable, and ebulliently manipulative. Pete is not a milquetoast like Bruce, but they share similar traits of naïveté, reserve, and frankness. Yet Pete also resembles Walter. We learn that Jefty has a reputation as a fickle womanizer, and Pete, conscientious manager and friend that he is, dutifully and routinely assumes the role of a big brother, rectifying Jefty's irresponsible flings. In this case, like Walter with Hildy, Pete tries to dissuade his friend from pursuing the relationship (the difference being that Pete speaks candidly to Jefty, while Walter acts furtively, using any devious means at his disposal).

Lily's first night singing in the bar is a success, although Road House employee Susie (Celeste Holm) offers the ironic observation, "She does more without a voice than anyone I've ever heard." In his eagerness to please her, Jefty orders Pete to teach her how to bowl. In the next scene, Pete demonstrates for her the proper technique for the sport—and the image of a bowling ball knocking down the hourglass-shaped bowling pins is laden with (supposedly) sexually charged symbolism.

From there, fate intervenes to move them closer together. Jefty takes a hiatus on a hunting trip, giving Pete and Lily the time they need to fall in love. Jefty returns, intending to marry Lily even though she never gave him cause to think she was in love with him. He sees her romance with Pete as a betrayal and he concocts a plan to frame Pete for theft of the Road House receipts. Pete is found guilty, but at Jefty's "considerate" request, he is paroled and released into Jefty's custody. Now in control of his nemesis, Jefty orders Pete to accompany him to his cabin in the woods. Lily and Susie go along. Jefty gets drunk and takes everyone outside to show how well he shoots. He gets belligerent with Lily. Pete fights with him and knocks him out. Pete and Lily flee into the forest to escape to Canada while Susie remains with Jefty. Susie discovers the payroll receipt that proves Pete's innocence. Jefty recovers and prepares to go after them, but Susie runs ahead, trying to warn Pete. Jefty shoots and wounds her. Pete wrestles Jefty for the gun, but Lily is able to get it first. Jefty coaxes Lily to give him the gun, moving ever closer toward her while she keeps warning him to stop. He grabs a rock and moves to hit her with it, forcing her to shoot him. Pete picks Susie up off the ground and starts to carry her back to the cabin, with Lily behind them.

Jefty's dictatorial complex and underhanded manipulations connect him with *His Girl Friday*'s Walter Burns. His framing Pete and trying to dominate him while he is in his custody, then taking the three friends out to the cabin where he controls the action, are behaviors that parallel the self-serving machinations of Walter Burns who frames Bruce for counterfeiting and lewdness and wheedles Hildy into writing the Earl Williams story. In playing Jefty, Widmark reprises his performance of the year before as the psychotic killer Tommy Udo in *Kiss of Death*, with his twisted smile, heckling laugh, and bipolar behavior. Jefty and Walter are amoral characters, but Walter is also more apathetic, his motives stemming not from any emotional source but from his selfish belief that the ends justify the means: that is, what is good for him and the newspaper excuses any actions he must take to get it. Jefty is identified with animal imagery, suggesting that he acts from bestial instincts. He has a reputation as a hunter and has his own cabin in the woods. His Road House is replete with stuffed trophy heads, particularly of deer. When he makes his first entrance, he stands in Pete's office with one of the trophy heads positioned directly behind him, the antlers seemed to sprout from his own head. (He is, in his own mind, later cuckolded by Lily.) One night while Lily is singing, a burly, brutish customer stands behind her while one of Jefty's trophy heads hangs on the wall above him. His bestial quality is manifested when he suddenly tries to take Lily by force and Pete has to fight him and subdue him. The brute is a doppelgänger of Jefty and his attack on Lily foreshadows Jefty's bestial behavior characterized by his savage laugh and his predatory pursuit of Pete and Lily through the woods until Pete is forced to fight him, and Lily is forced to shoot him down like a crazed, rabid animal.

Comparatively, Pete Morgan shares similarities with both Bruce Baldwin and Walter Burns. Like Bruce, he is naïve and trusting to the point where he can be duped and manipulated. For one thing, he is genuinely mystified that the weekly receipts are missing and never suspects Jefty as the culprit. He is also the more sensitive soul compared to his adversary. However, like Walter, he at first acts indifferently, even rudely, toward the woman, yet he wins her in the end.

Hildy, as pointed out in a previous chapter discussing the roles of the screwball female, is the Adversarial Partner. Even though she swears she is through with Walter and has already chosen a mate to replace him, the true bond—the real working relationship—is between the two of them. She recites a litany of reasons why Walter was a failure as a spouse and how leaving him was the sanest thing she ever did, but her resolve is mere fantasy. In the end, she must return to him and renew their marriage vows.

With Pete, Lily plays the noir version of screwball's Adversarial Partner. In their relationship, she adopts a contentious position when she fences verbally with him at their first meeting in his office. Pete takes her to the train station and tries to get her to leave town, but she slaps his face, and from then on he considers her Jefty's girl and so avoids her. The cigarette burns left on his desk and on the piano from lit cigarettes that she carelessly lays around symbolize the indelible impression she leaves on his psyche. Inevitably, the animosity in their battle of the sexes dissolves and they become lovers.

In noir terms, Lily is the Femme Blanche in relation to Pete and the Femme Fatale in relation to Jefty. She is devoted to Pete, advising him how to act under Jefty's restrictions and even rescuing him at the end when she gets the gun and shoots Jefty. From Jefty's distorted perspective, she is the Femme Fatale—devious, cunning, self-serving—and although objectively she does not possess an evil nature, she ironically is directly responsible for his death—hers is the hand that pulls the trigger.

Fate influences events in both *His Girl Friday* and *Road House*. Hildy's agreement to write one last story for Walter seems a matter of free choice, but it is a decision that involves her more deeply in the Earl Williams case and with Walter. By chance, she is alone in the press room when Williams enters after making his jail break, and this enables her to get the exclusive story that implicates the sheriff and mayor in a political scandal. It also reminds her that this is why she loves being a reporter and influences her decision to finally leave Bruce and return to Walter, both for professional and personal reasons.

Road House (1948, 20th Century–Fox; Jean Negulesco, director)—Lily Stevens
(Ida Lupino) and Pete Morgan (Cornel Wilde) both seem to be wondering what
Jefty (Richard Widmark) will do when he discovers that they have fallen in love.

In *Road House,* Fate is at work from the beginning: Jefty has already met Lily on one of his excursions and hired the piano-playing chanteuse for his road house. The job is just a ruse, however, for he soon reveals that he has had the ulterior motive all along to take her for his wife. His bringing her to his club enables her to meet Pete and leads to the central conflict for the three of them. Also coincidental is the fact that Jefty goes away on a hunting trip, giving Pete and Lily time to overcome their mutual animosity and discover their love. In the end, the fact that, of the three of them, Lily is the one who gets the gun is fittingly prophetic. For one thing, in an earlier scene, she had threatened to kill Jefty. Pete may appear to be the classic male protector (he did, after all, come to Lily's aid when the barroom brawler attacked her), but it is doubtful whether he could have shot his childhood friend. The gun had to end up in the hand of the cynical, streetwise Lily, who had the predisposition and the pluck to pull the trigger.

Obsession and alienation, two key elements of noir, are often present in screwball comedy. In *His Girl Friday,* the tonal quality of the film is borne out of the hectic pace of the dialogue, which reflects the main characters' high-strung emotions and gives the impression of dire urgency. There are the rapid-fire exchanges between Cary Grant and Rosalind Russell, of course, but in the jail's press room, the reporters, portrayed by the ensemble of seasoned character actors Porter Hall, Roscoe Karns, Regis Toomey, Ernest Truex, among others, bons mots and sarcasms fly around the room like bees in a rose garden. Added to this are the barbed projectiles that Clarence Kolb (the mayor) shoots at Gene Lockhart (his sheriff). The frenzy created by the quickly delivered lines enhances the resolve of the two main characters: Walter is determined to break up Hildy's engagement with Bruce and keep her on the job; Hildy appears determined to marry a man whose personality is contrary to Walter's, although her true motives may lie buried in her subconscious—without acknowledging it herself, she may have recruited Bruce to make Walter jealous because she never really wanted to leave him or the newspaper in the first place.

There are a few images of alienation in *His Girl Friday.* Earl Williams becomes a social pariah when he is singled out as a victim of a political conspiracy. The press room at the jail symbolizes an isolated world: the reporters form an autonomous social circle, siphoning the news from the outside and channeling it to the various outlets for dissemination. Walter may have his clique of associates, but he shows signs of alienation in that he separates himself from mainstream society and acts as a manipulative dictator in his private realm of the news media. In some ways, Hildy demonstrates exceptional strength and independence—after all, she competes with Walter toe-to-toe and holds her own against him. Yet, despite this, she seems to emerge as a pathetic and lonely figure. She is a competent woman in a man's world, which tends to alienate her from her own gender. Walter actually calls her a great "newspaperman" and the other male reporters respect her as one of their own. She is not fit for the traditional role of housewife—she knows this and everyone else knows it, so even if the ending has its romantic aspects, it also has its tragic aspects. Her projected remarriage to Walter is, in one respect, a redemption, but it is also a condemnation.

Obsession in *Road House* is evident from Jefty's behavior toward Lily. Contrary to his usual treatment of women, he dotes on her and, on one occasion even brings her breakfast in bed. He gets a marriage license without consulting her, expecting her to comply automatically with his proposal. He reacts hysterically to Pete's confession that he and Lily have fallen in love, and his final maniacal, animalistic outburst while held at gunpoint suggests that his jealous obsession has caused him to abandon any rational human thought.

The Road House is itself an ambiguous symbol of socialization and alienation. People gather here to escape their routines and find entertainment, excitement, and sport. Yet it is also a place aloof and remote from the ordinary world. Although Jefty owns the club and Pete runs it, the character most identified with it as a symbol of alienation is Lily. In her initial appearance, she sits behind the desk in Pete's office, the furniture acting like a wall isolating her from the rest of the world that she seems to view with a pessimistic, or at least fatalistic, attitude. She plays solitaire in that first scene, as she does in later scenes—sitting at the bar (the bartender cautions her against cheating, but she claims you have to cheat once in awhile) and sitting in the jeep, alienated from the fun that Pete and Susie are sharing while taking a swim. (As she does with her voice, making the most of the least, she converts two scarves into a bathing suit and dives into the water to join them.) Even at the very end, after she has shot Jefty, she lags behind Pete who has picked up the wounded Susie and is carrying her back to the cabin. We may assume that Lily and Pete will end up together, but the film concludes with Susie getting the protagonist's attention and this unsettling image of Lily looking dejected and rejected while walking alone behind them.

The image of the labyrinth is apparent in the final scenes of *Road House* when the lovers escape into the woods, and Jefty, transformed into a monster, bestial and irrationally vindictive, pursues his victims through the overgrown trails. The labyrinth may not be so obvious in *His Girl Friday*, but the action takes place in the city which routinely assumes the qualities of a labyrinth. On the city streets, Bruce, the outsider, becomes prey to Walter's wiles, twice getting framed for illegal activities. Hildy, however, is familiar with the crooked and misleading avenues of this maze, and although Walter gets his way with her in the end, it is because she surrenders willingly to her fate as a woman born to be a newspaperman.

Guilt is something that is both acknowledged and ignored in *His Girl Friday*. Hildy feels its twinges when Walter plays on her sensitive nature and tells her of the Earl Williams tragedy to inveigle one "last" story out of her before she goes off to marry Bruce. But while Walter knows how to use guilt to manipulate others, he himself is immune to it. For all the mischief he does, there is not one iota of remorse or regret, right to the end when he walks out of the press room and expects the tamed Hildy to carry her own suitcases.

Noir generally fuses guilt with motivation, and that is the case in *Road House*. Good-natured Pete feels guilty when he falls in love with Lily, knowing that she is "Jefty's girl." Love, however, is stronger than friendship, and he intends to run away with Lily after taking his usual salary out of the weekly receipts. Jefty frames him by making it seem that he took all the money, and Pete is found guilty by a court of law. There is the possibility that Pete surrenders so easily to the verdict and being released into Jefty's custody because he accepts this as punishment for this "betrayal." Jefty is, of course, the truly guilty party, framing Pete for stealing money he never stole, for intimidating the girls at his cabin by carelessly brandishing his gun carelessly around, for shooting innocent Susie, and for trying to kill Pete and Lily. His death signifies his being sentenced to execution for his guilt in these crimes.

Appendix A: Filmography of Screwball Comedies, 1934–1954

Besides being produced within the limited time frame of 1934 to 1954—the 20 years under the guardianship of Joseph I. Breen before he retired from the Production Code Administration (PCA)—the screwball comedy films in this filmography have been selected according to certain criteria that define the genre. These films may use most or all of the criteria, among them a conflict centered on a battle of the sexes that resolves itself in marriage or reconciliation, surprising plot twists, eccentric characters (main or minor), and sexual implications. Also noted here are several films of the early 1930s that prefigure many of the screwball elements.

1. *Adam's Rib* (George Cukor, 1949) Assistant district attorney Adam Bonner (Spencer Tracy) is assigned to prosecute Doris Attinger (Judy Holliday) for attempting to murder her philandering husband, Warren (Tom Ewell). Tracy's wife, lawyer Amanda Bonner (Katharine Hepburn), complicates their professional and personal lives when she volunteers to defend the woman.

2. *Adventure in Manhattan* (Edward Ludwig, 1936) In this screwball mystery, ace reporter George Melville (Joel McCrea) brags to colleagues that he will catch the perpetrator of recent art thefts. Stage actress Claire Peyton (Jean Arthur) supports him in his cat-and-mouse game with art thief Blackton Gregory (Reginald Owen).

3. *Affectionately Yours* (Lloyd Bacon, 1941) Reporter "Rickey" Mayberry (Dennis Morgan) welcomes his worldwide assignments because they enable him to live a double life as a married man and a womanizer. Wife Sue's (Merle Oberon) suit for divorce suddenly makes him re-assess his priorities.

4. *And So They Were Married* (Elliot Nugent, 1936) Widower Stephen Blake (Melvyn Douglas) and divorcée Edith Farnham (Mary Astor) fall in love while snowbound at a winter lodge. Douglas's son (Jackie Moran) and Astor's daughter (Edith Fellows) do not approve, and their antics lead to the couple's break-up. The children, however, realize their mistake and plot to reunite the lovers.

5. *Arsenic and Old Lace* (Frank Capra, 1944) Male chauvinist writer Mortimer Brewster (Cary Grant) renounces his sworn bachelorhood to marry Elaine Harper

(Priscilla Lane). Before he can proclaim his marriage, he learns that his two aunts (Josephine Hull, Jean Adair) share the hobby of poisoning tramps and burying their bodies in the basement. Grant's criminally insane brother Jonathan (Raymond Massey) arrives with Dr. Einstein (Peter Lorre) to menace the family and make matters more dangerous.

6. *The Awful Truth* (Leo McCarey, 1937) Considered one of the cornerstone screwball comedies, this film is a prime example of the remarriage motif. Suspicious that the other has been unfaithful, Jerry (Cary Grant) and Lucy Warriner (Irene Dunne) sue for divorce. Lucy meets oilman "Dan" Leeson (Ralph Bellamy) and Grant gets involved with heiress Barbara Vance (Molly Lamont), but neither affair takes root. Only at the Eleventh hour, minutes before the divorce is to take effect, does the couple reconcile.

7. *The Bachelor and the Bobby-Soxer* (Irving Reis, 1947) Teenager Susan (Shirley Temple), infatuated with artist-playboy Dick Nugent (Cary Grant), creates legal and personal problems for him. Placed in a compromising position, he is forced to get involved with her older sister, Judge Margaret Turner (Myrna Loy).

8. *Bachelor Mother* (Garson Kanin, 1939) Mistaken for the mother of an orphaned infant, Polly Parrish (Ginger Rogers) finds her life complicated even further when David Merlin (David Niven), son of Mr. Merlin (Charles Coburn), owner of Merlin's department store where she works, is accused of being the father.

9. *Ball of Fire* (Howard Hawks, 1941) To avoid testifying against gangster boyfriend Joe Lilac (Dana Andrews), nightclub singer Sugarpuss O'Shea (Barbara Stanwyck) hides out at the Totten Foundation where Prof. Bertram Potts (Gary Cooper) and his seven quirky colleagues are writing an encyclopedia. Potts soon becomes enamored with her. His kindnesses and Andrews' villainy soon convince her where to place her allegiance.

10. *Bedtime Story* (Alexander Hall, 1941) In this story of remarriage, stage actress Jane Drake (Loretta Young) has planned to retire to a farm, but learns that playwright husband Luke (Fredric March) has sold the property to finance his new play. She leaves for Reno to get a divorce, but he keeps using elaborate ploys to get her interested in his play, and eventually, he wins her over.

11. *Bluebeard's Eighth Wife* (Ernst Lubitsch, 1938) Millionaire Michael Brandon (Gary Cooper) first meets Nicole De Loiselle (Claudette Colbert) in a men's store where he wants to purchase only the pajama tops, and she is willing to purchase only the bottoms. This fortuitous liaison leads him to propose marriage, which seems natural enough until she learns that he has been married seven times before and has a habit of paying off his spurned spouses.

12. *Bombshell* (Pre-screwball—Victor Fleming, uncredited, 1933) Glamorous Jean Harlow unflinchingly takes center stage in this satire of the Hollywood filmmaking industry, exposing the artificial lifestyle of its denizens, the machinations of its publicity agents, and the triteness of its censorship rules.

13. *Breakfast for Two* (Alfred Santell, 1937) Heiress Valentine Ransome (Barbara Stanwyck) takes over the business of irresponsible playboy Jonathan Blair (Herbert Marshall) in order to save it and make it profitable. Blair misinterprets her intentions, failing to see that she has his interests in mind.

14. *The Bride Came C.O.D.* (William Keighley, 1941) Aviator Steve Collins (James Cagney) needs money to pay his creditors and save his airline. Millionaire Lucas K. Winfield (Eugene Pallette) offers him the money he needs if he will kidnap daughter Joan (Bette Davis) to keep her from marrying bandleader Allen Brice (Jack Carson).

15. *The Bride Walks Out* (Leigh Jason, 1936) Career girl Carolun Martin (Barbara Stanwyck) is used to financial independence. She marries engineer Michael Martin (Gene Raymond) who expects her to quit her job and let him act as sole breadwinner, even if it means living on a smaller salary. She prefers the freedom that money gives her.

16. *Bringing Up Baby* (Howard Hawks, 1938) One of screwball's cornerstone films, this story pits zany heiress Susan Vance (Katharine Hepburn) against stodgy archeologist Dr. David Huxley (Cary Grant). "Baby" is Hepburn's tame leopard that becomes confused with a dangerous wild leopard, disrupting Huxley's routine and creating mayhem for all the characters.

17. *Casanova Brown* (Sam Wood, 1944) Cass Brown (Gary Cooper) secretly marries Isabel Drury (Teresa Wright), then divorces her, only to learn that she has given birth to their child. He kidnaps the child from the hospital, fearing that the infant will be given to foster parents.

18. *Christmas in Connecticut* (Peter Godfrey, 1945) In a story where one lie leads to another and compounds the confusion, magazine columnist Elizabeth Lane (Barbara Stanwyck) feigns culinary expertise. The owner of the magazine, gourmand Alexander Yardley (Sydney Greenstreet), invites himself and recovering navy vet Jefferson Jones (Dennis Morgan) to her supposed chateau (actually owned by boyfriend John Sloan [Reginald Gardiner]) for a luxurious Christmas dinner.

19. *Come Live with Me* (Clarence Brown, 1941) Illegal immigrant Johnny Jones (Hedy Lamarr), in love with Barton Kendrick (Ian Hunter), a married man, prevents her deportation by approaching struggling American writer Bill Smith (James Stewart), with a proposal of marriage. Unaware of her dilemma, Smith falls in love with her and writes a novel inspired by their platonic situation. Kendrick, a publisher, happens to take an interest in his manuscript.

20. *Cross-Country Romance* (Frank Woodruff, 1940) In this "runaway bride" plot, Maggie Jones (Wendy Barrie) escapes an arranged marriage by hiding out in the mobile trailer of Dr. Larry Smith (Gene Raymond), who sets out on a westward journey. Their feuding along the way is the precursor to their romantic reconciliation in the end.

21. *Design for Living* (Pre-screwball—Ernst Lubitsch, 1933) Before the censorship code took stringent effect, Lubitsch managed to defy social mores with this racy film. Gilda Farrell (Miriam Hopkins) treads a seductive line between two close friends, marrying George Curtis (Gary Cooper), then committing adultery with Tom Chambers (Fredric March).

22. *Design for Scandal* (Norman Taurog, 1941) Reporter Jeff Sherman (Walter Pidgeon) tries to save his job by helping boss Judson M. Blair (Edward Arnold) get a reduced divorce settlement from Judge Cornelia C. Porter (Rosalind Russell). Sherman believes that, if he can trick her into a scandal, he can compromise her ethics and her decision. Porter, however, is not the romantic type, and Sherman has difficulty appealing to her softer female side.

23. *The Devil and Miss Jones* (Sam Wood, 1941) Department store magnate John P. Merrick (Charles Coburn) assumes the position of a lowly clerk to discover who among his employees are union organizers fomenting unrest. He is befriended by several employees (Jean Arthur, Robert Cummings, and Spring Byington), whose kindnesses change his original vengeful intention.

24. *The Doctor Takes a Wife* (Alexander Hall, 1940) Dr. Timothy Sterling (Ray Milland) forms a pact with feminist writer June Cameron (Loretta Young) to pose as her new husband. Their live-in arrangement leads to problems with his fiancée

(Gail Patrick), his recently acquired professorship, and June's boyfriend (Reginald Gardiner).

25. *Double Wedding* (Richard Thorpe, 1937) Charles Lodge (William Powell) leads a bohemian existence contrary to the orderly, sedate lifestyle of Margit Agnew (Myrna Loy). When Lodge appears to take an interest in her sister (Florence Rice), Margit reluctantly becomes involved with him.

26. *Easy Living* (Mitchell Leisen, 1937) Retaliating against wife Jenny's (Mary Nash) frivolous spending, financier J. B. Ball (Edward Arnold) throws her sable coat from their penthouse balcony. The fur lands fatefully on Mary Smith (Jean Arthur), leading her into a series of life-changing escapades, including losing her job, being mistaken for Ball's mistress, living in a luxury hotel, and meeting Ball's son (Ray Milland), her destined romantic partner.

27. *Ever Since Eve* (Lloyd Bacon, 1937) Attractive secretary Marjorie Winton (Marion Davies), to avoid advances from amorous bosses, disguises herself as a homely, bespectacled woman and applies as secretarial assistant to womanizing writer Freddy Matthews (Robert Montgomery). When he glimpses her as she really is, the result is multiple identity confusion since she uses the name of roommate, Sadie Day (Patsy Kelly). He forsakes fiancée Camille Lansing (Marcia Ralston) for the beautiful woman he does not even know.

28. *The Ex-Mrs. Bradford* (Stephen Roberts, 1936) Divorcée Paula Bradford (Jean Arthur) moves in with ex-husband Lawrence (William Powell) to help him solve the case of a murdered jockey.

29. *Fast and Furious* (Busby Berkeley, 1939) This is the third screwball mystery involving husband-and-wife detectives Joel and Garda Sloane, who are also rare book collectors. Mike Stevens (Lee Bowman) asks friend Sloane (Franchot Tone) for a loan to invest in a beauty pageant. He invites Sloane and Garda (Ann Sothern) to the event, where graft, jealousy, and in-fighting lead to a murder that the Sloanes must solve.

30. *Fast and Loose* (Edwin L. Marin, 1939) This is the second screwball mystery involving Joel and Garda Sloane, husband-and-wife detectives and experts in rare books. Christopher Oats (Etienne Girardot) hires Sloane (Robert Montgomery) to validate the authenticity of a lost Shakespeare manuscript before he buys it. The manuscript becomes central to the rivalries and intrigues that lead to murder. Sloane depends on Garda (Rosalind Russell) to help him unmask the murderer.

31. *Fast Company* (Edward Buzzell, 1938) This is the first screwball mystery involving Joel and Garda Sloane, husband and wife detectives also interested in collecting rare books. The mystery revolves around the rare book market and insurance scams. Sloane (Melvyn Douglas) and Garda (Florence Rice) must clear the wrongly accused man while solving a murder.

32. *The Feminine Touch* (W.S. Van Dyke II, 1941) College professor John Hathaway (Don Ameche) has written a book on jealousy. Wife Julie (Rosalind Russell) travels with him to meet his publisher Elliott Morgan (Van Heflin), a narcissistic womanizer. Morgan takes more interest in Julie than in the book, and his editor Nellie Woods (Kay Francis), who is in love with him, uses John to arouse Morgan's jealousy. John thinks he is above such base passions as jealousy, but circumstances eventually force him to feel this emotion, making him more human.

33. *5th Ave Girl* (Gregory La Cava, 1939) Businessman Mr. Borden (Walter Connolly) recruits unemployed Mary Grey (Ginger Rogers) to act as his nightly escort, hoping to make his wife (Verree Teasdale) jealous and rekindle their relationship.

34. *The Footloose Heiress* (William Clemens, 1937) In this revamping of Shakespeare's *The Taming of the Shrew*, advertising executive John C. Allyn (Hugh O'Connell) hires Bruce Baeder (Craig Reynolds), a supposed tramp, to "tame" his unruly daughter Kay (Ann Sheridan). Baeder is actually the resourceful son of a wealthy Boston family, who not only proves to be an adept Petruchio, but also helps Allyn with his stymied ad campaign.

35. *Footsteps in the Dark* (Lloyd Bacon, 1941) Rita Warren (Brenda Marshall) is not aware that her husband, businessman Francis Monroe Warren II (Erroll Flynn), leads a secret life as a mystery novelist. Helped by valet Mr. Wilfred (Allen Jenkins), Francis accidentally stumbles onto a real-life murder mystery.

36. *Four's a Crowd* (Michael Curtiz, 1938) Replicating the opening of *MGM's Libeled Lady* of two years earlier, this Warner Bros. film opens with its four major stars (Erroll Flynn, Rosalind Russell, Olivia de Havilland, and Patric Knowles) walking down the street, arms entwined. Their interlocked arms foreshadow their complex entanglements in the story. Newspaper editor Pat Buckley (Knowles) hires Bob Lansford (Flynn) as a marketing strategist to boost sales. Lansford succeeds, but his plan complicates his position between girlfriend Lorri Dillingwell (de Havilland) and admirer Jean Christy (Russell).

37. *Front Page Woman* (Michael Curtiz, 1935) Veteran newspaperman Curt Devlin (George Brent) mentors novice newspaperwoman Ellen Garfield (Bette Davis) when she first enters the business, but once she feels secure in her job, they become rivals.

38. *The Girl from Missouri* (Jack Conway, 1934) After seeing how economic desperation affected her mother, Eadie (Jean Harlow) pursues wealthy T.R. Paige (Lionel Barrymore) for financial security. She is staunchly chaste, however, and expects to marry without losing her virginity. She meets Paige's son (Franchot Tone), a more likely candidate, but she resists his advances. When the senior Paige frames her in a scandal, however, she gets revenge and justice, and marriage to the appropriate man.

39. *Hands Across the Table* (Mitchell Leisen, 1935) A manicurist (Carole Lombard) seeks a millionaire husband. A debonair loafer (Fred MacMurray) is engaged to a rich socialite (Astrid Allwyn). Their chance meeting leads to a change of plans for both.

40. *His Girl Friday* (Howard Hawks, 1940) Editor Walter Burns (Cary Grant) recognizes Hildy Johnson's (Rosiland Russell) value as a newspaperwoman and works to sabotage her pending marriage to an insurance salesman (Ralph Bellamy), supposedly rescuing her from the dull routine of a complacent housewife.

41. *Holiday* (George Cukor, 1938) Johnny Case (Cary Grant) is engaged to attractive socialite Julia Seton (Doris Nolan), but when he learns that she and her father are planning the rest of his life, he gravitates toward her more open-minded and fun-loving sister, Linda (Katharine Hepburn).

42. *I Love You Again* (W.S. Van Dyke II, 1940) Con man George Carey (William Powell) has been living life as dull pottery-maker Larry Wilson until a clunk on the heads wakes him from his years of amnesia. Enlisting Doc Ryan's (Frank McHugh) help, he expects to return home as Wilson and withdraw all the money from his bank accounts. However, when he meets Wilson's wife, (Myrna Loy), and learns she intends to divorce him, he alters his plans.

43. *I Married a Witch* (René Clair, 1942) Jonathan Wooley (Fredric March) is responsible for having Jennifer (Veronica Lake) and her father, Daniel (Cecil Kellaway), burned at the stake during the 17th century Salem witch trials. Their spirits

imprisoned in a tree until a bolt of lightning releases them, they accidentally encounter Wooley's descendant, politician Wallace Wooley (also March), and set out to get their revenge. Jennifer's vengefulness, however, evolves into love.

44. *I Was a Male War Bride* (Howard Hawks, 1949) French army officer Capt. Henri Rochard (Cary Grant) must submit to all kinds of humiliating military regulations if he wants to travel with his wife, Lt. Catherine Gates (Ann Sheridan), an officer in the U.S. Army.

45. *If You Could Only Cook* (William A. Seiter, 1935) Joan Hawthorne (Jean Arthur) meets automobile entrepreneur and designer Jim Buchanan (Herbert Marshall) on a park bench and mistakes him for an unemployed person like herself. In the classified ads, she finds an opening for a butler and a maid. They apply and end up working for a professional gangster (Leo Carrillo), who competes with Buchanan for Hawthorne's affections.

46. *The Impatient Years* (Irving Cummings, 1944) Hardly acquainted with each other because of war's intrusion, two newlyweds, young mother Janie (Jean Arthur) and returning G. I. Andy Anderson (Lee Bowman), feel like strangers when they reunite. They consider ending their relationship, but Janie's father, William Smith (Charles Coburn), convinces them to retrace their early steps when they met, so they can recapture their lost love.

47. *It Happened One Night* (Frank Capra, 1934) One of the prototypes of screwball comedy, Capra's film bonds a jobless newspaperman (Clark Gable) with a runaway heiress (Claudette Colbert), who make a pact for their mutual benefit, he to make money, she to reach her estranged husband. The long bus trip leads to many adventures, and by the time they reach their destination, the experience changes their feelings toward each other.

48. *It's a Wonderful World* (W.S. Van Dyke II, 1939) Private detective Guy Johnson (James Stewart) tries to hide his millionaire client Willie Hayward (Ernest Truex), who is wrongly accused of murder. For his effort, Johnson is sentenced to prison, but he escapes, and with a single clue, a half-dime, he sets out to vindicate himself and his client. Along the way, he becomes entangled with aspiring poetess Edwina Corday (Claudette Colbert), who, with her romantic inclinations, insists that they are destined to be together.

49. *Joy of Living* (Tay Garnett, 1938) Maggie Garret (Irene Dunne) is a talented, successful singer beleaguered by a deadbeat family (father Guy Kibbee, mother Alice Brady, and sister Lucille Ball). Dan Brewster (Douglas Fairbanks, Jr.), inspires her to break away from them and establish her own life—with him.

50. *The Lady Eve* (Preston Sturges, 1941) After a year on the Amazon, studying snakes, Charles (Henry Fonda), heir to the Pike's Pale Ale fortune, returns to civilization by boarding a cruise ship. Professional gamblers Col. Harrington (Charles Coburn) and daughter Jean (Barbara Stanwyck) target him as an easy mark, but then Jean falls in love. Charles learns of her notorious reputation and his rigid ideals cause him to end the affair. Extremely hurt, Jean changes her identity to the Lady Eve Sidwich, intending to seduce him into submission and avenge herself by humiliating him.

51. *Lady of Burlesque* (William A. Wellman, 1943) This screwball mystery is based on a story by Gypsy Rose Lee. Burlesque star Deborah Hoople, a.k.a. Dixie Daisy (Barbara Stanwyck) becomes a prime suspect when two of her rivals are murdered.

52. *Libeled Lady* (Jack Conway, 1936) Newspaper editor Haggerty (Spencer Tracy) postpones his wedding to Gladys (Jean Harlow) to defuse a multi-million-

dollar libel suit that could ruin his company. He hires Bill Chandler (William Powell) to mollify the plaintiffs, Connie Allenbury (Myrna Loy) and her father (Walter Connolly). Chandler gets caught between Gladys and Connie in a romantic triangle that has unpredictable consequences.

53. *Live, Love and Learn* (George Fitzmaurice, 1937) In this parable on the pitfalls of success, struggling artist Bob Graham (Robert Montgomery) meets and marries rich socialite Julie Stoddard (Rosalind Russell). Life in his squalid flat is ideally happy and carefree until art critic Mr. Bawltitude (Monty Woolley) validates his artistic worth, and his paintings begin to sell. Graham becomes vain, materialistic, and obnoxious, unpleasant qualities that, he learns, diminish his ability to paint artistically.

54. *Love Crazy* (Jack Conway, 1941) Steve and Susan Ireland (William Powell and Myrna Loy) have the perfect marriage. When Steve's domineering mother-in-law (Florence Bates) trips on a rug in his apartment and he gets trapped as her nursemaid, he concocts a story with former girlfriend Isabel (Gail Patrick) to escape his imprisonment. Susan thinks he was cheating on her and she wants a divorce. Lawyer George Renny (Sidney Blackmer) advises Steve to feign insanity to delay the proceedings, but Steve's quirky behavior suggests that he really is crazy. Placed in an asylum, he has to prove his sanity to get out.

55. *Love on the Run* (W.S. Van Dyke II, 1936) Michael Anthony (Clark Gable) tricks rival reporter Barnabus Pells (Franchot Tone) into switching assignments. Anthony ends up helping bride-to-be heiress Sally Parker (Joan Crawford) escape from her fiancé; Pells follows the story of a trans–European flight by Baron Otto Spandermann (Reginald Owen) and his wife, Baroness Hilda Spandermann (Mona Barrie). Anthony and Pells vie for Parker's attention while they grapple with the Spandermanns, who are actually Russian spies.

56. *The Mad Miss Manton* (Leigh Jason, 1938) In this screwball mystery, socialite Melsa Manton (Barbara Stanwyck) tries to solve a murder while coping with harassment from reporter Peter Ames (Henry Fonda).

57. *Maid's Night Out* (Ben Holmes, 1938) Bill Norman (Allan Lane) has grandiose dreams of becoming a famous ichthyologist, but his father, a successful dairyman (George Irving), wants him to settle down in the family business. He bets his son that, if he can work faithfully for one month, he can take the family yacht on one of his proposed scientific expeditions. While delivering milk, Bill mistakes Sheila Harrison (Joan Fontaine) for her family's maid. He gets entangled in her life, leading to issues of class conflict and mistaken relationships.

58. *The Major and the Minor* (Billy Wilder, 1942) Frustrated by city life, Susan Applegate (Ginger Rogers) wants to go home, but does not have enough money for adult train fare. She disguises herself as a 12-year-old and meets Major Kirby (Ray Milland) who befriends her and brings her to the military academy where he works. Kirby's fiancée, Pamela Hill (Rita Johnson) soon recognizes Susan as a romantic rival.

59. *Merrily We Live* (Norman Z. McLeod, 1938) This film borrows from *My Man Godfrey*. E. Wade Rawlins (Brian Aherne), a successful author, is driving near the Kilbourne estate when his car breaks down. Mrs. Kilbourne (Billie Burke), who has a penchant for hiring and reforming tramps, takes him in as a chauffeur. Rawlins influences everyone for the better, including daughter Jerry (Constance Bennett), who dislikes him at first, but cannot help changing her feelings.

60. *Midnight* (Mitchell Leisen, 1939) American blues singer Eve Peabody (Claudette Colbert) is stranded in Paris without clothes or money. Cab driver Tibor

Czerny (Don Ameche) tries to help her, but she prefers someone with greater financial stability, and she runs away. She becomes allied with Georges Flammarion (John Barrymore), who wants to use her to seduce rich, handsome Jacques Picot (Francis Lederer) from his wife Helene (Mary Astor), who is having an affair with him. When Tibor discovers her whereabouts, he arrives at the chateau, claiming to be her husband. The result is confusion for all the entangled parties.

61. *Million Dollar Baby* (Curtis Bernhardt, 1941) Wealthy Cornelia Wheelwright (May Robson) learns from lawyer Jim Amory (Jeffrey Lynn) that her fortune is the result of some skullduggery her father played on his partner. To set matters aright, she decides to bequeath money to each of the partner's descendents. The lone heir is department store clerk Pamela McAllister (Priscilla Lane), but the million dollars Robson gives her becomes a source of contention between her and her boyfriend, (Ronald Reagan), who adheres to conventional ideas about the man being the breadwinner in the family.

62. *A Millionaire for Christy* (George Marshall, 1951) Secretary Christabel Sloane (Eleanor Parker) is told to notify radio celebrity Peter Ulysses Lockwood (Fred MacMurray) that he has inherited $2 million. Her insistence in delivering the message (and his reluctance to believe her) produce an ongoing contention that kindles their romance and leads to misunderstandings with his fiancée, June Chandler (Kay Buckley).

63. *The Miracle of Morgan's Creek* (Preston Sturges, 1944) Trudy Kockenlocker (Betty Hutton) ignores the genuine affections of Norval Jones (Eddie Bracken) and takes a one-night fling with a group of transient G. I.'s. On a drunken binge, she marries one of them and becomes pregnant, but she cannot remember the soldier's name. Norval comes to her rescue by claiming to be the father of her child and bearing the brunt of her father's (William Demarest) wrath.

64. *Mr. & Mrs. Smith* (Alfred Hitchcock, 1941) David and Ann Smith (Robert Montgomery and Carole Lombard) learn that, due to a slight clerical error, their marriage is not legally valid. His delay in rectifying the oversight leads to a classic battle of the sexes.

65. *Mr. Blandings Builds His Dream House* (H. C. Potter, 1948) Jim Blandings (Cary Grant) and his wife (Myrna Loy) experience the exasperations of building a house.

66. *Monkey Business* (Howard Hawks, 1952) A laboratory monkey accidentally concocts a fountain-of-youth formula that plays havoc with the lives of scientist Dr. Barnaby Fulton (Cary Grant) and his wife (Ginger Rogers).

67. *The Moon's Our Home* (William A. Seiter, 1936) Film actress Cherry Chester (Margaret Sullavan) and writer Anthony Amberton (Henry Fonda), without knowing each other personally, develop a bitter rivalry based merely on loathing the other's reputation. They meet and marry, keeping their careers a secret and not realizing that the other is someone they despise.

68. *More Than a Secretary* (Alfred E. Green, 1936) Carol Baldwin (Jean Arthur) tries to prove her worth to her boss Fred Gilbert (George Brent), whose icy formality is slow to defrost.

69. *The More the Merrier* (George Stevens, 1943) Because of a housing shortage in Washington, D. C., during World War II, Benjamin Dingle (Charles Coburn) finagles his way into sharing an apartment with Connie Milligan (Jean Arthur). He then proceeds to play matchmaker between her and Joe Carter (Joel McCrea).

70. *My Favorite Wife* (Garson Kanin, 1940) Thinking that his first wife Ellen (Irene Dunne) has died at sea, Nick Arden (Cary Grant) marries Bianca Bates (Gail

Patrick), only to learn on his wedding day that Ellen has returned. Nick is confused on how to resolve this awkward situation.

71. *My Man Godfrey* (Gregory La Cava, 1936) Screwball socialite Irene Bullock (Carole Lombard), on a scavenger hunt, pulls derelict Godfrey (William Powell) out of the city dump. She hires him as the family butler, unaware that he is a blue blood who recently deserted society.

72. *Next Time I Marry* (Garson Kanin, 1938) A provision in her father's will states that heiress Nancy Cracker Fleming (Lucille Ball) cannot inherit his money unless she marries an American. She is in love with foreigner Count Georgi (Lee Bowman), so she marries American Tony Anthony (James Ellison) to gain the inheritance, expecting to divorce him quickly afterwards. Anthony learns of her deceit and kidnaps her on the way to Reno, locking her in his house trailer so he can be first to instigate divorce proceedings.

73. *A Night to Remember* (Richard Wallace, 1942) In this screwball mystery, Nancy Troy (Loretta Young) and husband Jeff (Brian Aherne), a mystery writer, move to a new apartment where they encounter an assortment of sinister and eccentric characters. A dead body shows up in their garden and they become enmeshed in the intrigue as they work toward the solution of the crime.

74. *No More Ladies* (Edward H. Griffith, 1935) Sheridan Warren (Robert Montgomery) has difficulty adhering to his promise to wife Marcia (Joan Crawford) that he will no longer flirt with other women. She tries to cure him by resurrecting a friendship with an old flame (Franchot Tone).

75. *Nothing Sacred* (William Wellman, 1937) Conniving reporter Wally Cook (Fredric March) tries to soothe cantankerous editor Oliver Stone (Walter Connolly) by exploiting the story of a small-town girl (Carole Lombard) dying of radiation poisoning. Unknown to Cook, an alcoholic country doctor (Charles Winninger) made the wrong diagnosis, and the girl, eager to see the big city, goes along with the mistake to take advantage of the compassionate but pretentious public.

76. *No Time for Comedy* (William Keighley, 1940) Veteran stage actress Linda Paige (Rosalind Russell) supports neophyte playwright Gaylord Esterbrook (James Stewart) in his first venture on Broadway. They marry, and after four successful comedies, he decides to turn to tragedy. Inspired by seductive Amanda Swift (Genevieve Tobin), wife of investor Philo Swift (Charlie Ruggles), he decides to leave Linda for his new supporter, and Linda becomes involved with Philo. However, Gaylord's tragedy flops and Amanda, unable to tolerate failure, runs out on him. When Philo also condemns Gaylord for his failure, Linda defends him and returns to him to reconcile.

77. *The Palm Beach Story* (Preston Sturges, 1942) Gerry (Claudette Colbert) deserts husband Tom (Joel McCrea), rationalizing that, without her, he can achieve greater success as an architect. On a train from New York to Palm Beach, she meets wealthy J.D. Hackensacker III (Rudy Vallee), who buys her clothes and invites her to his mansion. Tom coincidentally arrives to take his wife back, but Gerry pretends he is her brother. J.D.'s sister Princess Centimillia (Mary Astor) flirts with McCrea. McCrea and Colbert, however, reconcile their differences, and they appease J.D. and the princess by introducing them to each of their identical twins.

78. *Party Wire* (Erle C. Kenton, 1935) Matthew Putnam (Victor Jory) returns to the small town of his boyhood to claim the Putnam Dairy Fortune. He admires Marge Oliver (Jean Arthur) whom he has not seen since they were children, but she has a boyfriend, Roy Daniels (Robert Allen). Busybodies overhear snatches of conversation on the "party wire" and mistakenly conclude that Marge is pregnant

with Daniels's baby. The scandal makes her an outcast in town. When Putnam learns how the rumor got started, he punishes the town by firing all the employees at the dairy and later marrying Marge.

79. *People Will Talk* (Joseph L. Mankiewicz, 1951) Medical student Deborah Higgins (Jeanne Crain), unmarried, learns she is pregnant and tries to commit suicide because she is ashamed that her indiscretion will hurt her father, Arthur (Sidney Blackmer). Arthur, a penniless poet, depends on cantankerous brother John (Will Wright) for his necessities. Fearing she may try suicide again, Noah Praetorius (Cary Grant), a doctor and professor, marries her. His colleague (Hume Cronyn) is jealous of his popularity and unearths information from Praetorius's mysterious past to try to discredit him.

80. *Petticoat Fever* (George Fitzmaurice, 1936) Suffering from cabin fever in a Labrador telegraph outpost where he has worked for two years, Dascom Dinsmore (Robert Montgomery suddenly has two visitors, aviator Sir James Felton (Reginald Owen) and his fiancée, Irene Campton (Myrna Loy), who had to make an emergency landing nearby. Although slightly unbalanced, Dinsmore makes a favorable impression on Irene, who falls in love with him. They plan to marry, but then Clara Wilson (Winifred Shotter), Dinsmore's fiancée, arrives. Guilt forces him to do the right thing until a message notifying him of his rich uncle's recent death makes him realize Wilson's motives.

81. *Phffft!* (Mark Robson, 1954) Believing their marriage has declined into total ennui, married couple Robert and Nina Tracey (Jack Lemmon and Judy Holliday) divorce. Even as they experiment with other partners, Robert with Janis (Kim Novak) and Nina with Charlie (Jack Carson), they come to realize that routine can be a source of contentment.

82. *The Philadelphia Story* (George Cukor, 1940) Tracy Lord (Katharine Hepburn) and C.K. Dexter Haven (Cary Grant) divorce, and Tracy later plans to marry self-made businessman George Kittredge (John Howard). Dexter reappears with tabloid reporters Macaulay Connor (James Stewart) and Elizabeth Imbrie (Ruth Hussey) as unwelcome guests before the wedding. Their interactions produce a conversion in Tracy who realizes that her superior attitude prevents her not only from being tolerable of the flaws in others but also from seeing the foibles in herself.

83. *Platinum Blonde* (Pre-screwball—Frank Capra, 1931) Reporter Stew Smith (Robert Williams) forsakes his job and friendships to marry rich socialite Jean Harlow. In time, he realizes his mistake and especially that his association with fellow reporter Gallagher (Loretta Young) is more than a platonic relationship.

84. *Please Believe Me* (Norman Taurog, 1950) Englishwoman Alison Kirbe (Deborah Kerr) sails to America to claim her inherited Texas ranch, unaware that it is a desolate, worthless stretch of property. Aboard ship are bankrupt gambler Terence Keath (Robert Walker), millionaire playboy Jeremy Taylor (Peter Lawford), and attorney Matthew Kinston (Mark Stevens), all interested in her for different reasons. The three men vie for advantage, thinking that she is a wealthy heiress.

85. *Remember?* (Norman Z. McLeod, 1939) Sky Ames (Lew Ayres) introduces fiancée Linda Bronson (Greer Garson) to friend Jeff Holland (Robert Taylor) and the two strangers immediately fall in love. They marry, but Jeff gives priority to his advertising business, which interferes with their honeymoon plans. After several disappointments, Linda divorces him, but Sky, a scientist working on an amnesia formula, sneaks the potion into their drinks. They forget they met, and when they meet again, as if for the first time, their romance blossoms anew.

86. *Remember Last Night?* (James Whale, 1935) In this screwball mystery, Tony

and Carlotta Milburn (Robert Young and Constance Cummings) join friends to celebrate their six-month wedding anniversary in a "progressive party" that moves from house to house. They sleep the night at the Hulings (George Meeker, Sally Eilers), only to wake and find their host murdered. District Attorney Danny Harrison (Edward Arnold) arrives, but before he or Tony and Carlotta can solve the crime, several other people are murdered.

87. *Smartest Girl in Town* (Joseph Santley, 1935) Cookie (Ann Sothern) vows with her sister Gwen (Helen Broderick) to marry only a rich, eligible man. When Cookie mistakes millionaire Dick Smith (Gene Raymond) for an ordinary photographer's model, he becomes intrigued with her. Cookie has difficulty making up her mind about him, first reluctant to get involved, then ready to accept him, then shunning him and returning to her original marital plan.

88. *Sullivan's Travels* (Preston Sturges, 1941) Filmmaker John Sullivan (Joel McCrea) abandons the comedies for which he is famous to make a serious film on social consciousness. He dresses as a tramp to research ideas for his film, "O Brother, Where Art Thou?" He meets a girl (Veronica Lake), who accompanies him on his quest. Grateful for what the tramps taught him, he tries to distribute money among them. A greedy tramp waylays him, and the confused Sullivan slugs a railroad guard and winds up on a chain gang.

89. *Sylvia Scarlett* (George Cukor, 1935) Fleeing from Paris to London, con artist Henry Scarlett (Edmund Gwenn) and daughter Sylvia (Katharine Hepburn), disguised as a boy, meet fellow con man Jim Monkey (Cary Grant). Although he momentarily betrays them to customs, they reunite to tour the countryside as a harlequin group. At one stop, Sylvia meets bohemian artist Michael Fane (Brian Aherne). She becomes enamored of him, which puts her disguise in jeopardy as she switches between her male and female identities.

90. *Take a Letter, Darling* (Mitchell Leisen, 1942) Male and female stereotypes are inverted when an artist (Fred MacMurray) goes to work for a businesswoman (Rosalind Russell) as her subservient factotum. When he reaches his limit of tolerance, he quits, but circumstances create further encounters between them.

91. *The Talk of the Town* (George Stevens, 1942) Academic Prof. Michael Lightcap (Ronald Coleman) learns to compromise his rigid, lofty values when he meets a suspected criminal (Cary Grant) in the house he is renting from Nora Shelley (Jean Arthur).

92. *Tell It to the Judge* (Norman Foster, 1949) Because she had recently divorced lawyer Pete Webb (Robert Cummings) for what appeared to be a marital impropriety, lawyer Marsha Meredith (Rosalind Russell) finds her nomination for a judgeship in jeopardy. Webb explains to her that the "impropriety' was really a misunderstanding, and convinces her to remarry. Events, however, begin to repeat themselves and Webb seems to fall into the same extramarital misconduct that plagued him the first time.

93. *Theodora Goes Wild* (Richard Boleslawski,1936) To hide her identity from people in the provincial small town where she lives, Theodora Lynn (Irene Dunne) writes scandalous best-selling novels under the pseudonym Caroline Adams. New York City artist Michael Grant (Melvyn Douglas) urges her to stop living her two lives. She does, and when she visits Grant in the big city, she finds that he is also guilty of his own brand of hypocrisy and she works to cure him of it.

94. *There Goes My Heart* (Norman Z. McLeod, 1938) Following the formula of *It Happened One Night,* heiress Joan Butterfield (Virginia Bruce) runs away from home, but is recognized and pursued by news-hungry reporter Bill Spencer (Fredric

March). Peggy O'Brien (Patsy Kelly) befriends Joan, welcomes her as a roommate, and gets her a job at the department store where she works, ironically the same store owned by Joan's millionaire grandfather (Claude Gillingwater). Bill and Joan fall in love and have to prove to her family that he is worthy of her.

95. *There's Always a Woman* (Alexander Hall, 1938) In this screwball mystery, Bill Reardon (Melvyn Douglas), former investigator for the district attorney's office, decides to return to his old job because his new job as private detective cannot pay the bills. Wife Sally (Joan Blondell) manages to sign a client, Lola Fraser (Mary Astor), whose husband (Lester Matthews) is later murdered, and Sally and Bill become rivals trying to solve the mystery.

96. *The Thin Man* (W.S. Van Dyke II, 1934) The prototype of the screwball mystery, *The Thin Man* crosses lines with film noir, as most screwball mysteries do by tending to incorporate noir stylistics with screwball humor. (Ironically, both this film and the archetypical noir, *The Maltese Falcon*, were adapted from novels written by Dashiell Hammett.) Perpetually inebriated Nick Charles (William Powell) manages to run his wife Nora's (Myrna Loy) businesses while solving the mystery of a missing inventor.

97. *To Be or Not to Be* (Ernst Lubitsch, 1942) At the beginning of World War II, members of a Polish theater troupe use their acting abilities to keep a list of Polish underground names from the Nazis. Against this larger, more serious objective is the more personal story of ham actor Joseph Tura (Jack Benny) and wife Maria (Carole Lombard). Joseph is jealous of a young aviator (Robert Stack) who pays unusually close attention to his wife.

98. *Too Many Husbands* (Wesley Ruggles, 1940) When Bill Cardew (Fred Mac-Murray) returns home after being lost at sea and presumed dead, he discovers wife Vicky (Jean Arthur) has married his business partner, Henry (Melvyn Douglas). While they struggle through many trivial contests to prove who is superior to the other and deserving of their wife's sole fidelity, Vicky has difficulty choosing between them.

99. *Topper* (Norman Z. McLeod, 1937) Strait-laced banker Cosmo Topper (Roland Young) envies the loose lifestyle of his clients, George and Marion Kerby (Cary Grant, Constance Bennett). After the Kerbys die in a car crash, they return as ghosts intent on doing a good deed by reforming their friend.

100. *Topper Returns* (Roy Del Ruth, 1941) This third entry in the *Topper* series is a screwball mystery. While visiting wealthy girlfriend Ann Carrington (Carole Landis), Gail Richards (Joan Blondell) is mistakenly murdered in her place. Topper (Roland Young), coincidentally stops at the mansion and meets her ghost. Together, they uncover the murderer.

101. *Topper Takes a Trip* (Norman Z. McLeod, 1939) In this follow-up to the first *Topper*, righteous Mrs. Nancy Parkhurst (Verree Teasdale) encourages Mrs. Topper (Billie Burke) to instigate divorce proceedings against her husband (Roland Young) who seems either mad or adulterous. The judge's decision delayed, Mrs. Parkhurst takes Mrs. Topper to Paris to meet an eligible bachelor. The spirit of Marion Kerby (Constance Bennett) returns in time to help Topper reclaim his wife.

102. *Trouble in Paradise* (Pre-screwball—Ernst Lubitsch, 1932) Professional thief Gaston Monescu (Herbert Marshall) meets and falls in love with his female counterpart, Lily (Miriam Hopkins). Their perfect union is momentarily disrupted when Gaston begins to fall under the seductive spell of their latest target (Kay Francis).

103. *Turnabout* (Hal Roach, 1940) In this fantasy about gender reversal, husband and wife Tim and Sally Willows (John Hubbard, Carole Landis) squabble over

who has the harder job. They go to bed, each wishing to do the other's job, and when they wake, they have switched genders. Tim gets to live Sally's life as a house-wife and Sally goes to work as an advertising man. The experience teaches both of them something about respecting the other's role.

104. *Twentieth Century* (Howard Hawks, 1934) Megalomaniac Oscar Jaffe (John Barrymore) is a Broadway producer who nurtures protégée Mildred Plotka (Carole Lombard) to stardom. She leaves the stage to become a famous name in Hollywood while Jaffe's fame dims into oblivion. After a chance meeting on the Twentieth Century Limited, Jaffe tries to reverse his fortune by tricking her into returning to work for him.

105. *Two-Faced Woman* (George Cukor, 1941) When ski instructor Karin Borg (Greta Garbo) meets magazine publisher Larry Blake (Melvyn Douglas) for a skiing lesson, they fall in love and marry. Larry immediately expects to return to New York City to his job, but Karin is content to stay where she is. She later visits him in the city, but tests his fidelity by pretending to be her twin sister and seeing how he responds to her.

106. *Unfaithfully Yours* (Preston Sturges, 1948) Noted conductor Sir Alfred De Carter (Rex Harrison) suddenly suspects that wife Daphne (Linda Darnell) is cheat-ing on him with his secretary, Tony Windborn (Kurt Kreuger). Before his suspicions can be allayed, he fantasizes three possible scenarios where he gets revenge by killing either Daphne, Tony, or himself.

107. *Vivacious Lady* (George Stevens, 1938) While visiting the city, Prof. Peter Morgan (James Stewart) meets and marries Francey (Ginger Rogers) in one day. He takes her home to Old Sharon, but is reticent to tell conservative dad (Charles Coburn), president of the staid college where Peter teaches biology, of his hasty marriage to a nightclub singer. Peter's delay complicates life with his fiancée (Frances Mercer), his father, his job, and his wife.

108. *Without Love* (Harold S. Bucquet, 1945) A scientist (Spencer Tracy) and a widow (Katharine Hepburn) agree to a platonic marriage of convenience because of fears of being hurt by a failed or curtailed relationship. Gradually, they realize that their association is evolving into something more than mere companionship.

109. *The Whole Town's Talking* (John Ford, 1935) Edward G. Robinson plays two extreme characters, a milquetoast clerk and a ruthless gangster. Clerk Arthur Fer-guson Jones (Robinson) has a secret crush on Bill (Jean Arthur), a saucy, brash co-worker. When he gets mistaken for look-alike mobster Killer Mannion (also Robinson) and then becomes involved with Mannion himself, Jones is forced to do things that are completely out of character for him.

110. *Woman Chases Man* (John Blystone, 1937) Kenneth Nolan (Joel McCrea) is a tight-fisted, practical man who has inherited money from his mother. He has drifted away from his father, B.J. Nolan (Charles Winninger), a millionaire until his reckless schemes broke him. B.J. is confident that his latest housing project has fail-proof potential, if he can just get his son to invest in it. He hires architect Vir-ginia Travis (Miriam Hopkins) not only to design the development but also to trick his son into providing the capital.

111. *You Belong to Me* (Wesley Ruggles, 1941) Dr. Helen Hunt (Barbara Stan-wyck) treats wealthy idler Peter Kirk (Henry Fonda) after he has a skiing accident. They fall in love and marry. Passionate about her job, Helen feels fulfilled by it. Kirk grows extremely jealous of her male patients. Only after he gets a job as a department store clerk, and then invests in a hospital where his wife can resume her profession, does he prove himself a significant contributor to society.

112. *You Can't Beat Love* (Christy Cabanne, 1937) Trudy Olson (Joan Fontaine) and Jimmy Hughes (Preston Foster) meet as political competitors. She is daughter of the current mayor, and he has decided to run to eradicate corruption. Jimmy's political rivals try to entangle him in a variety of scandals, but with Trudy's help, he outsmarts them.

113. *You Can't Take It with You* (Frank Capra, 1938) Capra's film espouses an idealistic philosophy by suggesting that the "do-what-makes-you-happy" motto of eccentric Grandpa Vanderhof (Lionel Barrymore) far outweighs the "do-what-makes-you-money" viewpoint of banker Anthony P. Kirby, Sr. (Edward Arnold). The clash between classes is mirrored on a personal level in the relationship between Kirby's son (James Stewart) and Vanderhof's granddaughter (Jean Arthur), whose love signifies a way to overcome these philosophical differences.

Appendix B: Filmography of Films Noirs, 1941–1958

The following filmography is a partial listing of films noirs produced during those years that most film critics cite as the opening and closing dates of noir's classical period. Although Huston's *The Maltese Falcon*, with hard-boiled detective Sam Spade, receives bragging rights as the first true film noir, there are a number of "precursors," among them Lang's *Fury* (1936) and Ingster's *Stranger on the Third Floor* (1940). And although, by consensus, Welles's *Touch of Evil*, with corrupt detective Hank Quinlan, marks the close of the original cycle, noirs still emerged in the likes of Wise's *Odds Against Tomorrow* (1959), Hitchcock's trend-setting *Psycho* (1960), and Thompson's disturbing *Cape Fear* (1962). Yet, as Paul Schrader argues, noir was the product of a distinct time period in American history, and although filmmakers may still apply the formulas that designate their productions as noir— or preferably termed neo-noir to differentiate them from those of the original cycle— the classical films noirs were defined and shaped by the time period that gave them birth.

In *Film Noir: An Encyclopedic Reference to the American Style*, Alain Silver and Elizabeth Ward include synopses and critical comments for over 300 films. Spencer Selby lists over 400 films in *Dark City: The Film Noir*. The select filmography below lists many of the key films noirs mentioned throughout this book and compared with screwball comedy.

1. *Ace in the Hole* (a.k.a. *The Big Carnival*) (Billy Wilder, 1951) A big-city newsman (Kirk Douglas) comes to a small town where he selfishly exploits a local story, delaying its resolution and producing tragic consequences.

2. *The Accused* (William Dieterle, 1949) After accidentally killing her student in self-defense when he attempts to rape her, Professor Wilma Tuttle (Loretta Young), numbed by the tragedy, tries to cover up her crime.

3. *Act of Violence* (Fred Zinnemann, 1948) Engineer Frank Enley (Van Heflin) leads a settled and successful life, until Joe Parkson (Robert Ryan) suddenly appears to avenge Enley's betrayal of fellow soldiers while in a prisoner of war camp.

4. *Angel Face* (Otto Preminger, 1952) Beautiful but possessive Diane Tremayne

(Jean Simmons) lures ambulance driver Frank Jessup (Robert Mitchum) away from his girlfriend (Mona Freeman) with the promise of a more exciting relationship.

5. *The Asphalt Jungle* (John Huston, 1950) An ex-convict (Sam Jaffe) plans the perfect heist that goes wrong because of unforeseen accidents and human greed.

6. *Beware, My Lovely* (Harry Horner, 1952) Helen Gordon (Ida Lupino) is menaced by unstable handyman Howard Wilton (Robert Ryan) who holds her prisoner in her own house.

7. *Beyond a Reasonable Doubt* (Fritz Lang, 1956) To prove that innocent people can be convicted of crimes they did not commit, newspaper owner Austin Spencer (Sidney Blackmer) convinces Tom Garrett (Dana Andrews) to help him amass false evidence proving Garrett's guilt in a recent murder. Before they can discredit the evidence, Spencer is killed in a traffic accident and Garrett cannot prove their hoax.

8. *The Big Clock* (John Farrow, 1948) A magazine editor (Ray Milland) becomes the unwitting suspect in a murder that was actually committed by his boss (Charles Laughton).

9. *The Big Heat* (Fritz Lang, 1953) A police detective (Glenn Ford) seeks revenge on the criminal syndicate responsible for killing his wife (Jocelyn Brando).

10. *The Big Sleep* (Howard Hawks, 1946) Private detective Phillip Marlowe (Humphrey Bogart) tries to protect the wealthy Sternwood sisters (Lauren Bacall, Martha Vickers) while solving several murders.

11. *Black Angel* (Roy William Neill, 1946) Alcoholic pianist Martin Blair (Dan Duryea) falls in love with Catherine Bennett (June Vincent) while trying to help her clear her husband (John Phillips) of a murder he did not commit.

12. *The Blue Dahlia* (George Marshall, 1946) When Lieutenant-Commander Johnny Morrison (Alan Ladd) returns home after the war, his unfaithful wife (Doris Dowling) is murdered. Suspected of the crime, he relies on Joyce Harwood (Veronica Lake) and G. I. buddies (William Bendix and Hugh Beaumont) to help him.

13. *The Blue Gardenia* (Fritz Lang, 1953) After their date, sleazy Harry Prebble (Raymond Burr) invites telephone operator Norah Larkin (Anne Baxter) to his home, where he attacks her. Partially drunk, she knocks him out with a poker and passes out herself. When she revives, Prebble is dead and Larkin runs away, thinking she killed him.

14. *Body and Soul* (Robert Rossen, 1947) A fighter (John Garfield) grows from a young ambitious boxer to a vain, avaricious champion. After mistreating those closest to him, he redeems himself by placing ethical values above personal glory.

15. *Boomerang* (Elia Kazan, 1947) In a complex murder trial in which several witnesses accuse a man (Arthur Kennedy) of killing a priest, an attorney (Dana Andrews), against public opinion, doubts the man's guilt and fights for justice.

16. *Born to Kill* (Robert Wise, 1947) Even though divorcée Helen Brent (Claire Trevor) knows that brutish Sam Wild (Lawrence Tierney) has murdered two people, she has trouble repressing her attraction to him.

17. *Cape Fear* (J. Lee Thompson, 1962) Ex-convict Max Cady (Robert Mitchum) blames lawyer Sam Bowden (Gregory Peck) for sending him to jail. To get revenge, he harasses Peck, his wife (Polly Bergen), and his daughter (Lori Martin). Bowden tries to use legal means to thwart Cady, but eventually becomes just as ruthless and vindictive as his adversary.

18. *The Chase* (Arthur Ripley, 1946) Desperate for a job, ex-G. I. Chuck Scott (Robert Cummings) accepts an offer from racketeer Eddie Roman (Steve Cochran) to work as his chauffeur. Scott helps Roman's wife (Michèle Morgan) escape her sadistic husband.

19. *Clash by Night* (Fritz Lang, 1952) Cynical Mae Doyle (Barbara Stanwyck) marries soft-hearted Jerry D'Amato (Paul Douglas). When life becomes routine and dull, she has an affair with Jerry's friend Earl Pfeiffer (Robert Ryan). Earl gives her an ultimatum to run away with him, and she must choose between him and her husband and daughter.

20. *Cornered* (Edward Dmytryk, 1945) In postwar France, a veteran (Dick Powell) seeks revenge by looking for the elusive Nazi responsible for his wife's death.

21. *Criss Cross* (Robert Siodmak, 1949) After two years of drifting, Steve Thompson (Burt Lancaster) returns home. Ex-wife Anna (Yvonne De Carlo) is now married to racketeer Slim Dundee (Dan Duryea). Thompson helps the gang plot the heist of an armored car, only because he expects to reclaim Anna for himself.

22. *Dark City* (William Dieterle, 1950) Bookie Danny Haley (Charlton Heston) sets up a gambling scam with friends Barney (Ed Begley) and Augie (Jack Webb) to con businessman Arthur Winant (Don DeFore) out of his investment money. The plan works, but Winant, despondent, hangs himself, and his brother, psychotic Sidney Winant (Mike Mazurki), seeks out each of the three men to avenge his death.

23. *The Dark Corner* (Henry Hathaway, 1946) Private eye Bradford Galt (Mark Stevens) becomes a pawn in a series of frame-ups, first by former partner Jardine (Kurt Kreuger) and then by art dealer Hardy Cathcart (Clifton Webb) who plans to kill Jardine for flirting with his wife (Cathy Downs) and then framing Galt for the murder.

24. *Dead Reckoning* (John Cromwell, 1947) Ex-G. I. Capt. Rip Murdock (Humphrey Bogart) investigates the mysterious death of fellow paratrooper Johnny Drake (William Prince). He meets resistance from nightclub owner Martinelli (Morris Carnovsky), his bodyguard (Marvin Miller), and Johnny's wife (Lizabeth Scott).

25. *Deadline at Dawn* (Harold Clurman, 1946) Seaman Alex Winkley (Bill Williams) cannot recall how he got such a huge wad of money. At a dance hall, he meets taxi dancer June Goth (Susan Hayward), who helps him retrace his steps to a murdered woman. They have to prove whether Winkley or someone else killed her.

26. *Detour* (Edgar G. Ulmer, 1945) Musician Al Roberts (Tom Neal) hitchhikes cross-country to reunite with girlfriend Sue Harvey (Claudia Drake). A man (Edmund MacDonald) gives him a ride, but mysteriously dies. Roberts takes his car, until a former acquaintance (Ann Savage) recognizes the man's car and suspects foul play. In a bizarre accident, Roberts strangles her with a telephone cord. Ultimately, he finds himself stranded on the "highway of life" until police pick him up.

27. *D.O.A.* (Rudolph Maté, 1950) Accountant Frank Bigelow (Edmond O'Brien) becomes the innocent victim in a cover-up for a murder. After inadvertently taking a toxic poison, he sets out to catch his killer before the poison takes effect.

28. *Double Indemnity* (Billy Wilder, 1944) A prototype of the noir genre, *Double Indemnity* has insurance salesman Walter Neff (Fred MacMurray) falling under the spell of femme fatale Phyllis Dietrichson (Barbara Stanwyck). She seduces Neff into killing her husband (Tom Powers) for the insurance money, although it puts him in jeopardy with shrewd claims investigator Barton Keyes (Edward G. Robinson).

29. *A Double Life* (George Cukor, 1947) Stage actor Ronald Coleman decides to perform *Othello*, a play that has been a curse to him in the past. In the meantime, he meets Pat Kroll (Shelley Winters), a waitress who becomes an innocent victim of his psychological breakdown.

30. *Fallen Angel* (Otto Preminger, 1945) Drifter Eric Stanton (Dana Andrews) arrives in a small town where he meets and falls in love with diner waitress Stella (Linda Darnell). Stanton and several other men showing romantic designs on Stella become suspects when she is murdered.

31. *Fear in the Night* (1947) Vince Grayson (DeForest Kelley) wakes from a dream in which he killed a man. Objects in his pocket confirm the deed. He turns to brother-in-law Cliff Herlihy (Paul Kelly), a police detective, who discovers that a neighbor (Robert Emmett Keane) had hypnotized Grayson into committing murder for him.

32. *The File on Thelma Jordon* (Robert Siodmak, 1950) Assistant District Attorney Cleve Marshall (Wendell Corey), disenchanted with his marriage, is easily seduced by Thelma Jordon (Barbara Stanwyck), who uses him to cover up a jewel theft and murder she planned with boyfriend Tony Laredo (Richard Rober).

33. *Force of Evil* (Abraham Polonsky, 1948) Lawyer Joe Morse (John Garfield) works for the syndicate, favoring money over ethics. He tries to protect his brother Leo Morse (Thomas Gomez), who is in the numbers racket, but Leo rejects any help from him. Eventually, Joe must decide between personal gain and allegiance to family.

34. *Fury* (Pre-noir—Fritz Lang, 1936) Driving through a small town, Joe Wilson (Spencer Tracy) is arrested and jailed for a kidnapping-murder he knows nothing about. Angry vigilantes storm the jail to hang him. The jail is burned down, and Wilson escapes undetected. Leaders of the mob, now accused of murder, stand trial, and a vengeful Wilson must decide whether to intervene or let them face sentencing.

35. *Gilda* (Charles Vidor, 1946) Gilda Mundson (Rita Hayworth) and Johnny Farrell (Glenn Ford) have a puzzling love-hate relationship. After she marries his boss (George Macready), Ford assumes the job of restraining her sexual volatility, which she constantly flaunts in and teases him with her supposed extramarital exploits.

36. *The Guilty* (John Reinhardt, 1947) Mike Carr (Don Castle) and Johnny Dixon (Wally Cassell) are roommates dating twin sisters (both played by Bonita Granville). When one of the sisters disappears, Carr weighs all the tangible evidence and suspects that Dixon may have murdered her.

37. *Gun Crazy* (a.k.a. *Deadly Is the Female*) (Joseph H. Lewis, 1950) Gun enthusiast Barton Tare (John Dall) becomes enamored with carnival sharpshooter Annie Laurie Starr (Peggy Cummins), who marries him, then convinces him to pursue a career of robbing banks.

38. *He Ran All the Way* (John Berry, 1951) Thief Nick Robey (John Garfield) escapes police by befriending a girl (Shelley Winters) and forcing her family to take him in. Guilt and paranoia prevent him from trusting her as someone who might help him.

39. *The Hitch-Hiker* (Ida Lupino, 1953) Roy Collins (Edmond O'Brien) and Gilbert Bower (Frank Lovejoy) are carefree outdoorsmen taken hostage by escaped killer Emmett Myers (William Talman). Myers constantly harasses and belittles the two men, who know they must escape or he will kill them when he reaches his destination.

40. *I Wake Up Screaming* (H. Bruce Humberstone, 1941) Public relations agent Frankie Christopher (Victor Mature) furthers the career of Vicky Lynn (Carole Landis), but when someone murders her shortly after she announces she is leaving him, Christopher becomes a prime suspect.

41. *In a Lonely Place* (Nicholas Ray, 1950) Suspected of murder, quick-tempered screenwriter Dixon Steele (Humphrey Bogart) develops a romantic relationship with neighbor Laurel Gray (Gloria Grahame), but his unstable personality gradually erodes her confidence in his innocence.

42. *Kansas City Confidential* (Phil Karlson, 1952) Former detective Tim Foster (Preston Foster) plans the perfect bank heist, but implicates an innocent bystander,

ex-convict Joe Rolfe (John Payne). Although police finally prove that Payne is innocent, he loses his job and he takes it on himself to find the perpetrators of the robbery.

43. *The Killers* (Robert Siodmak, 1946) Insurance investigator Jim Reardon (Edmond O'Brien) explores the background of recently murdered Ole "Swede" Andreson (Burt Lancaster). He discovers that the dead man was involved in a payroll heist, and that a devious Kitty Collins (Ava Gardner) was one of the main reasons for betrayal among the thieves.

44. *Kiss Me Deadly* (Robert Aldrich, 1955) Private detective Mike Hammer (Ralph Meeker) is obsessed with locating what he believes is a valuable object, even though it costs the life of his friend (Nick Dennis) and places him and his girlfriend (Maxine Cooper) in jeopardy.

45. *Kiss of Death* (Henry Hathaway, 1947) Nick Bianco (Victor Mature) is arrested for a jewelry theft. He expects his family to be supported by the mob, but when his wife kills herself and his two daughters are placed in an orphanage, he decides to become an informer for the police. Bianco's testimony sends Tommy Udo (Richard Widmark) to prison, but when Udo gets out, Bianco cannot depend on the police to protect him and his new family, and he must confront Udo himself.

46. *Kiss the Blood Off My Hands* (Norman Foster, 1948) Suffering from post-traumatic stress disorder after the war, Bill Saunders (Burt Lancaster) lacks control over his bursts of violence, until he meets nurse Jane Wharton (Joan Fontaine), who has a calming influence on him. Saunders becomes involved with thief Harry Carter (Robert Newton) who intends to steal penicillin to sell on the black market, but his relationship with Wharton convinces him to reform.

47. *Ladies in Retirement* (Charles Vidor, 1941) Determined to protect her two deranged sisters (Elsa Lanchester, Edith Barrett) and keep the three of them together, a housekeeper (Ida Lupino) is forced to murder her employer (Isobel Elsom).

48. *The Lady from Shanghai* (Orson Welles, 1948) High-profile lawyer Arthur Bannister (Everett Sloane) hires adventurer Michael O'Hara (Orson Welles) to protect him from a supposed assassin. O'Hara takes the job, attracted to the lawyer's wife (Rita Hayworth), but he quickly realizes that his clients are not what they pretend to be.

49. *The Lady in the Lake* (Robert Montgomery, 1947) Searching for a missing woman, private detective Phillip Marlowe (Robert Montgomery) uncovers a complex web of adultery and murder.

50. *Laura* (Otto Preminger, 1944) While trying to solve the murder of a beautiful woman (Gene Tierney), a police detective (Dana Andrews) falls in love with her portrait.

51. *The Leopard Man* (Jacques Tourneur, 1943) As a publicity stunt, agent Jerry Manning (Dennis O'Keefe) gives entertainer Kiki Walker (Jean Brooks) a leopard but when the leopard escapes and several people are killed, doubts arise as to whether it is the work of the leopard or some man who can transform himself into one.

52. *Macao* (Josef von Sternberg. 1952) Fleeing New York because he had killed a man, Nick Cochran (Robert Mitchum) meets singer Julie Benson (Jane Russell) on a ship sailing to Macao. Once there, Benson gets a job working for racketeer Vincent Halloran (Brad Dexter). Cochran forms an alliance with undercover detective Lawrence C. Trumble (William Bendix), but Trumble is killed by Halloran's thugs. With Benson's help, Cochran turns Halloran over to authorities and expects to clear himself of his crime.

53. *The Maltese Falcon* (John Huston, 1941) Detective Sam Spade (Humphrey Bogart), trying to solve the mystery of the death of his partner (Jerome Cowan),

gets involved with a gaggle of unsavory characters looking for the jewel-encrusted figure of a black bird.

54. *The Mark of the Whistler* (William Castle, 1944) Having the same name as the owner of an unclaimed dormant bank account, jobless drifter Lee Nugent (Richard Dix) claims the money. His assumed identity is, coincidentally, that of the son of a thief who framed another man for his crime. The framed man lost his sanity in prison, and his son (John Calvert) now vows revenge on Nugent for what Nugent's father had done.

55. *Mildred Pierce* (Michael Curtiz,1945) Successful restaurateur Mildred Pierce (Joan Crawford) fails at marriage and motherhood, divorcing her husband (Bruce Bennett) and losing control of her spoiled daughter (Ann Blyth) who competes with her for the attention of a playboy (Zachary Scott).

56. *Murder, My Sweet* (Edward Dmytryk, 1944) Private detective Phillip Marlowe (Dick Powell) gets involved in a complex web of mystery, looking for the missing girlfriend of Moose Malloy (Mike Mazurki), recovering a stolen jade necklace for Mrs. Grayle (Claire Trevor), and solving several murders.

57. *The Naked City* (Jules Dassin, 1948) Shot on location in New York City, this film chronicles the realistic investigative methods used by police to track down criminals and administer justice.

58. *The Narrow Margin* (Richard Fleischer, 1952) Police detective Walter Brown (Charles McGraw) thinks he is protecting a gangster's girlfriend, when it turns out that she is a decoy for the real witness who needs to be protected from the mob.

59. *Night and the City* (Jules Dassin, 1950) Hustler Harry Fabian (Richard Widmark) thinks he has found the key to success when he sponsors a wrestling match between legitimate Greco–Roman wrestler Gregorius (Stanislaus Zbyszko) and commercial wrestler The Strangler (Mike Mazurki). Gregorius is fatally hurt in an altercation with The Strangler, and the wrestler's son (Herbert Lom), offers a reward to have Fabian executed.

60. *Nightmare* (Maxwell Shane, 1956) In this remake of *Fear in the Night*, Stan Grayson (Kevin McCarthy) turns to brother-in-law Rene Bressard (Edward G. Robinson), a police detective, to help him prove whether he had killed a man or only dreamt it.

61. *Nightmare Alley* (Edmund Goulding, 1947) A worker in a carnival sideshow (Tyrone Power) dreams of making the big time as a gifted mentalist. Greed and deceit undo his success.

62. *99 River Street* (Phil Karlson, 1953) Taxi driver Ernie Driscoll (John Payne) discovers that his wife (Peggie Castle) is having an affair with a man (Brad Dexter) who is involved in a jewel heist. The man kills Driscoll's wife and frames him for the murder. Stage actress Linda James (Evelyn Keyes), a friend of Driscoll's, helps him catch up with the killer to vindicate himself.

63. *No Man of Her Own* (Mitchell Leisen, 1950) Helen Ferguson (Barbara Stanwyck), deserted and pregnant, assumes the identity of a well-to-do married woman who was killed when their train crashed. The dead woman's family, who had not yet met their daughter-in-law, believes Ferguson is she. Ferguson, for the sake of her child, accepts their mistake. Everything goes smoothly until her baby's father (Lyle Bettger) shows up to blackmail her.

64. *No Way Out* (Joseph L. Mankiewicz. 1950) Luther Brooks (Sidney Poitier) is a young doctor who contends with racial prejudice from a bigoted patient (Richard Widmark).

65. *Notorious* (Alfred Hitchcock, 1946) American agent Devlin (Cary Grant)

asks Alicia Huberman (Ingrid Bergman), daughter of a convicted Nazi, to become the mistress of a man (Claude Rains) working in a Nazi cabal in post-war South America. Devlin, however, has fallen in love with her, and the question of duty over personal interest complicates their relationship.

66. *Odds Against Tomorrow* (Robert Wise, 1959) In this heist film, Dave Burke (Ed Begley) recruits Earle Slater (Robert Ryan) and Johnny Ingram (Harry Belafonte) to execute his perfect plan to rob a bank. Racial tensions and bad luck sabotage their success.

67. *On Dangerous Ground* (Nicholas Ray, 1952) Jim Wilson (Robert Ryan) is a hardened, sadistic police detective whose brutality mars his reputation and results in his being assigned to a rural community. While on the trail of a suspect, he meets the man's blind sister (Ida Lupino) who transforms his life.

68. *Out of the Past* (Jacques Tourneur, 1947) Private detective Jeff Bailey (Robert Mitchum) thinks he has escaped the indiscretions of his past, but a chance encounter with a former acquaintance (Paul Valentine) forces him to resume business with the villainous femme fatale (Jane Greer) and gangster (Kirk Douglas) he thought he had escaped.

69. *Phantom Lady* (Robert Siodmak, 1944) Civil engineer Scott Henderson (Alan Curtis) is convicted of murdering his wife. His alibi is that a woman (Fay Helm) accompanied him that night, but she seems to be a "phantom lady" who does not exist. His secretary, Carol Richman (Ella Raines), sets out to find the woman and prove his innocence.

70. *Pitfall* (André de Toth, 1948) Insurance man John Forbes (Dick Powell) is disenchanted with his routine existence. On the pretext of company business, he visits model Mona Stevens (Lizabeth Scott) to discuss items her boyfriend (Byron Barr) purchased with embezzled money. Forbes has an affair with her, cheating on his wife (Jane Wyatt). Private investigator MacDonald (Raymond Burr) had already told Forbes of his interest in Stevens, and when he discovers Forbes's deceit, he sets him up to be murdered by Steven's boyfriend.

71. *Possessed* (Curtis Bernhardt, 1947) Although married to Dean Graham (Raymond Massey), Louise (Joan Crawford) is obsessed with David Sutton (Van Heflin), who treats her with casual indifference. Her monomania drives her to madness.

72. *The Postman Always Rings Twice* (Tay Garnett, 1946) Drifter Frank Chambers (John Garfield) stops at a diner owned by Nick Smith (Cecil Kellaway). After one look at Smith's wife (Lana Turner), Chambers becomes obsessed with her. Together, they plot to kill her husband, but all their well-planned designs become foiled by circumstances.

73. *Pushover* (Richard Quine, 1954) Police detective Paul Sheridan (Fred MacMurray) falls for Lona McLane (Kim Novak), girlfriend of gangster Harry Wheeler (Paul Richards), and together they plot to steal the gangster's money while misleading authorities.

74. *Raw Deal* (Anthony Mann, 1948) Convict Joe Sullivan (Dennis O'Keefe) discovers that the prison break planned by gangster Rick Coyle (Raymond Burr) was a trap to kill him, but he escapes anyway. With help from girlfriend Pat Cameron (Claire Trevor) and his lawyer's assistant (Marsha Hunt), he heads toward Coyle's residence to seek revenge.

75. *Rear Window* (Alfred Hitchcock, 1954) Photographer L.B. Jeffries (James Stewart), his leg broken, is confined to a wheelchair. He passes the time looking out his window and watching his neighbors. The sudden disappearance of Lars Thorwald's (Raymond Burr) wife (Irene Winston) makes Jeffries suspicious that he killed her.

76. *Return of the Whistler* (D. Ross Lederman, 1948) Their marriage delayed by a storm, Ted Nichols (Michael Duane) and fiancée Alice Barkley (Lenore Aubert) are forced to sleep in different hotels. The next day he cannot find her, and private detective Gaylord Traynor (Richard Lane) offers his assistance. Alice Barkley is a widow, and her dead husband's family has kidnapped her, planning to commit her to a sanitarium so they can claim her former husband's inheritance.

77. *Road House* (Jean Negulesco, 1948) Proprietor of a road house, Jefty Robbins (Richard Widmark) is infatuated with singer-pianist Lily Stevens (Ida Lupino). He hires her to entertain at his club, but when she falls in love with manager Pete Morgan (Cornel Wilde), Robbins becomes dangerously unstable and threatening.

78. *Scarlet Street* (Fritz Lang, 1945) When he meets beautiful Kitty March (Joan Bennett), henpecked Chris Cross (Edward G. Robinson) finds an outlet for his love of painting and his dream of having an ideal woman who loves him. March, however, loves con artist Johnny Prince (Dan Duryea). She rejects Cross, which drives him to madness and produces dire consequences for all three characters.

79. *The Set-Up* (Robert Wise, 1949) A boxer (Robert Ryan) defends his integrity by opposing the racketeers and winning the bout he was supposed to throw.

80. *711 Ocean Drive* (Joseph M. Newman, 1950)A telephone repairman (Edmond O'Brien) learns that he can get rich if he applies his electrical expertise to bookmaking and gambling schemes. His creative skills make him rich, but his involvement with murder leads to his downfall.

81. *Shadow of a Doubt* (Alfred Hitchcock, 1943) Charles Oakley (Joseph Cotten) is the Merry Widow Murderer who visits his sister and her family in small town Santa Rosa. Niece Charlie (Teresa Wright) initially welcomes him, but then starts to suspect his evil duplicity.

82. *Shanghai Gesture* (Joef von Sternberg, 1941) Mother Gin Sling (Ona Munson) runs a notorious casino in an area of Shanghai where her former husband Guy Charteris (Walter Huston) is trying to eradicate gambling. She blames her husband for deserting her and tries to get revenge on him by having her henchman Doctor Omar (Victor Mature) lure Charteris' daughter Poppy (Gene Tierney) into a life of gambling and drug addiction. Too late she learns that Poppy is also her daughter who she thought died in childbirth.

83. *Side Street* (Anthony Mann, 1950) A mail carrier (Farley Granger) is resigned to his stagnant existence. On his route, he enters an office and finds an envelope full of money. He takes it, not knowing it is blackmail money, and even though he tries to give it back later, his action has enmeshed him in a dangerous scheme.

84. *Somewhere in the Night* (Joseph L. Mankiewicz, 1946) Suffering from amnesia, a G. I. (John Hodiak) returns to civilian life and follows clues that lead him to believe he was involved in murder and the transfer of illegal funds.

85. *Sorry, Wrong Number* (Anatole Litvak, 1948) Invalid Leona Stevenson (Barbara Stanwyck) uses her ill health to manipulate husband Henry (Burt Lancaster). On the phone, her outlet to the outside world, she hears snippets of conversation suggesting that someone is planning to murder her. Confined to her room, she tries desperately to get help.

86. *Spellbound* (Alfred Hitchcock, 1945) Psychiatrist Constance Petersen (Ingrid Bergman) suspects that Dr. Edwardes (Gregory Peck), sent to replace Dr. Murchison (Leo G. Carroll) as head of the sanitarium, is not who he says he is. She learns that he suffers from amnesia, and although he believes he murdered the real Dr. Edwardes, she helps him discover the truth.

87. *The Spiral Staircase* (Robert Siodmak, 1945) A mute (Dorothy McGuire)

lives as a servant girl in a household plagued by a phantom murderer. A country doctor (Kent Smith) tries to cure her, but cannot find the answer to her malady. When the murderer finally confronts her, fear overpowers her and she screams, finding her voice once more.

88. *Stranger on the Third Floor* (Pre-noir—Boris Ingster, 1940) When a newspaper reporter (John McGuire) is arrested for a murder he did not commit, his girlfriend (Margaret Tallichet) investigates on her own and uncovers the real murderer.

89. *Strangers on a Train* (Alfred Hitchcock, 1951) Psychopath Bruno Antony (Robert Walker) kills Guy Haines's (Farley Granger) estranged wife (Kasey Rogers), thinking Haines had agreed to kill Antony's father (Jonathan Hale) in return. When Antony decides that Haines does not intend to go through with their pact, he plans to frame him for his wife's murder.

90. *Street of Chance* (Jack Hively, 1942) Amnesiac Frank Thompson (Burgess Meredith) searches for his lost identity. Ruth Dillon (Claire Trevor) appears to be helping him, but may have some ulterior motive in mind.

91. *Sunset Boulevard* (Billy Wilder, 1950) Screenwriter Joe Gillis (William Holden) gets a job as editor for silent movie star Norma Desmond (Gloria Swanson) who is writing a script for her return to the screen. Gillis accepts the lifestyle of a gigolo until his relationship with Betty Schaefer (Nancy Olson) makes him aware of his phoniness. His attempt to leave the possessive Desmond, however, is not so easy.

92. *Suspicion* (Alfred Hitchcock, 1941) Heiress Lina (Joan Fontaine) is in a quandary about her irresponsible husband Johnnie (Cary Grant). She does not know what to make of his lying and his careless handling of money, until she begins to fear that he may want to kill her to collect the insurance money he took out on her life.

93. *Tension* (John Berry, 1949) Pharmacist Warren Quimby (Richard Basehart), ever submissive to his wife's (Audrey Totter) whims, learns she is cheating on him and he plans to murder her lover (Lloyd Gough). However, someone else murders her lover first, and Quimby, although innocent, looks like the guilty party.

94. *They Live by Night* (Nicholas Ray, 1948) Keechie (Cathy O'Donnell) falls in love with young bank robber Bowie Bowers (Farley Granger). Although fugitives, they try to live a normal existence until authorities catch up with them.

95. *They Won't Believe Me* (Irving Pichel, 1947) Larry Ballentine (Robert Young), accused of murdering his wife (Rita Johnson), takes the witness stand and tells his story. He admits staying in his loveless marriage because his wife controlled the money. He had affairs with Janice Bell (Jane Greer) and Verna Carlson (Susan Hayward), and when his wife suffered a mysterious death, he was arrested as the most likely suspect.

96. *This Gun for Hire* (Frank Tuttle, 1942) An assassin (Alan Ladd) is betrayed by the man who hired him. Seeking revenge, he meets a nightclub magician (Veronica Lake). He develops a liking for her and he convinces him to help her stop a chemical company from selling its poison gas to the Germans.

97. *Touch of Evil* (Orson Welles, 1958) Corrupt police captain Hank Quinlan (Orson Welles) plants evidence that can convict a young Mexican (Victor Millan) of murdering an American construction company mogul with a car bomb. Mexican narcotics agent Mike Vargas (Charlton Heston) suspects Welles of planting evidence, and while trying to protect his new wife (Janet Leigh), he carries out his own investigation.

98. *The Two Mrs. Carrolls* (Peter Godfrey, 1947) Painter Geoffrey Carroll (Humphrey Bogart) is married, but meets Sally Morton (Barbara Stanwyck) and

falls in love. He poisons his wife to marry Morton. Then, when he meets Ceily Latham (Alexis Smith), he thinks he can repeat his crime.

99. *Undercurrent* (Vincente Minnelli, 1946) Reserved Ann Hamilton (Katharine Hepburn) marries gregarious industrialist Alan Garroway (Robert Taylor) before she realizes he may be a psychotic killer. Garroway's brother (Robert Mitchum) intervenes to save her.

100. *The Unsuspected* (Michael Curtiz, 1947) Victor Grandison (Claude Rains), impresario of a murder mystery radio show, murders his secretary (Barbara Woodell). Unannounced, Steven Howard (Ted North) abruptly arrives at Grandison's mansion, claiming to be the husband of Grandison's niece (Joan Caulfield). Howard, who is actually the brother of the dead secretary, is suspicious of the coroner's conclusion that she hanged herself. He falls in love with Grandison's niece, but his arrival places her in danger.

101. *Vertigo* (Alfred Hitchcock, 1957) Retired police detective Scottie Ferguson (James Stewart) accepts Gavin Elster's (Tom Helmore) request to follow his wife, Madeleine, (Kim Novak) who he thinks is possessed by a dead woman. After several days of surveillance, Scottie falls in love with Madeleine, who is not who or what she seems to be.

102. *Where Danger Lives* (John Farrow, 1950) Physician Jeff Cameron (Robert Mitchum) gets involved with psychotic Margo (Faith Domergue), not realizing she is married to the elderly Mr. Lannington (Claude Rains). In an altercation, Lannington hits Cameron on the head with a poker, and while recovering, Cameron does not realize that Margo has killed her husband. Letting Cameron think that he killed Lannington, Margo uses his guilt to make him flee with her to Mexico.

103. *Where the Sidewalk Ends* (Otto Preminger, 1950) Police detective Mark Dixon (Dana Andrews) has a violent temper. In a fight with a suspect (Craig Stevens), Dixon accidentally kills him, then works to cover up his crime while trying to solve another one.

104. *While the City Sleeps* (Fritz Lang, 1956) A news reporter (Dana Andrews) endangers the life of his girlfriend (Sally Forrest) when he uses her as bait to catch a serial killer (John Barrymore, Jr.).

105. *The Whistler* (William Castle, 1944) Earl C. Conrad (Richard Dix) suffers from intense guilt that he did not save his wife when their cruise ship sank. He plots his own death, hiring an assassin to kill him. When he learns that his wife is alive, however, he changes his mind about dying, but cannot find the man with whom he made the contract.

106. *The Window* (Ted Tetzlaff, 1949) Young Tommy Woodry (Bobby Driscoll) witnesses his neighbors (Paul Stewart, Ruth Roman) committing a murder. Because he has a reputation for extravagant storytelling, the police and his parents (Arthur Kennedy, Barbara Hale) do not believe him. When the murderers realize he knows of their crime, they come after him to kill him.

107. *Witness to Murder* (Roy Rowland, 1954) Cheryl Draper (Barbara Stanwyck) witnesses a murder in an apartment across from hers. Neo-Nazi Albert Richter (George Sanders) covers up his crime, making Draper look neurotic, so that police detective Lawrence Mathews (Gary Merrill) has difficulty believing her story.

108. *The Woman in the Window* (Fritz Lang, 1944) After his wife and children leave for a vacation, Richard Wanley (Edward G. Robinson) falls asleep in a chair at his private club and dreams of meeting the woman (Joan Bennett) whose portrait he saw earlier in a window. She leads him into a dangerous intrigue involving murder and blackmail.

Bibliography

Balio, Tino, ed. *History of the American Cinema*. Charles Harpole, gen. ed. New York: Scribner's, 1993. 270.

Belton, John. *American Cinema/American Culture*. 3rd ed. New York: McGraw-Hill, 2009.

Bergman, Andrew. *We're in the Money: Depression America and Its Films*. New York: New York University Press, 1971.

Borde, Raymond, and Étienne Chaumeton. *A Panorama of American Film Noir, 1941–1953*. Trans. Paul Hammond. San Francisco: City Lights Books, 2002.

Byron, Stuart, and Elisabeth Weis, eds. *The National Society of Film Critics on Movie Comedy*. New York: Penguin Books, 1977.

Capra, Frank. *The Name Above the Title*. New York: Macmillan, 1971.

Carney, Raymond. *American Vision: The Films of Frank Capra*. London: Cambridge University Press, 1986.

Cavell, Stanley. *Pursuits of Happiness: The Hollywood Comedy of Remarriage*. Cambridge, MA: Harvard University Press, 1981.

Cook, David A. *A History of Narrative Film*. 3rd ed. New York: W. W. Norton, 1996.

Dickos, Andrew. *Street with No Name: A History of the Classic American Film Noir*. Lexington: University Press of Kentucky, 2002.

Durgnat, Raymond. "Paint It Black: The Family Tree of the *Film Noir*." *Film Noir Reader*. Eds. Alain Silver and James Ursini. New York: Limelight Editions, 1998. 37–51.

Ellis, Jack C. *A History of Film*. Boston: Allyn and Bacon, 1995.

Everson, William K. *Hollywood Bedlam: Classic Screwball Comedies*. New York: Citadel Press, 1994.

Frank, Nino. "A New Kind of Police Drama: The Criminal Adventure." *Film Noir Reader 2*. Eds. Alain Silver and James Ursini. New York: Limelight Editions, 1999. 15–19.

Gehring, Wes D. *Screwball Comedy: A Genre of Madcap Romance*. Westport, CT: Greenwood Press, 1986.

_____. *Screwball Comedy: Defining a Film Genre*. Muncie, IN: Ball State University, 1983.

_____. *Romantic vs. Screwball Comedy: Charting the Difference.* Lanham, MD: Scarecrow Press, 2002.

Harvey, James. *Romantic Comedy in Hollywood from Lubitsch to Sturges.* New York: Da Capo Press, 1987.

Haskell, Molly. *From Reverence to Rape: The Treatment of Women in the Movies.* New York: Holt, Rinehart and Winston, 1974.

Hirsch, Foster. *The Dark Side of the Screen: Film Noir.* New York: Da Capo Press, 1981.

Internet Movie Database. N.p. N.d. Web. March 2011.

Jacobs, Lewis. *The Rise of the American Film: A Critical History.* New York: Teachers College Press, 1971.

Kaplan, E. Ann, ed. *Women in Film Noir.* London: British Film Institute, 1980.

Maltby, Richard. "The Production Code and the Hays Office." *Vol. 5: Grand Design: Hollywood as a Modern Business Enterprise, 1930–1939.* Ed. Tino Balio (*History of the American Cinema,* gen. ed. Charles Harpole). New York: Scribner's, 1993. 37–72.

Mast, Gerald. *A Short History of the Movies.* Indianapolis: Pegasus, 1971.

Phillips, William H. *Film: An Introduction.* Boston: Bedford/St. Martin's, 1999.

Renzi, Thomas C. *Cornell Woolrich from Pulp Noir to Film Noir.* Jefferson, NC: McFarland, 2006.

Sarris, Andrew. *"You Ain't Heard Nothin' Yet": The American Talking Film, History and Memory, 1927–1949.* New York: Oxford University Press, 1998.

Schatz, Thomas. *Hollywood Genres: Formulas, Filmmaking, and the Studio System.* Philadelphia: Temple University Press, 1981.

Selby, Spencer. *Dark City: The Film Noir.* Jefferson, NC: McFarland, 1984.

Sikov, Ed. *Screwball: Hollywood's Madcap Romantic Comedies.* New York: Crown, 1989.

Silver, Alain, and James Ursini. *Film Noir Reader.* 4th ed. New York: Limelight Editions, 1998.

_____. *Film Noir Reader 2.* New York: Limelight Editions, 1999.

_____. *Film Noir Reader 3.* New York: Limelight Editions, 2002.

_____. *Film Noir Reader 4.* New York: Limelight Editions, 2004.

_____, and Elizabeth Ward, eds. *Film Noir: An Encyclopedic Reference to the American Style,* 3rd ed. Woodstock, New York: The Overlook Press, 1992.

Turner Sports and Entertainment Digital Network. Turner Classic Movies. N.d. Web. March 2011.

Index

Numbers in **bold italics** indicate pages with photographs.

Lightning Source UK Ltd.
Milton Keynes UK
UKHW011313080720
366217UK00003B/782